Stress Information for Teens

First Edition

Stress Information for Teens

Health Tips about the Mental and Physical Consequences of Stress

Including Information about the Different Kinds of Stress, Symptoms of Stress, Frequent Causes of Stress, Stress Management Techniques, and More

◆

Edited by Sandra Augustyn Lawton

Omnigraphics

P.O. Box 31-1640, Detroit, MI 48231

Bibliographic Note

Because this page cannot legibly accommodate all the copyright notices, the Bibliographic Note portion of the Preface constitutes an extension of the copyright notice.

Edited by Sandra Augustyn Lawton

Teen Health Series
Karen Bellenir, *Managing Editor*
David A. Cooke, M.D., *Medical Consultant*
Elizabeth Collins, *Research and Permissions Coordinator*
Cherry Stockdale, *Permissions Assistant*
EdIndex, Services for Publishers, *Indexers*

***

Omnigraphics, Inc.
Matthew P. Barbour, *Senior Vice President*
Kevin M. Hayes, *Operations Manager*

***

Peter E. Ruffner, *Publisher*

Copyright © 2008 Omnigraphics, Inc.

ISBN 978-0-7808-1012-9

Library of Congress Cataloging-in-Publication Data

Stress information for teens : health tips about the mental and physical consequences of stress including information about the different kinds of stress, symptoms of stress, frequent causes of stress, stress management techniques, and more / Edited by Sandra Augustyn Lawton.
   p. cm. -- (Teen health series)
  Includes bibliographical references and index.
   Summary: "Provides basic consumer health information for teens about common causes of stress, the effects of stress on the body and mind, and coping strategies. Includes index, resource information and recommendations for further reading"--Provided by publisher.
   ISBN 978-0-7808-1012-9 (hardcover : alk. paper) 1. Stress management for teenagers. 2. Stress (Psychology) I. Lawton, Sandra Augustyn.
  RA785.S766 2008
  616.9'800835--dc22
                                                                    2008015151

Electronic or mechanical reproduction, including photography, recording, or any other information storage and retrieval system for the purpose of resale is strictly prohibited without permission in writing from the publisher.

The information in this publication was compiled from the sources cited and from other sources considered reliable. While every possible effort has been made to ensure reliability, the publisher will not assume liability for damages caused by inaccuracies in the data, and makes no warranty, express or implied, on the accuracy of the information contained herein.

This book is printed on acid-free paper meeting the ANSI Z39.48 Standard. The infinity symbol that appears above indicates that the paper in this book meets that standard.

Printed in the United States

Table of Contents

Preface ix

Part One: Understanding Stress

Chapter 1—Teens And Stress: An Overview 3

Chapter 2—Can Stress Actually Be Good For You? 9

Chapter 3—How People Experience Stress 13

Chapter 4—Differences Between Acute And Chronic Stress 21

Part Two: Common Causes Of Stress In Teens

Chapter 5—Are You Overbooked? 31

Chapter 6—Sleep-Deprived Teens Are More Stressed 35

Chapter 7—News Reports Can Bring On Stress 39

Chapter 8—School Can Cause Stress 43

Chapter 9—The Effects Of School Violence 47

Chapter 10—Consequences Of Bullying 51

Chapter 11—How To Make Homework Less Stressful 59

Chapter 12—Test Anxiety 63

Chapter 13—Young, Gifted, And Stressed 69

Chapter 14—Sports Pressure And Competition 73

Chapter 15—Handling Peer Pressure 77

Chapter 16—Relationships Can Be Stressful 85

Chapter 17—Dealing With Pressure To Have Sex 93

Chapter 18—Getting Over A Break-Up 97

Chapter 19—Keeping Your Cool Under Prom Pressure 101

Chapter 20—When Your Family Has To Move 107

Chapter 21—When Your Parents Fight 113

Chapter 22—When Your Parent Has A Substance
　　　　　　 Abuse Problem 117

Chapter 23—Family Violence 121

Chapter 24—Dealing With Divorce 127

Chapter 25—Stepfamilies: Adjusting To Change 133

Chapter 26—Living With A Chronic Illness Or Disability 143

Chapter 27—Chronic Pain And Psychological Stress
　　　　　　 Go Hand In Hand 151

Chapter 28—Dealing With Grief 155

Part Three: How Stress Affects Your Body And Mind

Chapter 29—Stress And Disease: What's The Connection? 161

Chapter 30—Stress And The Immune System 173

Chapter 31—Stress And Insomnia 181

Chapter 32—Chronic Fatigue Syndrome 185

Chapter 33—Fibromyalgia 191

Chapter 34—Irritable Bowel Syndrome 199

Chapter 35—Stress And Weight Gain: Is There A Link? 207

Chapter 36—Stress And Your Skin 211

Chapter 37—Stress And Hair Loss 219

Chapter 38—Headaches And Facial Tics 223

Chapter 39—Does Stress Really Cause Heart Disease? 229

Chapter 40—Adolescent Stress And Depression 235

Chapter 41—Stress, Depression, And Suicide:
    Helping A Friend In Trouble 243

Chapter 42—Anxiety Disorders 249

Chapter 43—Posttraumatic Stress Disorder (PTSD) 261

Chapter 44—Stress, Substance Abuse, And Addiction 269

Chapter 45—Eating Disorders 277

Chapter 46—Self-Harm 287

Part Four: Managing Stress

Chapter 47—Fitting In And Finding Yourself 295

Chapter 48—The Importance Of Emotional And Social Support 301

Chapter 49—Tips For Dealing With Stress 305

Chapter 50—Build Resilience 309

Chapter 51—Boost Your Self-Esteem 313

Chapter 52—Control Your Anger 317

Chapter 53—Proper Nutrition And Exercise
    Can Help Relieve Stress 321

Chapter 54—The Benefits Of Journaling, Stress Logs,
    And Other Action Plans For Stress Management 325

Chapter 55—Owning A Dog Or Cat Can Reduce Stress 331

Chapter 56—Using Your Senses To Relieve Stress:
    Aromatherapy And Music 335

Chapter 57—Breathing Techniques For Stress Management 341

Chapter 58—Massage Therapy 347

Chapter 59—Mind-Body Therapies: Guided Imagery,
　　　　　　Meditation, Progressive Muscle Relaxation,
　　　　　　Yoga, And Spirituality And Religion 351

Part Five: If You Need More Information

Chapter 60—Directory Of Stress And Stress
　　　　　　Management Resources 367

Chapter 61—Additional Reading About Stress
　　　　　　And Stress Management 371

Index 379

Preface

About This Book

Teens often struggle to balance their own desires with the demands placed upon them by parents and others in positions of authority over them, including teachers, coaches, and employers. They may face internal pressures from the urge to achieve independence and external pressures from their peers. Puberty's hormones can bring confusing emotional and physical changes. Furthermore, in today's fast-paced world, many may find that every minute of the day is filled with constant activity. All this can lead to significant amounts of stress. Some stress is good, and most stress is only temporary; but when stress becomes chronic, it can lead to mental and physical consequences that are unhealthy.

Stress Information For Teens describes the difference between good stress (sometimes called eustress) and the kinds of stress that can lead to symptoms such as impaired concentration, appetite changes, headaches, insomnia, gastrointestinal problems, depression, anger, anxiety, and other physical and mental concerns. The most common causes of stress in teens are described, and facts are provided about a broad variety of techniques that can be used for stress management, including nutrition, exercise, journaling, breathing techniques, and massage therapy. The book concludes with a directory of stress and stress management resources and suggestions for additional reading.

How To Use This Book

This book is divided into parts and chapters. Parts focus on broad areas of interest; chapters are devoted to single topics within a part.

Part One: Understanding Stress provides an overview of stress, including how some stress can actually be good and how it can be used to one's advantage. It discusses the diverse ways in which people experience stress, and it contrasts the differences between acute (short-term) and chronic (long-term) stress.

Part Two: Common Causes Of Stress In Teens examines the various reasons why teens experience stress. Some causes of stress in teens, such as schedules that are too busy, relationship problems, and family issues, are the same as for adults. Others, including bullying, school violence, test anxiety, and peer pressure, are more closely associated with the adolescence. The individual chapters in this part examine these sources of stress and provide suggestions for overcoming the related challenges.

Part Three: How Stress Affects Your Body And Mind explains how stress can lead to insomnia, chronic fatigue, weight gain, headaches, skin conditions, and other physical ailments. The mental consequences of chronic stress, including depression, anxiety disorders, posttraumatic stress disorder, eating disorders, and self-harm, are also described.

Part Four: Managing Stress suggests several ways teens can cope with stress by building resilience and boosting self-esteem. It describes how eating well and getting sufficient exercise can help keep stress levels reduced, and it also provides information on some commonly used techniques for stress management, including journaling, aromatherapy, music, massage therapy, and mind-body therapies such as meditation, progressive muscle relaxation, and spirituality.

Part Five: If You Need More Information offers a directory of stress and stress management resources and suggestions for further reading.

Bibliographic Note

This volume contains documents and excerpts from publications issued by the following government agencies: Center for Disease Control and Prevention (CDC); Federal Trade Commission (FTC); National Cancer Institute (NCI); National Center for Complementary and Alternative Medicine (NCCAM); National Center for Posttraumatic Stress Disorder (NCPTSD);

National Clearinghouse on Families and Youth; National Institute of Arthritis and Musculoskeletal and Skin Diseases (NIAMS); National Institute of Diabetes and Digestive and Kidney Diseases (NIDDK); National Institutes of Health (NIH); National Institute of Mental Health (NIMH); National Institute on Drug Abuse (NIDA); National Women's Health Information Center (NWHIC); National Youth Violence Prevention Resource Center; Substance Abuse and Mental Health Services Administration; U.S. Department of Labor; and the U.S. Department of Veterans Affairs.

In addition, this volume contains copyrighted documents and articles produced by the following organizations and individuals: A.D.A.M., Inc.; About, Inc.; Academy of General Dentistry; American Human Association; American Institute of Stress; American Lung Association; American Osteopathic College of Dermatology; American Psychiatric Association; American Psychological Association; Boys Town; Children, Youth and Women's Health Service, Government of South Australia; Clemson University Cooperative Extension Service; Counseling Center at the University of Massachusetts, Lowell; Duke University Talent Identification Program; Richard N. Fogoros, M.D.; Hartford Hospital; Long Beach VA Healthcare System; MSNBC Interactive News, LLC; Maine Youth Suicide Prevention Program; National Center on Addiction and Substance Abuse (CASA) at Columbia University; National Headache Foundation; National Jewish Medical and Research Center; National Sleep Foundation; Nemours Foundation; New Zealand Dermatological Society; Elizabeth Scott, M.S.; Wesley E. Sime, Ph.D.; Students Against Destructive Decisions (SADD); Texas A&M University; University of Minnesota Extension; University of New Hampshire Health Services; University of South Florida, Lakeland; Wake Forest University Baptist Medical Center; and the Wellness Council of Arizona.

Full citation information is provided on the first page of each chapter. Every effort has been made to secure all necessary rights to reprint the copyrighted material. If any omissions have been made, please contact Omnigraphics to make corrections for future editions.

The photograph on the front cover is from photos.com/Jupiterimages.

Acknowledgements

In addition to the organizations listed above, special thanks are due to the *Teen Health Series* research and permissions coordinator, Elizabeth Collins, and to its managing editor, Karen Bellenir.

About the *Teen Health Series*

At the request of librarians serving today's young adults, the *Teen Health Series* was developed as a specially focused set of volumes within Omnigraphics' *Health Reference Series*. Each volume deals comprehensively with a topic selected according to the needs and interests of people in middle school and high school.

Teens seeking preventive guidance, information about disease warning signs, medical statistics, and risk factors for health problems will find answers to their questions in the *Teen Health Series*. The *Series*, however, is not intended to serve as a tool for diagnosing illness, in prescribing treatments, or as a substitute for the physician/patient relationship. All people concerned about medical symptoms or the possibility of disease are encouraged to seek professional care from an appropriate health care provider.

If there is a topic you would like to see addressed in a future volume of the *Teen Health Series*, please write to:

Editor
Teen Health Series
Omnigraphics, Inc.
P.O. Box 31-1640
Detroit, MI 48231

A Note about Spelling and Style

Teen Health Series editors use *Stedman's Medical Dictionary* as an authority for questions related to the spelling of medical terms and the *Chicago Manual of Style* for questions related to grammatical structures, punctuation, and other editorial concerns. Consistent adherence is not always possible, however, because the individual volumes within the *Series* include many documents from a wide variety of different producers and copyright holders, and the editor's primary goal is to present material from each source as accurately as is possible following the terms specified by each document's producer. This sometimes means that information in different chapters or sections may follow other guidelines and alternate spelling authorities. For example, occasionally a copyright holder may require that eponymous terms be shown in possessive forms (Crohn's disease *vs.* Crohn disease) or that British spelling norms be retained (leukaemia *vs.* leukemia).

Locating Information within the *Teen Health Series*

The *Teen Health Series* contains a wealth of information about a wide variety of medical topics. As the *Series* continues to grow in size and scope, locating the precise information needed by a specific student may become more challenging. To address this concern, information about books within the *Teen Health Series* is included in *A Contents Guide to the Health Reference Series*. The *Contents Guide* presents an extensive list of more than 13,000 diseases, treatments, and other topics of general interest compiled from the Tables of Contents and major index headings from the books of the *Teen Health Series* and *Health Reference Series*. To access *A Contents Guide to the Health Reference Series*, visit www.healthreferenceseries.com.

Our Advisory Board

We would like to thank the following advisory board members for providing guidance to the development of this *Series*:

Dr. Lynda Baker, Associate Professor of Library and Information Science, Wayne State University, Detroit, MI

Nancy Bulgarelli, William Beaumont Hospital Library, Royal Oak, MI

Karen Imarisio, Bloomfield Township Public Library, Bloomfield Township, MI

Karen Morgan, Mardigian Library, University of Michigan-Dearborn, Dearborn, MI

Rosemary Orlando, St. Clair Shores Public Library, St. Clair Shores, MI

Medical Consultant

Medical consultation services are provided to the *Teen Health Series* editors by David A. Cooke, M.D. Dr. Cooke is a graduate of Brandeis University, and he received his M.D. degree from the University of Michigan. He completed residency training at the University of Wisconsin Hospital and Clinics. He is board-certified in internal medicine. Dr. Cooke currently works as part of the University of Michigan Health System and practices in Ann Arbor, MI. In his free time, he enjoys writing, science fiction, and spending time with his family.

Part One

Understanding Stress

Chapter 1

Teens And Stress: An Overview

Feeling like there are too many pressures and demands on you? Losing sleep worrying about tests and schoolwork? Eating on the run because your schedule is just too busy? You're not alone. Everyone experiences stress at times—adults, teens, and even kids. But there are things you can do to minimize stress and manage the stress that's unavoidable.

What Is Stress?

Stress is a feeling that's created when we react to particular events. It's the body's way of rising to a challenge and preparing to meet a tough situation with focus, strength, stamina, and heightened alertness.

The human body responds to stressors by activating the nervous system and specific hormones. The hypothalamus signals the adrenal glands to produce more of the hormones adrenaline and cortisol and release them into the bloodstream. These hormones speed up heart rate, breathing rate, blood pressure, and metabolism. Blood vessels open wider to let more blood flow to large muscle groups, putting our muscles on alert. Pupils dilate to improve vision. The liver releases some of its stored glucose to increase the body's energy. And

---

About This Chapter: Information in this chapter is from "Stress," July 2007, reprinted with permission from www.kidshealth.org. Copyright © 2007 The Nemours Foundation. This information was provided by KidsHealth, one of the largest resources online for medically reviewed health information written for parents, kids, and teens. For more articles like this one, visit www.KidsHealth.org, or www.TeensHealth.org.

sweat is produced to cool the body. All of these physical changes prepare a person to react quickly and effectively to handle the pressure of the moment.

This natural reaction is known as the stress response. Working properly, the body's stress response enhances a person's ability to perform well under pressure. But the stress response can also cause problems when it overreacts or fails to turn off and reset itself properly.

> ♣ **It's A Fact!!**
> The events that provoke stress are called stressors, and they cover a whole range of situations—everything from outright physical danger to making a class presentation or taking a semester's worth of your toughest subject.

Good Stress And Bad Stress

The stress response (also called the fight or flight response) is critical during emergency situations, such as when a driver has to slam on the brakes to avoid an accident. It can also be activated in a milder form at a time when the pressure's on but there's no actual danger—like stepping up to take the foul shot that could win the game, getting ready to go to a big dance, or sitting down for a final exam. A little of this stress can help keep you on your toes, ready to rise to a challenge. And the nervous system quickly returns to its normal state, standing by to respond again when needed.

But stress doesn't always happen in response to things that are immediate or that are over quickly. Ongoing or long-term events, like coping with a divorce or moving to a new neighborhood or school, can cause stress, too. Long-term stressful situations can produce a lasting, low-level stress that's hard on people. The nervous system senses continued pressure and may remain slightly activated and continue to pump out extra stress hormones over an extended period. This can wear out the body's reserves, leave a person feeling depleted or overwhelmed, weaken the body's immune system, and cause other problems.

What Causes Stress Overload?

Although just enough stress can be a good thing, stress overload is a different story—too much stress isn't good for anyone. For example, feeling a

Teens And Stress: An Overview

little stress about a test that's coming up can motivate you to study hard. But stressing out too much over the test can make it hard to concentrate on the material you need to learn.

Pressures that are too intense or last too long, or troubles that are shouldered alone, can cause people to feel stress overload. Here are some of the things that can overwhelm the body's ability to cope if they continue for a long time:

- being bullied or exposed to violence or injury
- relationship stress, family conflicts, or the heavy emotions that can accompany a broken heart or the death of a loved one
- ongoing problems with schoolwork related to a learning disability or other problems, such as attention deficit hyperactivity disorder (ADHD) (usually once the problem is recognized and the person is given the right learning support the stress disappears)
- crammed schedules, not having enough time to rest and relax, and always being on the go

Some stressful situations can be extreme and may require special attention and care. Posttraumatic stress disorder is a very strong stress reaction that can develop in people who have lived through an extremely traumatic event, such as a serious car accident, a natural disaster like an earthquake, or an assault like rape.

Some people have anxiety problems that can cause them to overreact to stress, making even small difficulties seem like crises. If a person frequently feels tense, upset, worried, or stressed, it may be a sign of anxiety. Anxiety problems usually need attention, and many people turn to professional counselors for help in overcoming them.

Signs Of Stress Overload

People who are experiencing stress overload may notice some of the following signs:

- anxiety or panic attacks
- a feeling of being constantly pressured, hassled, and hurried

- irritability and moodiness
- physical symptoms, such as stomach problems, headaches, or even chest pain
- allergic reactions, such as eczema or asthma
- problems sleeping
- drinking too much, smoking, overeating, or doing drugs
- sadness or depression

Everyone experiences stress a little differently. Some people become angry and act out their stress or take it out on others. Some people internalize it and develop eating disorders or substance abuse problems. And some people who have a chronic illness may find that the symptoms of their illness flare up under an overload of stress.

Keep Stress Under Control

What can you do to deal with stress overload or, better yet, to avoid it in the first place? The most helpful method of dealing with stress is learning how to manage the stress that comes along with any new challenge, good or bad. Stress management skills work best when they're used regularly, not just when the pressure's on. Knowing how to "de-stress" and doing it when things are relatively calm can help you get through challenging circumstances that may arise. Here are some things that can help keep stress under control:

- **Take a stand against overscheduling.** If you're feeling stretched, consider cutting out an activity or two, opting for just the ones that are most important to you.

- **Be realistic.** Don't try to be perfect—no one is. And expecting others to be perfect can add to your stress level, too (not to mention put a lot of pressure on them!). If you need help on something, like schoolwork, ask for it.

- **Get a good night's sleep.** Getting enough sleep helps keep your body and mind in top shape, making you better equipped to deal with any negative stressors. Because the biological "sleep clock" shifts during adolescence, many teens prefer staying up a little later at night and sleeping a little later in the morning. But if you stay up late and still need to get up early for school, you may not get all the hours of sleep you need.

- **Learn to relax.** The body's natural antidote to stress is called the relaxation response. It's your body's opposite of stress, and it creates a sense of well-being and calm. The chemical benefits of the relaxation response can be activated simply by relaxing. You can help trigger the relaxation response by learning simple breathing exercises and then using them when you're caught up in stressful situations. And ensure you stay relaxed by building time into your schedule for activities that are calming and pleasurable: reading a good book or making time for a hobby, spending time with your pet, or just taking a relaxing bath.

- **Treat your body well.** Experts agree that getting regular exercise helps people manage stress. (Excessive or compulsive exercise can contribute to stress, though, so as in all things, use moderation.) And eat well to help your body get the right fuel to function at its best. It's easy when you're stressed out to eat on the run or eat junk food or fast food. But under stressful conditions, the body needs its vitamins and minerals more than ever. Some people may turn to substance abuse as a way to ease tension. Although alcohol or drugs may seem to lift the stress temporarily, relying on them to cope with stress actually promotes more stress because it wears down the body's ability to bounce back.

- **Watch what you're thinking.** Your outlook, attitude, and thoughts influence the way you see things. Is your cup half full or half empty? A healthy dose of optimism can help you make the best of stressful circumstances. Even if you're out of practice, or tend to be a bit of a pessimist, everyone can learn to think more optimistically and reap the benefits.

- **Solve the little problems.** Learning to solve everyday problems can give you a sense of control. But avoiding them can leave you feeling like you have little control and that just adds to stress. Develop skills to calmly look at a problem, figure out options, and take some action toward a solution. Feeling capable of solving little problems builds the inner confidence to move on to life's bigger ones—and it and can serve you well in times of stress.

Build Your Resilience

Ever notice that certain people seem to adapt quickly to stressful circumstances and take things in stride? They're cool under pressure and able to handle problems as they come up. Researchers have identified the qualities that make some people seem naturally resilient even when faced with high levels of stress. If you want to build your resilience, work on developing these attitudes and behaviors:

- Think of change as a challenging and normal part of life.
- See setbacks and problems as temporary and solvable.
- Believe that you will succeed if you keep working toward your goals.
- Take action to solve problems that crop up.
- Build strong relationships and keep commitments to family and friends.
- Have a support system and ask for help.
- Participate regularly in activities for relaxation and fun.

☞ Remember!!
Learn to think of challenges as opportunities and stressors as temporary problems, not disasters. Practice solving problems and asking others for help and guidance rather than complaining and letting stress build. Make goals and keep track of your progress. Make time for relaxation. Be optimistic. Believe in yourself. Be sure to breathe. And let a little stress motivate you into positive action to reach your goals.

Chapter 2

Can Stress Actually Be Good For You?

As a yoga instructor in New York City, Jennifer Parmelee knows what to do to find her inner calm when hit with daily stresses. Instead of feeling overwhelmed by pressures or annoyances like being stuck in the subway, Parmelee uses them to keep her motivated.

"You need stress to a certain degree," she says. "You just try not to let it take control of you," she says.

For her, the idea is to turn a stressful situation into "fierceness or fun." Stress ... fun? Could stress actually be good for you?

In small doses, yes.

We may talk about cutting the stress from our lives, but we need those precious, powerful fight-or-flight hormones our bodies produce when we're about to be hit by a car or when confronted with an unexpected, needed-it-yesterday deadline at work. When the brain perceives physical or psychological stress, it starts pumping the chemicals cortisol, epinephrine (adrenaline), and norepinephrine into the body. Instantly, the heart beats faster, blood pressure increases, senses sharpen, a rise in blood glucose invigorates us, and we're ready to rock. Or leap away from the car.

> About This Chapter: Information in this chapter is from "Can stress actually be good for you?" by Jane Weaver. Copyright 2006 by MSNBC Interactive News, LLC. Reproduced with permission from MSNBC Interactive News, LLC.

"Stress is a burst of energy," says psychiatrist Dr. Lynne Tan of Montefiore Medical Center in New York City. "It's our body telling us what we need to do."

Moderate amounts of stress—the kind of short-term buzz we get from a sudden burst of hormones—can help people perform tasks more efficiently and can improve memory. Good stress is the type of emotional challenge where a person feels in control and provides some sense of accomplishment. It can improve heart function and make the body resistant to infection, experts say. Far from being something we need to eliminate from our lives, good stress stimulates us.

"Think about your daily life—when do you get things done?" asks Janet DiPietro, a developmental psychologist at the Johns Hopkins Bloomberg School of Public Health in Baltimore. "When you have a deadline, when you have to perform. You want some stress to help you do your best."

The Upside Of Stress

Increasingly, researchers are probing the upside of stress. Some believe short-term boosts of it can strengthen the immune system and protect against some diseases of aging, like Alzheimer disease, by keeping the brain cells working at peak capacity. People who experience moderate levels of stress before surgery have a better recovery than those with high or low levels, another study showed. Recently, a study suggested that stress could help prevent breast cancer because it suppresses the production of estrogen. Research out of Johns Hopkins found that children of mothers who had higher levels of the stress hormone cortisol during pregnancy were developmentally ahead of those of women with lower levels.

"Those powerful chemicals are there, first and foremost, to help you survive," says Monika Fleshner, a neuroimmunophysiologist at the University of Boulder, Colorado who has studied stress' effect on the immune system. "It's only under the circumstances of chronic stress or extreme, severe stress that we suffer negative effects."

Of course, there's the rub. Stress can be positive, but get too much of it—when the flood of hormones bombards your body longer than 24 hours, doctors say—and all kinds of bad things start to happen. Long-term, chronic

> ✔ **Quick Tip**
>
> **Harnessing Good Stress**
>
> Stress is not always a bad thing—it's what you do with it that's key. Here are some ways to avoid the pitfalls of pressure overload:
>
> - Think of the glass as half full. We can't make stress go away, but we can change how our brains react to it. An optimistic look at life can give more of a feeling of personal control and help limit the elevation of stress hormones.
>
> - Focus on the task at hand. An unexpected deadline at work or home can give a burst of hormone-related energy, but don't feel you have to do everything at once. If you feel overwhelmed, say "no" to taking on more tasks.
>
> - Fight the urge to be a superman or wonder woman. You're not perfect, so don't expect it from others. Prioritize and be realistic about work deadlines. Don't hesitate to ask for help.
>
> - Exercise. Regular, moderate exercise helps make your body more resistant to the negative effects of psychological stress.
>
> - Meditate. Try to think of pleasant moments or nothing at all. Just 10 minutes to 20 minutes of quiet time can relax you and increase your tolerance to chronic stress.
>
> - Be alert to stress clues. Frequent colds, cold sores, backaches, headaches, difficulty thinking clearly, irritability, or insomnia are signals that your body and immune system are suffering from too much stress.
>
> MSNBC; National Mental Health Association

emotional stress that lasts weeks or months is blamed for high blood pressure, heart disease, exhaustion and depression.

"Over time, if you're constantly in fight-or-flight, if your heart muscles and valves are awash in the epinephrine, it causes changes in the arteries and in the way that cells are able to regenerate," says Tan.

The problem is, it's difficult to shut off the onslaught of stress hormones when they become harmful. People can't control how high their hormones go when they experience a difficult situation.

The body does give off signals when healthy tension has tipped over into bad stress. Mental fogginess, frequent colds, increased sensitivity to aches and pains are all signs of an overwhelmed immune system. Autoimmune diseases like psoriasis, arthritis, and inflammatory bowel disease often flare up.

"What we can do is change the way our brains respond to stress with coping techniques such as deep breathing, meditation, and exercise," says Dr. Bruce Rabin, a professor of pathology and psychiatry at the University of Pittsburgh Medical Center.

Moderate exercise elevates stress hormones in the body and, through its cardiovascular benefits, actually makes the brain and body more resistant to psychological stress, he explains.

Matter Of Perception

Indeed, stress is a doubled-edged sword that affects everyone differently. It's mostly a matter of perception. A speeding ride on a roller coaster is torture for some, while others race for the next ride. Multi-tasking or living in a hectic urban environment is a thrill for some, a confusing sensory overload for others.

The goal isn't an absence of stress. It's an unavoidable reality. Besides, without it, life would be a pretty dull existence. The key is channeling stress energy into productive action instead of feeling overwhelmed, experts say.

"Focus the energy like a laser beam on what you need to do," says Tan. "Very successful people, rather than feeling disempowered, take the extra stress energy ... and make it into a high-energy, positive situation."

Dr. Paul J. Rosch, president of the American Institute of Stress, compares stress to the tension in a violin string.

"Not enough produces a dull, raspy noise and too much results in an annoying shrill or snaps the string. However, just the right amount of stress creates pleasing sounds," he says.

Chapter 3

How People Experience Stress

Definition Of Stress

If you were to ask a dozen people to define stress, or explain what causes stress for them, or how stress affects them, you would likely get 12 different answers to each of these requests. The reason for this is that there is no definition of stress that everyone agrees on. What is stressful for one person may be pleasurable or have little effect on others, and we all react to stress differently.

Stress is not a useful term for scientists because it is such a highly subjective phenomenon that defies definition. And if you can't define stress, how can you possibly measure it? The term "stress," as it is currently used, was coined by Hans Selye in 1936, who defined it as "the non-specific response of the body to any demand for change." Selye had noted in numerous experiments, that laboratory animals subjected to acute but different noxious physical and emotional stimuli (blaring light, deafening noise, extremes of heat or cold, perpetual frustration), all exhibited the same pathologic changes of stomach ulcerations, shrinkage of lymphoid tissue, and enlargement of the adrenals. He later demonstrated that persistent stress could cause these

---

About This Chapter: Information under the heading "Definition Of Stress" is from "Stress, Definition of Stress, Stressor, What Is Stress?, Eustress?" Text under the heading "Effects Of Stress" is from "Effects of Stress," © 2006 The American Institute of Stress (www.stress.org). Reprinted with permission.

animals to develop various diseases similar to those seen in humans, such as heart attacks, stroke, kidney disease, and rheumatoid arthritis. At the time, it was believed that most diseases were caused by specific but different pathogens. Tuberculosis was due to the tubercle bacillus, anthrax by the anthrax bacillus, syphilis by a spirochete, etc. What Selye proposed was just the opposite, namely that many different insults could cause the same disease, not only in animals, but in humans as well.

> ♣ **It's A Fact!!**
> The term "stress," as it is currently used, was coined by Hans Selye in 1936, who defined it as "the non-specific response of the body to any demand for change."
>
> Source: Excerpted from "Stress, Definition of Stress, Stressor, What Is Stress?, Eustress?" © 2006 The American Institute of Stress (www.stress.org). Reprinted with permission.

Selye's theories attracted considerable attention, and stress soon became a popular buzzword that completely ignored Selye's original definition. Some people used stress to refer to an overbearing or bad boss or some other unpleasant situation they were subjected to. For many, stress was their reaction to this in the form of chest pain, heartburn, headache, or palpitations. Others used stress to refer to what they perceived as the end result of these repeated responses, such as an ulcer or heart attack. Many scientists complained about this confusion, and one physician concluded in a 1951 issue of the British Medical Journal that, "Stress in addition to being itself, was also the cause of itself, and the result of itself."

Unfortunately, Selye was not aware that stress had been used for centuries in physics to explain elasticity, the property of a material that allows it to resume its original size and shape after having been compressed or stretched by an external force. As expressed in Hooke's Law of 1658, the magnitude of an external force, or stress, produces a proportional amount of deformation, or strain, in a malleable metal. This created even more confusion when his research had to be translated into foreign languages. There was no suitable word or phrase that could convey what he meant, since he was really describing strain. In 1946, when he was asked to give an address at the prestigious Collège de France, the academicians responsible for maintaining the purity of the French language struggled with this problem for several days and subsequently decided that a new word would have to be created. Apparently, the male chauvinists prevailed, and le stress was born, quickly followed by el stress, il stress, lo stress, der stress in other European languages, and similar neologisms in Russian, Japanese, Chinese, and Arabic. Stress is one of the very few words you will see preserved in English in these and other languages that do not use the Roman alphabet.

Because it was apparent that most people viewed stress as some unpleasant threat, Selye subsequently had to create a new word, stressor, to distinguish stimulus from response. Stress was generally considered as being synonymous with distress, and dictionaries defined it as "physical, mental, or emotional strain or tension" or "a condition or feeling experienced when a person perceives that demands exceed the personal and social resources the individual is able to mobilize." Thus, stress was put in a negative light and its positive effects ignored. However, stress can be helpful and good when it motivates people to accomplish more.

Any definition of stress should therefore also include good stress, or what Selye called eustress. For example, winning a race or election can be just as stressful as losing, or more so. A passionate kiss and contemplating what might follow is stressful, but hardly the same as having a root canal procedure.

Selye struggled unsuccessfully all his life to find a satisfactory definition of stress. In attempting to extrapolate his animal studies to humans so that people would understand what he meant, he redefined stress as "The rate of wear and tear on the body." This is actually a pretty good description of biological aging so it is not surprising that increased stress can accelerate many aspects of the aging process. In his later years, when asked to define stress, he told reporters, "Everyone knows what stress is, but nobody really knows."

As noted, stress is difficult to define because it is so different for each of us. A good example is afforded by observing passengers on a steep roller coaster ride. Some are hunched down in the back seats, eyes shut, jaws clenched, and white knuckled with an iron grip on the retaining bar. They can't wait for the ride in the torture chamber to end so they can get back on solid ground and scamper away. But up front are the wide-eyed thrill seekers, yelling and relishing each steep plunge, who race to get on the very next ride. And in between you may find a few with an air of nonchalance that borders on boredom. So, was the roller coaster ride stressful?

The roller coaster analogy is useful in explaining why the same stressor can differ so much for each of us. What distinguished the passengers in the back from those up front was the sense of control they had over the event. While neither group had any more or less control, their perceptions and expectations were quite different. Many times we create our own stress because of faulty perceptions you can learn to correct. You can teach people to move from the back of the roller coaster to the front, and, as Eleanor Roosevelt noted, nobody can make you feel inferior without your consent. While everyone can't agree on a definition of stress, all of our experimental and clinical research confirms that the sense of having little or no control is always distressful—and that's what stress is all about.

♣ It's A Fact!!

Stress is difficult for scientists to define because it is a highly subjective phenomenon that differs for each of us. Things that are distressful for some individuals can be pleasurable for others.

Source: Excerpted from "Effects of Stress," © 2006 The American Institute of Stress (www.stress.org). Reprinted with permission.

Effects Of Stress

We also respond to stress differently. Some people blush, some eat more, while others grow pale or eat less. There are numerous physical as well as emotional responses as illustrated by the following list of some 50 common signs and symptoms of stress.

1. Frequent headaches, jaw clenching or pain

How People Experience Stress

2. Gritting, grinding teeth

3. Stuttering or stammering

4. Tremors, trembling of lips, hands

5. Neck ache, back pain, muscle spasms

6. Light headedness, faintness, dizziness

7. Ringing, buzzing or popping sounds

8. Frequent blushing, sweating

9. Cold or sweaty hands, feet

10. Dry mouth, problems swallowing

11. Frequent colds, infections, herpes sores

12. Rashes, itching, hives, "goose bumps"

13. Unexplained or frequent "allergy" attacks

14. Heartburn, stomach pain, nausea

15. Excess belching, flatulence

16. Constipation, diarrhea

17. Difficulty breathing, sighing

18. Sudden attacks of panic

19. Chest pain, palpitations

20. Frequent urination

21. Poor sexual desire or performance

22. Excess anxiety, worry, guilt, nervousness

23. Increased anger, frustration, hostility

24. Depression, frequent or wild mood swings

25. Increased or decreased appetite

26. Insomnia, nightmares, disturbing dreams

27. Difficulty concentrating, racing thoughts

28. Trouble learning new information

29. Forgetfulness, disorganization, confusion

30. Difficulty in making decisions

31. Feeling overloaded or overwhelmed

32. Frequent crying spells or suicidal thoughts

33. Feelings of loneliness or worthlessness

34. Little interest in appearance, punctuality

35. Nervous habits, fidgeting, feet tapping

36. Increased frustration, irritability, edginess

37. Overreaction to petty annoyances

38. Increased number of minor accidents

39. Obsessive or compulsive behavior

40. Reduced work efficiency or productivity

41. Lies or excuses to cover up poor work

42. Rapid or mumbled speech

43. Excessive defensiveness or suspiciousness

44. Problems in communication, sharing

45. Social withdrawal and isolation

46. Constant tiredness, weakness, fatigue

47. Frequent use of over-the-counter drugs

48. Weight gain or loss without diet

49. Increased smoking, alcohol or drug use

50. Excessive gambling or impulse buying

As demonstrated in the above list, stress can have wide-ranging effects on emotions, mood, and behavior. Equally important, but often less appreciated, are effects on various systems, organs, and tissues all over the body.

There are numerous emotional and physical disorders that have been linked to stress including depression, anxiety, heart attacks, stroke, hypertension, immune system disturbances that increase susceptibility to infections, a host of viral linked disorders ranging from the common cold and herpes to acquired immune deficiency syndrome (AIDS) and certain cancers, as well as autoimmune diseases like rheumatoid arthritis and multiple sclerosis. In addition, stress can have direct effects on the skin (rashes, hives, atopic dermatitis, the gastrointestinal system (gastroesophageal reflux disease, peptic ulcer, irritable bowel syndrome, and ulcerative colitis), and can contribute to insomnia and degenerative neurological disorders like Parkinson disease. In fact, it's hard to think of any disease in which stress cannot play an aggravating role or any part of the body that is not affected. This list will undoubtedly grow as the extensive ramifications of stress are increasingly being appreciated.

Chapter 4

Differences Between Acute And Chronic Stress

What Is Acute (Short-Term) Stress?

Have you ever started a new school, argued with your best friend, or moved? Do you have to deal with the ups and downs of daily life—like homework or your parents' expectations? Then you already know about stress. In fact, everyone experiences stress. Your body is pre-wired to deal with it—whether it is expected or not. This response is known as the stress response, or fight or flight.

The fight or flight response is as old as the hills. In fact, when people used to have to fight off wild animals to survive, fight or flight is what helped them do it. Today, different things cause stress (when was the last time you had to fend off a grizzly bear?), but we still go through fight or flight. It prepares us for quick action, which is why the feeling goes away once whatever was stressing you out passes. It can also happen when something major happens, like if you change schools or have a death in your family.

Everyone has weird feelings when they are stressed. Fight or flight can cause things like sweaty palms or a dry mouth when you are nervous or knots

> About This Chapter: Information in this chapter is from "Got Butterflies? Find Out Why," BAM! Body and Mind, Your Life, Centers for Disease Control and Prevention, 2003.

in your stomach after an argument with someone. This is totally normal and means that your body is working exactly like it should. There are lots of signs of stress—common types are physical (butterflies in your stomach), emotional (feeling sad or worried), behavioral (you do not feel like doing things), and mental (you cannot concentrate).

So, when you feel stress, what happens to make your body do the things it does? According to the experts, three glands "go into gear" and work together to help you cope with change or a stressful situation. Two are in your brain and are called the hypothalamus (hipe-o-thal-a-mus) and the pituitary (pi-to-i-tary) gland. The third, the adrenal (a-dree-nal) glands, are on top of your kidneys. The hypothalamus signals your pituitary gland that it is time to tell your adrenal glands to release the stress hormones called epinephrine (ep-in-efrin), norepinephrine (nor-ep-in-efrin), and cortisol (cor-ti-sol). These chemicals increase your heart rate and breathing and provide a burst of energy, which is useful if you are trying to run away from a bear. These chemicals can also control body temperature (which can make you feel hot or cold), keep you from getting hungry, and make you less sensitive to pain. Because everyone is different, everyone will have different signs. Not to worry—everyone experiences these physical signs of stress sometimes. The good news is that, once things return to normal, your body will turn off the stress response. After some rest and relaxation, you will be good as new.

♣ **It's A Fact!!**
Most physical signs of stress usually do not last that long and can help you perform better, if you manage them right.

Source: Centers for Disease Control and Prevention

What Is Chronic (Long-Term) Stress?

What happens when life continues to throw curves at you and if you have one stressful event after another? Your stress response may not be able to stop itself from running overtime, and you may not have a chance to rest, restore, and recuperate. This can add up and, suddenly, the signs of overload hit you—turning short-term stressors into long-term stress. This means that you may have even more physical signs of stress. Things like a headache, eating too much or not at all, tossing and turning all night, or feeling down

Differences Between Acute And Chronic Stress 23

and angry all the time, are all signs of long-term stress. These signs start when you just cannot deal with any more.

Long-term stress can affect your health and how you feel about yourself, so it is important to learn to deal with it. No one is completely free of stress, and different people respond to it in lots of different ways. The most important thing to learn about long-term stress is how to spot it. You can do that by listening to your body signals and learning healthy ways to handle it.

Cold Hands, Dry Mouth, And Pounding Heart

You are about to take a big test or star in the school play, and you have cold hands, a mouth as dry as the desert, and your heart is pounding.

Cold Hands

Because you are nervous and under pressure to perform, your body has kicked the stress response into high gear. The stress hormones are shooting through your bloodstream and moving your blood away from your skin. This can give your heart and muscles more strength, which you would really need if you were trying to run away. Because your blood is going to the places that really need it (like your heart, lungs, and liver), your hands can be left feeling like ice.

Dry Mouth

Once that stress response is running full force, your body sends your blood to only those parts that are truly necessary for you to survive. Lots of the fluid in your body goes to really important places (like your organs) and can leave you with a mouth as dry as the desert. Because your blood is busy with your organs and not your muscles, your throat (which is made of muscle) can tighten, making it hard to swallow.

Pounding Heart

When you are starring in the school play, your body wants to give you what you need to succeed, which goes back to the fight or flight response. Your heart will start pounding to help you out. In fact, it is one of the first signs of the stress response. It happens because the release of stress hormones can speed up the flow of your blood by 300–400 percent. Your heart has to beat much faster to move all of that blood to your organs and your muscles. This provides a burst of energy that can help you get through backstage jitters and the first few minutes of your play.

Everyone experiences stress. If you have any of these signs of stress, it means that your body is dong its job.

Butterflies And Knots

It is your first day back at school, or maybe you are starting a new school, and you have got butterflies in your stomach.

Stomachaches, or a queasy feeling, happen all the time in stressful situations like this, and it is no wonder. Once the stress response kicks into high gear, one of the stress hormones (cortisol) shuts the stomach down and will not let food digest. It can also put your digestive tract into high speed, making you feel nauseated.

Can't Concentrate?

You have so much to do, but you just cannot seem to concentrate.

Got too much to do? You know how it goes—you have tons of homework to do right now, you have a game this afternoon, your little brother is annoying you, and your mom is insisting that you clean your room—but you just cannot seem to focus on any one thing. You feel like you have no energy to finish all that you have to do. This is because the stress hormones fill up your short-term memory with the immediate demands of dealing with stress. They also signal your brain to store the memory of the stressful event in your long-term memory so you know how to respond the next time something stressful happens. All of this means you are more likely to forget something, feel like you cannot concentrate, snap at your family, be mean to a friend, or feel tongue-tied.

Headache

It has been a long, tense day, and you feel like you have a rubber band squeezing around your head that just will not stop.

Headaches are one of the most common signs of long-term stress. They can feel dull and achy, just like a rubber band tightening around your head. Although

Differences Between Acute And Chronic Stress

it is unclear what exactly causes these headaches, tight head and neck muscles are generally thought to be to blame. The chemical messengers in your brain get really busy and tell your blood vessels to get really small. This means that less blood is getting to your head, and that can cause a headache. Your eyes, forehead, or the top of your head will be the first places you feel the pain.

Sleeplessness

You are exhausted, but when you try to sleep, you lie awake for hours.

During the day, the levels of hormones that give you energy (epinephrine and norepinephrine) and those that help you stay happy (called dopamine) stay consistent. Towards the end of a normal day, these hormones begin to decrease, and the hormone that helps you sleep (called serotonin) kicks into high gear; but if you have been trapped in a stress cycle, your body continues to produce those stress hormones from the adrenal glands. They "rev" up your body and block out the serotonin, making it hard to sleep even if you feel tired.

Change In Appetite

You just had a fight with your best friend, and eating is the only thing that makes you feel better; or maybe you feel like you could never eat again.

While you might become ravenous after a stressful event, your best friend might be grossed out by the thought of food. It just depends on how your body reacts to stress. If you get hungry, you may crave comfort foods (like candy bars, soda, or ice cream) because they increase the levels of a feel-good hormone called serotonin in the body—meaning that you will be in a better mood. Keep in mind that your body is just responding to the stress you are feeling and that your appetite will go back to normal.

On the other hand, your best friend might lose her appetite because the stress hormones make it difficult for her to eat. If you cannot eat when you are stressed, try something small like peanut butter on toast or a piece of fruit.

Overwhelmed?

You are starting to feel overwhelmed by it all, and you do not know if you can handle it.

♣ **It's A Fact!!**

Symptoms Of Stress

Physical signs and symptoms of stress include, but are not limited to: increased heart rate; pounding heart; elevated blood pressure; sweaty palms; tightness of the chest, neck, jaw, and back muscles; headache; diarrhea; constipation; urinary hesitancy; trembling, twitching; stuttering and other speech difficulties; nausea; vomiting; sleep disturbances; fatigue; shallow breathing; dryness of the mouth or throat; susceptibility to minor illness; cold hands; itching; being easily startled; chronic pain.

Emotional signs and symptoms of stress include, but are not limited to: irritability, angry outbursts, hostility, depression, jealously, restlessness, withdrawal, anxiousness, diminished initiative, feelings of unreality or over-alertness, reduction of personal involvement with others, lack of interest, tendency to cry, being critical of others, self-deprecation, nightmares, impatience, decreased perception of positive experience opportunities, narrowed focus, obsessive rumination, reduced self-esteem, insomnia, changes in eating habits, and weakened positive emotional response reflexes.

Cognitive/perceptual signs and symptoms of stress include, but are not limited to: forgetfulness, preoccupation, blocking, blurred vision, errors in judging distance, diminished or exaggerated fantasy life, reduced creativity, lack of concentration, diminished productivity, lack of attention to detail, orientation to the past, decreased psychomotor reactivity and coordination, attention deficit, disorganization of thought, negative self-esteem, diminished sense of meaning in life, lack of control/need for too much control, negative self-statements, and negative evaluation of experiences.

Behavioral signs and symptoms of stress include, but are not limited to: increased smoking, aggressive behaviors (such as driving), increased alcohol or drug use, carelessness, under-eating, over-eating, withdrawal, listlessness, hostility, accident-proneness, nervous laughter, compulsive behavior, and impatience.

Source: Excerpted from "Stress—A Conceptual Understanding," by Wesley E. Sime, Ph.D., Professor, Department of Health and Human Performance, University of Nebraska Lincoln. © 2006 Wesley E. Sime. Reprinted with permission. The complete text of this document is available at http://cehs.unl.edu/stress/workshop/concept.html.

Differences Between Acute And Chronic Stress

Everyone has different ideas of what you should be doing, and it feels like you have so many different roles to play—good student, kid, brother, sister, and friend—that things can sometimes seem out of control. It can make you tired just thinking about all you have to do. If you are feeling overwhelmed, you may notice that you cannot sleep, which makes you tired and cranky. Then, you realize that you do not feel like doing the things you like to do, and you feel a little bit sad or anxious. You may begin to feel achy and tired all over. These are signs of being stressed out. Your stress response system is having a hard time turning off. Do not panic; your body is just trying to tell you something. Take the time to figure out what is stressing you out and try to lessen the load you are carrying.

Anger

Things are crazy right now, and you just do not have any patience with anyone. You feel angry at someone at the drop of a hat.

Anger is another common response to stress. Often, people who have been locked into a stress cycle feel helpless and overwhelmed. Once this happens, they can get angry much more quickly, and they lash out at anyone that gets in their way. In fact, everyone at one point or another gets angry because they are stressed out.

Part Two

Common Causes Of Stress In Teens

Chapter 5

Are You Overbooked?

"How much stress is normal? It's hard for me to go even a day without stressing about everything from writing a paper to making the soccer team."

"I couldn't handle all my honors classes last year, but I know colleges love AP credits, and my parents want me to go to a good school. How can I explain that I can't do it all anymore?"

"I'm like a juggler who's afraid to drop one of the million balls I've got up in the air. I can't relax without feeling like everything will come crashing down on me."

Do you recognize these feelings of being stressed and overbooked? What conscientious teen hasn't felt overwhelmed by expectations at some point or another? It's important to know that there are different types of stress, and not all stress is bad. Having some degree of stress in your life can be motivating; it may push you to achieve things you never before thought you were capable of accomplishing. When you find yourself saddled with too much stress, however, you may be tempted to give up on everything, even those activities and challenges you enjoy.

About This Chapter: Information in this chapter is from "Teens and Stress: Are You Overbooked?" *Decisions Newsletter*, Winter 2005. © 2005 SADD (Students Against Destructive Decisions). Reprinted with permission.

According to Benjamin Hunnicutt, professor of leisure studies at the University of Iowa, "Overbooked kids are a real danger in a society where work is taking on more and more importance in adults' lives." Children watch their parents go about their daily schedules, and they can't help but notice when work starts to sap the time that used to go to family and community activities. "We're living in a time when adults' lives have become more scheduled and more hectic, and children seem to be encouraged to join the pace at an earlier age than ever before," says Hunnicutt. No wonder many teens are feeling burned out by the time they reach high school!"

It's certainly important to find activities you enjoy and to commit to them. Whether it's a part-time job after school, community service through your church, or playing varsity sports, learning to be a responsible member of a group is part of growing up and can be a lot of fun. When you find that your schedule has crossed the line from rewarding to completely overwhelming, however, you may find you are doing yourself more harm than good.

Often the difference between successful and unsuccessful people is their ability to manage time. There is no magic formula to knowing just how many activities are appropriate; that depends on how you deal with the pressures and commitment each one requires. If you're a person who values free time above other endeavors, you need to remember this when you're choosing your commitments. Perhaps adding another night of drama practice won't bring you as much enjoyment as having a free night to chill out on your own. On the other hand, if you're a person who thrives in structured scheduling, you might be able to handle joining the choir when you're already treasurer of Students Against Destructive Decisions (SADD) and captain of the swimming team. The secret to being happy, healthy, and successful during these important years is finding your own way to balance the things you need to do with the things you enjoy doing.

Parents need to take responsibility, too. Millions of children and teens across the country feel overwhelmed and pressured. Psychologist Alvin Rosenfield, M.D., author of *The Over-Scheduled Child: Avoiding the Hyper-Parenting Trap*, believes that enrolling kids in too many activities is a trend that has spread nationwide. "Over-scheduling our children is not only a widespread phenomenon, it's also how we parent today," he says. "Parents think

Are You Overbooked?

that they're not being good parents if their kids aren't in all kinds of activities. Children are under pressure to achieve, to be competitive. I know sixth graders who are already working on their resumes so they'll have an edge when they apply to college." In fact, colleges do not want students who "dabble" in many activities. They want students who are committed to school and to those activities that they do best.

Other experts echo Rosenfield's observations. "Kids in America are so over-scheduled that they have no [free] time. They have no time to call on their own resources and be creative. Creativity is making something out of nothing, and it takes time for that to happen," says Diane Ehrensaft, Ph.D., of the Wright Institute. "In our efforts to raise Renaissance children who are competitive in all areas, we squelch creativity." This type of pressure can leave kids feeling overwhelmed and stressed out.

A pioneer in the field of stress research, Hans Selye, M.D., describes two different types of stress that teens feel: eustress and distress. Eustress is the pleasant stress we feel when we confront the normal challenges of life. A teen who loves basketball may thrive on the pressures of practices and games. Distress, on the other hand, occurs when we feel overwhelmed. The same kid who loves basketball may start to see it as a burden when it becomes one of four or five other activities.

The key to solving this problem seems to lie in one word: balance. Finding the happy medium between scheduled activities and free time will keep most teens on an even keel. If you find yourself overbooked, take a serious look at where your time is going. Prioritize things that you must do (for example, going to school) and then find some time for the one or two things you most want to do. If hockey is fun but it takes time away from your real passion, playing drums in a band, it might be time to hang up your skates.

> **Remember!!**
> Enjoying a few activities and doing them well will always bring you more satisfaction than stretching yourself too thin by trying to do everything.

Chapter 6

Sleep-Deprived Teens Are More Stressed

Six in ten American students in grades 9 to 12 average less than eight hours of sleep on school nights, according to the National Sleep Foundation (NSF) 2006 Sleep in America poll.

"Poll data confirm and extend what we've learned about adolescent sleep patterns and problems over the past few decades," said Mary Carskadon, Ph.D., poll task force chair. She directs the E.P. Bradley Hospital sleep and chronobiology research laboratory at Brown University.

Poll takers surveyed by telephone a randomly selected sample of the U.S. population: 1,602 adult caregivers of teenagers, and separately, their children aged 11 to 17 in grades 6 to 12. The combined adult/child interviews took about 25 minutes and were conducted between September 19, 2005 and November 29, 2005. The poll has a margin of error of 2.4 percentage points.

Carskadon's summer sleep camp studies in the 1970s show pubertal changes prompt an increased need for sleep. She later found a delay in the timing of the body's biological clock also kicks in at puberty, shifting adolescents' physiological readiness for sleep to 11 p.m. or later.

About This Chapter: Information in this chapter is from "Sleep-Deprived Teens Report Stress, Mood Disorders" by Lynne Lamberg, Psychiatric News, Volume 41, Number 10, May 19, 2006. Reprinted with permission. Copyright 2006 American Psychiatric Association.

As students get older, homework, extracurricular activities, jobs, and socializing push bedtimes even later. "Many teenagers' bedrooms are a technological playground, with access to a radio, television, telephone, computer, and the internet," Carskadon said. The poll found 97 percent of adolescents have at least one electronic item in their bedroom. Sixth graders usually have two; 12th graders have four. Those with four or more items reported about 30 minutes less sleep than those with fewer devices.

"Talking with friends and instant messaging keep adolescents from feeling tired in the evening," Carskadon noted. "But they must get up around 6:30 a.m. to get ready for school." Most high schools in the U.S. open slightly before 8 a.m., and most middle schools open slightly after 8 a.m., too early for most teens, Carskadon maintained.

At least once a week, 1 in 4 students in grades 9 to 12 dozes in class, and 1 in 7 oversleeps and arrives at school late or misses school. Among those who drive, 51 percent admit driving while drowsy in the past year, and 15 percent report fighting sleepiness while driving at least once a week.

Sixth graders average 8.4 hours of sleep on school nights, and students in grade 12, only 6.9 hours. Taking naps and sleeping longer on weekends disrupts body clocks and does not adequately replace lost sleep, Carskadon said.

While only 9 percent of high school students get the optimal nine hours of sleep on school nights, 80 percent of these students report getting As and Bs. Less than half of those who average eight hours or less report such high grades.

Using a validated instrument for depressive mood in adolescents, researchers asked adolescents how often different mood states had bothered or troubled them "much," "somewhat," or "not at all" in the past two weeks.

In every instance, students in grades 9 to 12 reported greater mood disturbance than those in grades 6 to 8. Nearly two-thirds of high school students reported being bothered "much" or "somewhat" by worrying too much about things and/or being stressed out or anxious in the previous two weeks. One-half similarly endorsed feeling nervous or tense; 4 in 10, feeling unhappy, sad, or depressed; and 1 in 4, feeling hopeless about the future.

Students with the highest depressive mood scores were more likely than those with lower scores to report getting less than eight hours sleep, having trouble falling and staying asleep, and feeling sleepy in the daytime. They also were more apt to report trouble getting along with their family, feeling cranky and irritable, feeling too tired to exercise, and consuming two or more caffeinated beverages each day. The poll did not ask about alcohol or drug use.

Poll findings hold implications for psychiatric practice, said Jodi Mindell, Ph.D., co-chair of the NSF task force. "Any time an adolescent is being evaluated for depression, sleep should be in the equation," said Mindell, a professor of psychology at St. Joseph's University and associate director of the sleep center at the Children's Hospital of Philadelphia.

✔ **Quick Tip**

Try these ideas to make sure you are not losing out on the sleep you need:

- Wake up at the same time each morning and go to bed at the same time each night.

- Relax before bedtime. A bath, a book, or a little TV can mellow you out, but do not watch TV in bed.

- Try a small snack with milk to bring on the zzzs. Pigging out before bed can make it harder to doze off.

- Make sure your room is dark, quiet, cool, and comfortable.

- Do not drink beverages with caffeine (like colas, coffee, and tea) from afternoon until bedtime.

- Do homework and study earlier in the evening. A good night's sleep is the best way to get ready for an important test or quiz.

- Finish exercising at least three hours before bedtime.

Source: Excerpted from *Teen Survival Guide: Health Tips for On-the-go Girls*, GirlsHealth.gov, U.S. Department of Health and Human Services, Office on Women's Health, June 2007.

"Improving sleep with basic sleep hygiene often substantially benefits mood," she said. "That means forgo caffeine after lunch, take television and computers out of the bedroom, and regularize sleep schedules."

The 1,271 members of the American Academy of Child and Adolescent Psychiatry who responded to a survey by Mindell and colleagues said insomnia was a major problem in 32 percent of their adolescent patients. More than half said they used a prescription or nonprescription medication to manage insomnia at least half or more of the time when treating primary insomnia; depression; bipolar, anxiety, and posttraumatic stress disorders; delayed sleep phase; and attention-deficit/hyperactivity disorder.

Chapter 7

News Reports Can Bring On Stress

The news can be full of stories about unexpected or bad things like tornadoes or hurricanes, disease threats, bombings, kidnappings, and war. The scary thing is that it may seem like these things are happening all around you, even in places where you feel secure like school, the mall, and at home. Seeing these things on television, or even experiencing them first hand (like being in a tornado), can cause you to feel uncertain, worried, or scared. These feelings may last even after the event is over.

Here are some tips to understanding the news and what you see and hear:

- The news does not talk about everyday activities. Instead, the news talks about things that are out of the ordinary—both good and bad. Sometimes it seems like the news shows more of the bad stuff—things like tragedies and crime. For example, if a plane crashes, it will get a lot of attention in the news—so much so, that you may think planes crash all the time. In fact, thousands of planes take off and land safely each day. The news just does not talk about it.

- Sometimes you see stories over and over about tragic events like bombings, or disasters such as floods, earthquakes, or hurricanes. This does not mean these things are happening all the time. It just means that the news is talking about it again. The news will cover something when

---

About This Chapter: Information in this chapter is from "News You Can Use," BAM! Body and Mind: Your Life, Centers for Disease Control and Prevention, 2003.

it first happens and then repeat the story, so you may see it on the news when you get home from school and then again before you go to bed. After the first day, the news may do what is called a "follow-up" story to tell you what happened after the event. So you may hear about the same thing for a few days, even though it only happened once.

- Bad things in the news can alert you to what is going on around you. For example, a news story could tell you about someone in your community who is breaking into homes. While this may scare you, just remember that even though it is on the news, it does not mean it will happen to you. Stories like this can help make you aware of your surroundings and of things you can do to protect yourself (like locking your doors).

- Disasters or tragic events can bring out the best in people. Firemen and policemen are doing their jobs (like saving people) and volunteers and everyday citizens also are there to help. You will see people in your community volunteering to bring food and clothing to help people who are affected, families coming together to help each other out, and shelters being put into place to give people a place to stay. You can get involved too.

> **Remember!!**
> It is normal to be concerned about what you hear in the news, but it is important to know that while things may seem uncertain for a while, your life usually will return to normal fairly soon.

Weave Your Own Safety Net

Following these tips can help you get on with your day-to-day life, even during stressful times.

Talk to your friends and your family and spend time with them. If you find yourself feeling unsafe, uncertain, worried, or scared, or if you do not understand what is going on around you, talk to your parents, teachers, or a school counselor. Your parents or other adults can help explain these events so you can understand things better. By talking with your friends and your family, you can share your feelings and know you are not alone. Plus, spending time with them may help you feel more safe and secure.

News Reports Can Bring On Stress

Help out others. Sometimes when you are concerned about what is going on around you, it is helpful to give others support. You can help out by raising money, donating clothes, or organizing an event like a food drive at your school to collect food and/or supplies for an organization that helps people affected by war, terrorism, or natural disasters. Even if you and your family are the ones who are affected by a disaster, helping others can help you deal with your own stress. It may make you feel a little more in control.

Write your feelings down. Writing your feelings down in a diary, a journal, or even on a piece of scrap paper, is a great way to get things off of your chest. You can write down how you feel, what is going on in your life, or anything else.

Stick to your normal routine. There is comfort in the little things you do every day, so keep on doing them and take care of yourself. Get lots of sleep, eat well, and be physically active.

Take a break from the television news and watch a funny movie, play some games, or read a funny book or magazine. Too much information about disasters can get you down, so change your pace and read a joke book, or even make up your own. Did you know that smiling has been proven to improve your mood? That can help you feel like new and take your mind off things for a while.

Sometimes things happen that we just cannot anticipate. A few things (like hurricanes, tornadoes, or forest fires) occur in certain areas of the country during certain seasons. If you live in areas where weather "can take you by storm," you can take a few steps to help prepare in case of an emergency. Being prepared can help you feel like you have more control in an emergency and help you feel less stressed.

Make a plan. Talk to your parents about being prepared. Just like your family should have a plan to get out of the house in case of a fire, make a plan in case bad weather strikes. Choose a place to go, who you would call, or what you would do. Make sure to talk about what you should do if you are at school, or a friend's house, or if your parents are at work.

Have an emergency supply kit. During or after a storm, you may be without power for a few days, or you may not be able to leave your home. Work with your parents to put together a supply kit for such emergencies. Some things to have on hand include water, and non-perishable (that means they will not spoil) foods such as crackers, peanut butter, and canned food (soup, fruit, veggies, etc.). Make sure to have a battery-powered radio, flashlights, and extra batteries on hand. A first aid kit, facial tissue, and toilet paper are good things to consider packing. Lanterns (lamp oil) or candles for light are good things to have, too. Also, do not forget about your family pet. Pack extra water and food for your four-legged friends.

Put together an activity survival kit. Having some favorite books and games on hand will keep you interested and help pass the time. While you may not want to live without power forever, being without it for a few days may be fun. It could give you an idea of what life was like before electricity.

Chapter 8

School Can Cause Stress

"I hate school, and I'm not going back!"

Have you ever had that thought? Lots of kids do. Usually this feeling doesn't last long. But what happens if you feel this way too much? School is a fact of life and getting an education can help you build the kind of future life you want. So let's talk about school and what to do when you don't like it.

Signs Of School Stress

When you worry about school, it can affect your body. A kid who feels stressed about school might have headaches or stomachaches. You might feel "butterflies" or like you have to throw up.

Having trouble sleeping is also a sign of stress. And if you're not getting enough sleep, you probably feel grouchy and tired during the day. Feeling tired can make your school day seem even worse.

If you're stressed out, you might have a hard time making decisions. In the morning, you can't decide what to eat, what to wear, or what to pack for

---

About This Chapter: Information in this chapter is from "What to Do if You Don't Like School," November 2007, reprinted with permission from www.kidshealth.org. Copyright © 2007 The Nemours Foundation. This information was provided by KidsHealth, one of the largest resources online for medically reviewed health information written for parents, kids, and teens. For more articles like this one, visit www.KidsHealth.org, or www.TeensHealth.org.

lunch. You don't want to go to school, so you put off getting your stuff together. And now you're not prepared to go to school, and you've just missed the bus—again! Staying home may seem like a good choice, but it just makes it harder to go to school the next day.

Why Do Some Kids Dislike School?

If you don't like school, the first step is finding out why. You might not like school because a bully is bothering you, or because a kid you don't like wants to hang around with you. Or maybe you don't get along with your teacher. You might feel different or worry that you don't have enough friends.

Sometimes it's a problem with your classes and schoolwork. Maybe the work is too easy and you get bored. Or maybe the work is too hard, or you don't feel as smart as the other kids. Reading may be difficult for you, but you're expected to do a lot of it. You may be getting farther and farther behind, and it may seem like you'll never catch up.

When you know why you don't like school, you can start taking steps to make things better.

Finding Help

It's a good idea to talk to someone about your problems with school. Your mom, dad, relative, teacher, or school counselor will be able to help you. It's especially important to tell an adult if the problem is that you're being bullied or someone hurts you physically.

Another good idea is to write down your feelings about school in a journal. You can use a journal or diary or just write in an ordinary notebook. It's a great way to let out emotions that may be stuck inside you. And you don't have to share what you've written with others.

If you feel disorganized or like you can't keep up with your schoolwork, your teachers and school counselors want to help. Teachers want and expect you to ask for help learning stuff. If all of your subjects seem really hard, a school counselor can help you sort things out. Special help is available if you need it.

Feeling Better About School

The next time you find yourself disliking school, try this:

- First, write down everything you don't like about school.

- Then make a list of the good things you enjoy (even if it's only recess and lunch, that's a start).

- Now, what can you change on the "don't like" list? Would remembering to do your homework help you feel more confident if you're called on in class? Could you find a way to show off your special interests and talents? If you made just one new friend, would you feel less alone? If you helped someone else feel less alone, would you feel even better? Which activities could you try that would help you meet new friends?

Of course, you may not be able to change everything on your "don't like" list. A bully may not simply disappear. Reading may always be a challenge. But that's OK. Focus on what you can change and you might be able to put the cool back in school!

☞ **Remember!!**
Try not to let the problems go on too long.
It's easier to catch up on one chapter
than the whole book!

Chapter 9

The Effects Of School Violence

School shootings are sobering and tragic events that cause much concern about the safety of children. Despite these events, schools remain a very safe place for children to spend their days.

Common Reactions To Tragedies Vary

Tragedies, including school shootings, affect different people in different ways. Understanding how this traumatic event may affect you can be useful as you begin to get back to your typical routines and relationships. Keep in mind that returning to your normal routine can take some time.

You may have witnessed the loss of life, experienced feelings of grief, sadness, and suffering, experienced separation or lack of communication with family, friends, and co-workers. At some point you may have felt that your own health and safety or the health and safety of someone you care about was in danger.

It is common for people who experience a tragedy to:

- feel a sense of loss, sadness, frustration, helplessness, or emotional numbness;

About This Chapter: Information in this chapter is excerpted from "School Violence: Tips for Coping with Stress," Centers for Disease Control and Prevention, April 2007.

- experience troubling memories from that day;
- have nightmares or difficulty falling or staying asleep;
- have no desire for food or a loss of appetite;
- have difficulty concentrating; or
- feel nervous or on edge.

Some people may notice positive changes as a result of this situation, such as increased respect for life and personal relationships.

Talk about your experiences and get support from your family, friends, and co-workers. Other places to seek support can include faith-based or volunteer organizations, such as the local American Red Cross.

It is important to take care of yourself by keeping your normal routine. Avoid using alcohol and drugs, which can suppress your feelings rather than letting them come out. Helping other people or volunteering in your community can help you feel better as well. Keep in mind that returning to the way you felt before the event may take some time.

Tips For Teens

A great deal of media attention has been focused on school shootings. Whether or not you were directly affected by a violent event, it is normal to feel anxious about your own safety and to want to make sense of the situation. Here are some suggestions to help teens cope with the aftermath of a traumatic event.

- **Talk to an adult you trust.** This might be your parent, another relative, a friend, neighbor, teacher, coach, school nurse, guidance counselor, member of the clergy, or family doctor. If you have witnessed or experienced violence of any kind, not talking about it can make feelings build up inside and cause problems. If you are not sure where to turn, call your local crisis intervention center or a national hotline.
- **Stay active.** Go for a walk, volunteer with a community group, play sports, write a play or poem, play a musical instrument, or join a club or after-school program. Trying any of these can be a positive way to handle your emotions.

The Effects Of School Violence

- **Take the initiative to make your school or community safer.** Join an existing group that is promoting non-violence in your school or community or launch your own effort. Safeyouth.org (www.safeyouth.org) can connect you with national organizations and provide you with information and resources to take action in your community.

- **Stay in touch with family.** If possible, stay in touch with trusted family, friends, and neighbors to talk things out and help deal with any stress or worry.

Each person's response to stress from traumatic situations varies. Some people might experience stress immediately, while others may not experience stress until later. You may not recognize these reactions as related to your recent experience. Getting support and talking to people can be helpful. Possible sources of support may include your family, friends, co-workers, faith-based or voluntary organizations, along with state and local government organizations. If you are troubled by these experiences, talking to a professional counselor can help.

♣ **It's A Fact!!**
The vast majority of children and youth homicides occur outside school hours and property.

Chapter 10

Consequences Of Bullying

In the United States, bullying among children and teenagers has often been dismissed as a normal part of growing up. Little attention has been paid to the devastating effects of bullying or to the connection between bullying and other forms of violence. In recent years, however, students and adults around the country have begun to make a commitment to stop bullying in their schools and communities.

What is bullying?

Bullying includes a wide variety of behaviors, but all involve a person or a group repeatedly trying to harm someone who is weaker or more vulnerable. It can involve direct attacks (such as hitting, threatening or intimidating, maliciously teasing and taunting, name-calling, making sexual remarks, and stealing or damaging belongings) or subtler, indirect attacks (such as spreading rumors or encouraging others to reject or exclude someone).

How common is bullying?

Almost 30 percent of teens in the United States (or over 5.7 million) are estimated to be involved in bullying as either a bully, a target of bullying, or

---

About This Chapter: Information in this chapter is from "Bullying," National Youth Violence Prevention Resource Center, 2002.

both. In a recent national survey of students in grades six to ten, 13 percent reported bullying others, 11 percent reported being the target of bullies, and another 6 percent said they bullied others and were bullied themselves.

Limited available data suggest that bullying is much more common among younger teens than older teens. As teens grow older, they are less likely to bully others and to be the targets of bullies.

Bullying occurs more frequently among boys than girls. Teenage boys are much more likely to bully others and to be the targets of bullies. While both boys and girls say others bully them by making fun of the way they look or talk, boys are more likely to report being hit, slapped, or pushed. Teenage girls are more often the targets of rumors and sexual comments. While teenage boys target both boys and girls, teenage girls most often bully other girls, using subtler and indirect forms of aggression than boys. For example, instead of physically harming others, they are more likely to spread gossip or encourage others to reject or exclude another girl.

How does bullying affect teens that are the targets of bullies?

Bullying can lead teenagers to feel tense, anxious, and afraid. It can affect their concentration in school and can lead them to avoid school in some cases. If bullying continues for some time, it can begin to affect teens' self-esteem and feelings of self-worth. It also can increase their social isolation, leading them to become withdrawn and depressed, anxious and insecure. In extreme cases, bullying can be devastating for teens, with long-term consequences. Some

♣ It's A Fact!!

Almost 75 percent of students who use violent weapons at school (for example, guns or knives) to attack others felt persecuted, bullied, threatened, attacked, or injured by others prior to the incident.

Source: Excerpted from "The Consequences of Bullying," from the online course titled "The ABCs of Bullying: Addressing, Blocking, and Curbing School Aggression," Substance Abuse and Mental Health Services Administration, U.S. Department of Health and Human Services, May 2004.

Consequences Of Bullying

> **♣ It's A Fact!!**
>
> Bullying can distract bullies, victims, and witnesses from learning. Bullies who are plotting their next attack or victims who are consumed with anxiety and fear about their next encounter with a bully will have difficulty focusing on the lesson at hand.
>
> Source: Excerpted from "Impact on Learning," from the online course titled "The ABCs of Bullying: Addressing, Blocking, and Curbing School Aggression," Substance Abuse and Mental Health Services Administration, U.S. Department of Health and Human Services, May 2004.

teens feel compelled to take drastic measures, such as carrying weapons for protection or seeking violent revenge. Others, in desperation, even consider suicide. Researchers have found that years later, long after the bullying has stopped, adults who were bullied as teens have higher levels of depression and poorer self-esteem than other adults.

Can bullying also affect those teens that witness the bullying?

In one study of junior high and high school students, over 88 percent said they had witnessed bullying in their schools. Teens who witness bullying can feel guilty or helpless for not standing up to a bully on behalf of a classmate or friend or for not reporting the incident to someone who could help. They may experience even greater guilt if they are drawn into bullying by pressure from their peers. Some teens deal with these feelings of guilt by blaming the victim and deciding that he or she deserved the abuse. Teens sometimes also feel compelled to end a friendship or avoid being seen with the bullied teen to avoid losing status or being targeted themselves.

Which teens are most likely to become bullies?

While many people believe bullies act tough in order to hide feelings of insecurity and self-loathing, in fact, bullies tend to be confident, with high self-esteem. They are generally physically aggressive, with pro-violence attitudes, and are typically hot-tempered, easily angered, and impulsive, with a low tolerance for frustration. Bullies have a strong need to dominate others and usually have little empathy for their targets. Male bullies are often physically bigger and stronger than their peers. Bullies tend to get in trouble more often and to dislike and do more poorly in school than teens that do not bully others. They are also more likely to fight, drink, and smoke than their peers.

Teens who come from homes where parents provide little emotional support for their children, fail to monitor their activities, or have little involvement in their lives, are at greater risk for engaging in bullying behavior. Parents' discipline styles are also related to bullying behavior. An extremely permissive or excessively harsh approach to discipline can increase the risk of teenage bullying.

Surprisingly, bullies appear to have little difficulty in making friends. Their friends typically share their pro-violence attitudes and problem behaviors (such as drinking and smoking) and may be involved in bullying as well. These friends are often followers who do not initiate bullying but participate in it.

As mentioned above, some teenagers not only bully others but are also the targets of bullies themselves. Like other bullies, they tend to do poorly in school and engage in a number of problem behaviors. They also tend to be socially isolated, with few friends and poor relationships with their classmates.

♣ **It's A Fact!!**

The effects of bullying extend beyond the school years. Bullying may lead to criminal behavior for those who bully and future health and mental health problems for both the bully and the victims.

Source: Excerpted from "Bullying's Long-Term Effects," from the online course titled "The ABCs of Bullying: Addressing, Blocking, and Curbing School Aggression," Substance Abuse and Mental Health Services Administration, U.S. Department of Health and Human Services, May 2004.

Consequences Of Bullying

What are the long-term consequences of bullying behavior?

Bullying is often a warning sign that children and teens are heading for trouble and are at risk for serious violence. Teens (particularly boys) who bully are more likely to engage in other antisocial/delinquent behavior (for example, vandalism, shoplifting, truancy, and drug use) into adulthood. They are four times more likely than nonbullies to be convicted of crimes by age 24, with 60 percent of bullies having at least one criminal conviction.

What can schools do to stop bullying?

Effective programs have been developed to reduce bullying in schools. Research has found that bullying is most likely to occur in schools where there is a lack of adult supervision during breaks, where teachers and students are indifferent to or accept bullying behavior, and where rules against bullying are not consistently enforced.

While approaches that simply crack down on individual bullies are seldom effective, when there is a school-wide commitment to end bullying, it can be reduced by up to 50 percent. One effective approach focuses on changing school and classroom climates by raising awareness about bullying, increasing teacher and parent involvement and supervision, forming clear rules and strong social norms against bullying, and providing support and protection for all students. This approach involves teachers, principals, students, and everyone associated with the school, including janitors, cafeteria workers, and crossing guards. Adults become aware of the extent of bullying at the school, and they involve themselves in changing the situation, rather than looking the other way. Students pledge not to bully other students, to help students who are bullied, and to make a point to include students who are left out.

What You Can Do If You Are Being Bullied

Talk to your parents or an adult you can trust, such as a teacher, school counselor, or principal. Many teens that are targets of bullies do not talk to adults because they feel embarrassed, ashamed, or fearful, and they believe they should be able to handle the problem on their own. Others believe that involving adults will only make the situation worse. While in some cases it is possible to end bullying without adult intervention, in other more extreme cases, it is necessary to involve school officials and even law enforcement. Talk to a trusted adult who can help you develop a plan to end the bullying and provide you with the support you need. If the first adult you approach is not receptive, find another adult who will support and help you.

It is not useful to blame yourself for a bully's actions. You can do a few things, however, that may help if a bully begins to harass you. Do not retaliate against a bully or let the bully see how much he or she has upset you. If bullies know they are getting to you, they are likely to torment you more. If at all possible, stay calm and respond evenly and firmly or else say nothing and walk away. Sometimes you can make a joke, laugh at yourself, and use humor to defuse a situation.

Act confident. Hold your head up, stand up straight, make eye contact, and walk confidently. A bully will be less likely to single you out if you project self-confidence.

Try to make friends with other students. A bully is more likely to leave you alone if you are with your friends. This is especially true if you and your friends stick up for each other.

Avoid situations where bullying can happen. If at all possible, avoid being alone with bullies. If bullying occurs on the way to or from school, you may want to take a different route, leave at a different time, or find others to walk to and from school with. If bullying occurs at school, avoid areas that are isolated or unsupervised by adults, and stick with friends as much as possible.

If necessary, take steps to rebuild your self-confidence. Bullying can affect your self-confidence and belief in yourself. Finding activities you enjoy and are good at can help to restore your self-esteem. Take time to explore new interests and develop new talents and skills. Bullying can also leave you feeling rejected, isolated, and alone. It is important to try to make new friendships with people who share your interests. Consider participating in extracurricular activities or joining a group outside of school, such as an after-school program, church youth group, or sports team.

Do not resort to violence or carry a gun or other weapon. Carrying a gun will not make you safer. Guns often escalate conflicts and increase the chances

Consequences Of Bullying

you will be seriously harmed. You also run the risk that the gun may be turned on you or an innocent person will be hurt, and you may do something in a moment of fear or anger you will regret for the rest of your life. Finally, it is illegal for a teen to carry a handgun; it can lead to criminal charges and arrest.

What You Can Do If Someone Else Is Being Bullied

Refuse to join in if you see someone being bullied. It can be hard to resist if a bully tries to get you to taunt or torment someone, and you may fear the bully will turn on you if you do not participate, but try to stand firm.

Attempt to defuse bullying situations when you see them starting up. For example, try to draw attention away from the targeted person, or take the bully aside and ask him/her to "cool it." Do not place yourself at risk, however.

If you can do so without risk to your own safety, get a teacher, parent, or other responsible adult to come help immediately.

Speak up and/or offer support to bullied teens when you witness bullying. For example, help them up if they have been tripped or knocked down. If you feel you cannot do this at the time, privately support those being hurt with words of kindness or condolence later.

Encourage the bullied teen to talk with parents or a trusted adult. Offer to go with the person if it would help. Tell an adult yourself if the teen is unwilling to report the bullying. If necessary for your safety, do this anonymously.

Chapter 11

How To Make Homework Less Stressful

Do algebra problems 15 through 25. Conjugate the verbs on page 50 of your French workbook. Read pages 12 through 20 of the Shakespeare play, and when you're finished with that, don't forget to fill in the missing chemical symbols on the Periodic Table of Elements worksheet.

Sound like a roster of your homework for the next few nights—or maybe even just for tonight? Homework is a major part of going to school. It's your teachers' way of evaluating how much you understand of what's going on in class, and it helps reinforce important concepts.

Create A Homework Plan

Luckily, there are several things you can do to make homework less work.

First, be sure you understand the assignment. Write it down in your notebook or day planner if you need to, and don't be afraid to ask questions about what's expected. It's much easier to take a minute to ask the teacher during or after class than to struggle to remember later that night. If you want, you

---

About This Chapter: Information in this chapter is from "How to Make Homework Less Work," November 2007, reprinted with permission from www.kidshealth.org. Copyright © 2007 The Nemours Foundation. This information was provided by KidsHealth, one of the largest resources online for medically reviewed health information written for parents, kids, and teens. For more articles like this one, visit www.KidsHealth.org, or www.TeensHealth.org.

can also ask how long the particular homework assignment should take to complete so you can budget your time.

Second, use any extra time you have in school to work on your homework. Many schools have study halls that are specifically designed to allow students to study or get homework done. It's tempting to hang out with friends during study periods or unstructured time, but the more work you can get done in school, the less you'll have to do that night.

Third, pace yourself. If you don't finish your homework during school, think about how much you have left and what else is going on that day, and then budget your time. Most high school students have between one and three hours of homework a night. If it's a heavy homework day and it seems like you've got an assignment in every subject but gym and lunch, you'll need to devote more time to homework.

Watch Where You Work

When you settle down to do homework or to study, where do you do it? Parked in front of the TV? In the kitchen, with the sound of dishes being cleared and your brothers and sisters fighting?

These places may have worked when you were younger and your assignments didn't require as much skill and concentration. But now that you're older, a bedroom, study, or any other room where you can get away from noise and distractions is the best place to get homework done. But don't study on your comfy bed—opt for a desk or table that you can set your computer on and is comfortable to work at. It doesn't need to be large, just big enough to spread out your stuff.

> ✔ **Quick Tip**
> It's a good idea to come up with some kind of homework schedule, especially if you are involved in sports or activities or have an after-school job.

Get To Work

When you start your homework, tackle the hardest assignments first. It's tempting to start with the easy stuff to get it out of the way, but you'll have the most energy and focus when you begin, so it's best to use this mental power on the subjects that are most challenging. Later, when you're more tired, you can focus on the simpler things.

If you get stuck on a problem, try to figure it out as best you can—but don't obsess and spend too much time on it because this can mess up your homework schedule for the rest of the night. If you need to, ask an adult or older sibling for help, or call or email a classmate for advice. But don't pick someone you'll be up all night chatting with, or you'll never get it done.

Take A Break

Most people's attention spans aren't very long, so take some breaks while doing your homework. Sitting for too long without stretching or relaxing will make you less productive than if you stop every so often. Taking a 15-minute break every hour is a good idea for most people. (But if you're really concentrating, wait until it's a good time to stop.)

Once your homework is done, you can check over it if you have extra time. Be sure to put it safely away in your backpack—there's nothing worse than having a completed assignment that you can't find the next morning or that gets ruined by a careless brother or sister. (And no teacher still believes that "chewed by the dog" line—even when it's true.) Now you're free to hang out.

Get Help When You Need It

Sometimes even though you're paying attention in class, studying for tests, and doing your homework, certain classes seem too hard. Although you may hope that things will get easier or that the explanation to the geometry theorems will magically appear in your dreams, most of the time this doesn't happen.

What does happen for many people is that they work harder and harder as they fall further and further behind. Naturally, this makes them hate a class and everything to do with it. If you need extra help, the most important thing to know is that there's nothing weird or embarrassing about it. No one is expected to understand everything, and people have very different learning styles.

The first place to turn for help is your teacher. He or she may be able to work with you before or after school and explain things more clearly. But what if you don't feel comfortable with your teacher? If you're in a big enough school, there may be other teachers who teach the same subject. Speak to a guidance counselor or to the other teacher directly, and you may be in luck. Sometimes it just helps to have someone new explain something in a different way.

You may also be able to get some help from another student. If there's someone you like who's a good student, think about asking that person if you can study together. This might help because you'll be hearing the information from the perspective of one of your peers. However, keep in mind that this might not get you the results you need. Lots of people understand something perfectly without being able to explain it.

Another option for extra help is a tutor, either after school, on weekends, or in the evening. You'll need to talk to an adult about this because it costs money to hire a tutor. Tutors sometimes come to your home, but there are also tutoring centers across the country. A tutor may have broad knowledge of many things or may be trained in just one subject. Tutors work with you one on one, helping review and further explain things taught in the classroom. The advantage of having a tutor is that it gives you the opportunity to ask questions directly and work at your own pace.

If you're interested in a tutor, check the yellow pages of your phone book or get a referral from a teacher, or friend, or classmate who has a tutor. And if you live in or near a town with a college or university, you may find tutors there. Often college students will tutor high school students in their areas of study to help cover the costs of school.

Chapter 12

Test Anxiety

You've participated in class, done all of your homework, studied hard, and you think you have a grip on the material. But then the day of the test comes. Suddenly, you blank out, freeze up, zone out, or feel so nervous that you can't get it together to respond to those questions you knew the answers to just last night.

If this sounds like you, you may have a case of test anxiety—that nervous feeling that people sometimes get when they're about to take a test.

It's pretty normal to feel a little nervous and stressed before a test. Just about everyone does. And a touch of nervous anticipation can actually help you get revved and keep you at peak performance while you're taking the test. But for some people, this normal anxiety is more intense. The nervousness they feel before a test can be so strong that it interferes with their concentration or performance.

What is test anxiety?

Test anxiety is actually a type of performance anxiety—a feeling someone might have in a situation where performance really counts or when the

> About This Chapter: Information in this chapter is from "Test Anxiety," February 2007, reprinted with permission from www.kidshealth.org. Copyright © 2007 The Nemours Foundation. This information was provided by KidsHealth, one of the largest resources online for medically reviewed health information written for parents, kids, and teens. For more articles like this one, visit www.KidsHealth.org, or www.TeensHealth.org.

pressure's on to do well. For example, a person might experience performance anxiety when he or she is about to try out for the school play, sing a solo on stage, get into position at the pitcher's mound, step onto the platform in a diving meet, or go into an important interview.

Like other situations in which a person might feel performance anxiety, test anxiety can bring on "butterflies," a stomachache, or a tension headache. Some people might feel shaky, sweaty, or feel their heart beating quickly as they wait for the test to be given out. A student with really strong test anxiety may even feel like he or she might pass out or throw up.

Test anxiety is not the same as doing poorly on a certain test because your mind is on something else. Most people know that having other things on their minds—such as a breakup or the death of someone close—can also interfere with their concentration and prevent them from doing their best on a test.

What causes it?

All anxiety is a reaction to anticipating something stressful. Like other anxiety reactions, test anxiety affects the body and the mind. When you're under stress, your body releases the hormone adrenaline, which prepares it for danger (you may hear this referred to as the "fight or flight" reaction). That's what causes the physical symptoms, such as sweating, a pounding heart, and rapid breathing. These sensations might be mild or intense.

Focusing on the bad things that could happen also fuels test anxiety. For example, someone worrying about doing poorly might think thoughts like, "What if I forget everything I know?" or "What if the test is too hard?" Too many thoughts like these leave no mental space for thinking about the test questions. People with test anxiety can also feel stressed out by their physical reaction and think things like "What if I throw up?" or "Oh no, my hands are shaking."

Just like other types of anxiety, test anxiety can create a vicious circle. The more a person focuses on the bad things that could happen, the stronger the feeling of anxiety becomes. This makes the person feel worse and, because his or her head is full of distracting thoughts and fears, it can increase the possibility that the person will do worse on the test.

Test Anxiety

Who's likely to have test anxiety?

People who worry a lot or who are perfectionists are more likely to have trouble with test anxiety. People with these traits sometimes find it hard to accept mistakes they might make or to get anything less than a perfect score. In this way, even without meaning to, they might really pressure themselves. Test anxiety is bound to thrive in a situation like this.

Students who aren't prepared for tests, but who care about doing well, are also likely to experience test anxiety. If you know you're not prepared, it's a no-brainer to realize that you'll be worried about doing poorly. People can feel unprepared for tests for several reasons: They may not have studied enough; they may find the material difficult; or perhaps they feel tired because they didn't get enough sleep the night before.

What can you do?

Test anxiety can be a real problem when someone is so stressed out over a test that he or she can't get past the nervousness to focus on the test questions and do his or her best work. Feeling ready to meet the challenge, though, can keep test anxiety at a manageable level.

> ♣ **It's A Fact!!**
>
> *Can sleep help you do better on tests?*
>
> A recent study found that people who got eight hours of sleep before taking a math test were nearly three times more likely to figure out the problem than people who stayed awake all night.

Use a little stress to your advantage. Stress is your body's warning mechanism. It's a signal that helps you prepare for something important that's about to happen. So use it to your advantage. Instead of reacting to the stress by dreading, complaining, or fretting about the test with friends, take an active approach. Let stress remind you to study well in advance of a test. Chances are, you'll keep your stress from spinning out of control. After all, nobody ever feels stressed out by thoughts that they might do well on a test.

Ask for help. Although a little test anxiety can be a good thing, an overdose of it is another story entirely. If sitting for a test gets you so stressed out that your mind goes blank and causes you to miss answers that you know, then your level of test anxiety probably needs some attention. Your teacher, your school guidance counselor, or a tutor can be useful resources to talk to if you always get extreme test anxiety.

Be prepared. Some students think that going to class is all it should take to learn and do well on tests. But there's much more to learning than just hoping to soak everything up in class. That's why good study habits and skills are so important—and why no amount of cramming or studying the night before a test can take the place of the deeper level of learning that happens over time with regular study.

Many students find that their test anxiety is reduced when they start to study better or more regularly. It makes sense—the more you know the material, the more confident you'll feel. Having confidence going into a test means you expect to do well. When you expect to do well, you'll be able to relax into a test after the normal first-moment jitters pass.

Watch what you're thinking. If expecting to do well on a test can help you relax, what about when people expect they won't do well? Watch out for any negative messages you might be sending yourself about the test. They can contribute to your anxiety.

If you find yourself thinking negative thoughts ("I'm never any good at taking tests," or "It's going to be terrible if I do badly on this test"), replace them with positive messages. Not unrealistic positive messages, of course, but ones that are practical and true, such as "I've studied hard, and I know the material, so I'm ready to do the best I can." (Of course, if you haven't studied, this message won't help.)

Accept mistakes. Another thing you can do is to learn to keep mistakes in perspective—especially if you're a perfectionist or you tend to be hard on yourself. Everyone makes mistakes, and you may have even heard teachers or coaches refer to mistakes as "learning opportunities." Learning to tolerate small failures and mistakes—like that one problem you got wrong in the math pop quiz—is a valuable skill.

Take care of yourself. It can help to learn ways to calm yourself down and get centered when you're tense or anxious. For some people, this might mean

Test Anxiety

learning a simple breathing exercise. Practicing breathing exercises regularly (when you're not stressed out) helps your body see these exercises as a signal to relax.

And, of course, taking care of your health—such as getting enough sleep, exercise, and healthy eats before a test—can help keep your mind working at its best.

> ### ☞ Remember!!
> Everything takes time and practice, and learning to beat test anxiety is no different. Although it won't go away overnight, facing and dealing with test anxiety will help you learn stress management, which can prove to be a valuable skill in many situations besides taking tests.

Chapter 13
Young, Gifted, And Stressed

I used to think that it helped someone who felt stressed to be told to "chill out" or that "everything will seem better in the morning." On reflection, however, I realized that when someone uttered those words to me, they did not help at all. By downplaying the raw feeling of powerlessness that often accompanies stress, we merely discount the reality of this corrosive condition. Nothing changes; the stress remains.

And who knows stress better than gifted kids? They are supposed to know it all and be it all: make perfect grades, show exemplary behavior, and set and reach ambitious goals. Just imagine the reaction when the school's top achiever gets an average score on the SAT, or the kid who appears to have it all together breaks down when his girlfriend dumps him. The people who matter most—parents, teachers, classmates—often reveal shock or disappointment that "someone so smart" fell short of the mark or had an emotional reaction that would be "natural" for anyone else.

Joanne Rand Whitmore has proposed that two overlooked qualities of gifted people are super-sensitivity and perfectionism. Ironically, these traits appear in both high and low achievers. The super-sensitivity often shows itself in acute awareness of others' expectations and in profound disappointment when these

> About This Chapter: Information in this chapter is reprinted with permission from the Duke Gifted Letter (www.dukegiftedletter.com). Copyright © 2003 Duke University Talent Identification Program.

standards are not met. Its corollary, perfectionism, is the gifted student's attempt to avoid this disappointment by not allowing himself or herself to be less than number one. The perceptive student realizes that it is often preferable to fail outright by not turning in homework than to fail to attain maximum success on that homework—say, by earning only a B—even after giving it the most strenuous effort.

Although there are no easy solutions to the problem of stress, there are ways to lessen the toll it takes.

Have Fun With Stress

I often ask my students to write down all of the things in life that cause them stress: relationships, grades, their physical appearance, their athletic performance, and so on. Then I ask them to wad up the paper on which they have just written and throw it at me. (They love this part.) Why does that last part feel so good? I ask. Because, they say, it allows them to do something with their stress, if only temporarily, by tossing it away in some concrete action. Next, we compile lists of things we can do when stress is at a peak, from listening to music to taking deep breaths to stroking a cat to screaming into a pillow. The students copy these lists and keep them in their notebooks. This accomplishes three things. First, it shows them that the stresses they feel are common. Second, it gives them some realistic, though temporary, ways to manage stress. Third, it begins a discussion of such time-tested techniques as doing the hardest project first, limiting the time spent on a project, and taking a stretch break every 30 minutes or so.

☞ Remember!!

It is important for gifted children, regardless of their abilities, and for their parents to bear in mind that few people are exceptional at everything they turn their hand to. Rather, most people succeed by identifying their strengths and weaknesses, making the most of the one, and finding ways to compensate for the other.

Source: Excerpted with permission from the Duke Gifted Letter (www.dukegiftedletter.com). Copyright © 2003 Duke University Talent Identification Program.

Review The Intensities That Gifted People Feel

The loneliest feeling in the world is to think that you are the first and only person to feel intense pressure. There are emotional commonalities among the gifted and all famous people have made mistakes along the way.

Confront The Sources Of Stress

Students who feel that their parents consider them failures because they have made only the junior varsity team, or who believe that their algebra teacher expects them to know everything, even without instruction, need to have a heart-to-heart talk. Role-playing in a school setting (preferably with older gifted students playing the part of the adult) can suggest strategies that students need to face their "accuser" in a non-threatening way.

It is probably impossible not be stressed to some degree. Whether the demon we fear is across the globe or in our psyche, the stress it causes is still stress. By addressing the reality of everyday stressors and then focusing on some of the ones that tend to be more visible in the gifted, we open a door to dialogue about this vital issue. That in itself is a relief.

—James R. Delisle, PhD

James R. Delisle is professor of education at Kent State University and a part-time teacher of gifted students in Twinsburg, Ohio.

Chapter 14

Sports Pressure And Competition

Most people play a sport for the thrill of having fun with others who share the same interest, right? But it's not always fun and games. Most student athletes who play competitive sports have had thoughts that go like this at one time or another: "Man, I can't believe I let the ball in the goal, and I know from the look in coach's eyes he wasn't happy."

There can be a ton of pressure in high school sports. A lot of the time it comes from the feeling that a parent or coach expects you to always win. But sometimes it comes from inside, too. Some players are just really hard on themselves. And individual situations can add to the stress. Maybe there's a recruiter from your number one college scouting you on the sidelines. Whatever the cause, the pressure to win can sometimes stress you to the point where you just don't know how to have fun anymore. Perhaps it could even be the reason why you haven't been playing as well lately.

How Can Stress Affect Sports Performance?

Stress is a feeling that's created when we react to particular events. It's the body's way of rising to a challenge and preparing to meet a tough situation

> About This Chapter: Information in this chapter is from "Handling Sports Pressure and Competition," August 2007, reprinted with permission from www.kidshealth.org. Copyright © 2007 The Nemours Foundation. This information was provided by KidsHealth, one of the largest resources online for medically reviewed health information written for parents, kids, and teens. For more articles like this one, visit www.KidsHealth.org, or www.TeensHealth.org.

with focus, strength, stamina, and heightened alertness. A little stress or the right kind of positive stress can help keep you on your toes, ready to rise to a challenge.

The events that provoke stress are called stressors, and they cover a whole range of situations—everything from outright danger to stepping up to take the foul shot that could win the game. Stress can also be a response to change or anticipation of something that's about to happen—good or bad. People can feel stress over positive challenges, like making the varsity team, as well as negative ones.

Distress is a bad type of stress that arises when you must adapt to too many negative demands. Suppose you had a fight with a close friend last night, you forgot your homework this morning, and you're playing in a tennis match this afternoon. You try to get psyched for the game but can't. You've hit stress overload. Continuous struggling with too much stress can exhaust your energy and drive.

Eustress is the good type of stress that stems from the challenge of taking part in something that you enjoy but have to work hard for. Eustress pumps you up, providing a healthy spark for any task you undertake.

What Can I Do To Ease Pressure?

When the demands of competition start to get to you, try these relaxation techniques:

- **Deep Breathing:** Find a quiet place to sit down. Inhale slowly through your nose, drawing air deep into your lungs. Hold your breath for about five seconds, then release it slowly. Repeat the exercise five times.

✎ What's It Mean?

Distress: A bad type of stress that arises when you must adapt to too many negative demands.

Eustress: The good type of stress that stems from the challenge of taking part in something that you enjoy but have to work hard for.

Sports Pressure And Competition

- **Muscle Relaxation:** Contract (flex) a group of muscles tightly. Keep them tensed for about five seconds, then release. Repeat the exercise five times, selecting different muscle groups.

- **Visualization:** Close your eyes and picture a peaceful place or an event from your past. Recall the beautiful sights and the happy sounds. Imagine stress flowing away from your body. You can also visualize success. People who advise competitive players often recommend that they imagine themselves completing a pass, making a shot, or scoring a goal over and over. Then on game day, you can recall your stored images to help calm nerves and boost self-confidence.

- **Mindfulness:** Watch out for negative thoughts. Whether you're preparing for a competition or coping with a defeat, repeat to yourself: "I learn from my mistakes." "I'm in control of my feelings." "I can make this goal."

When sports become too stressful, get away from the pressure. Go to a movie or hang out with friends. Put your mind on something completely different.

How Can I Keep Stress In Check?

If sports make you so nervous that you get headaches, become nauseated, or can't concentrate on other things, you're experiencing symptoms of unhealthy, potentially chronic (which means long-lasting and continuous) stress. Don't keep such stress bottled up inside you; suppressing your emotions might mean bigger health troubles for you later on.

Talk about your concerns with a friend. Simply sharing your feelings can ease your anxiety. Sometimes it may help to get an adult's perspective—someone who has dealt with stress over and over like your coach or fitness instructor. Here are some other things you can do to cope with stress:

- Treat your body right. Eat well and get a good night's sleep, especially before games where the pressure's on.
- Learn and practice relaxation techniques, like those described in the previous section.

- Get some type of physical activity other than the sport you're involved in. Take a walk, ride your bike, and get completely away from the sport that's stressing you out.

- Don't try to be perfect—everyone flubs a shot or messes up from time to time (so don't expect your teammates to be perfect either). Forgive yourself, remind yourself of all your great shots, and move on.

It's possible that some anxiety stems only from uncertainty. Meet privately with your coach or instructor. Ask for clarification if his or her expectations seem vague or inconsistent. Although most instructors do a good job of fostering athletes' physical and mental development, you may need to be the one who opens the lines of communication. You may also want to talk with your parents or another adult family member.

If you're feeling completely overscheduled and out of control, review your options on what you can let go. It's a last resort, but if you're no longer enjoying your sport, it may be time to find one that's less stressful. Chronic stress isn't fun—and fun is what sports are all about.

Recognizing when you need guidance to steer yourself out of a stressful situation doesn't represent weakness; it's a sign of courage and wisdom. Don't stop looking for support until you've found it.

Enjoy The Game

Winning is exhilarating. But losing and some amount of stress are part of almost any sports program—as they are in life. Sports are about enhancing self-esteem, building social skills, and developing a sense of community. And above all, sports are about having fun.

Chapter 15

Handling Peer Pressure

The very first thing you should do when kids are trying to talk you into doing something is think. Too many times, kids get into trouble by just going along with the crowd. Your generation is no different from any generation before you. There is something about the teenage years that make kids think they are invincible, that nothing can hurt them. And, to many teenagers, the worst four-letter word adults can say is "don't."

Here's a list of suggestions that might help:

1. **Think about what the group is asking you to do.** Is it wrong? Is it illegal? Why are you tempted to go along? Is it status? Are you afraid to "lose face?" Are you too weak to stand up and say, "I think this is wrong?" Do you know these people well enough to trust them?

If you have an uneasy feeling in your stomach, something is probably wrong. Use the skills of looking and listening. If a group of kids is talking about surrounding a carload of kids from another school in a parking lot, it's probably not because they're going to invite them to a picnic. Regardless of what they tell you, don't act on impulse. Think about the real message behind their words.

> About This Chapter: Information in this chapter is from *What's Right for Me? Making Good Choices in Relationships*, by Ron Herron and Val J. Peter, published by Boys Town Press, copyright © 1998. Reprinted with permission. Despite the older date of this document, the information presented is still appropriate for readers seeking to understand this issue.

And think about your motivation. If you rely too much on the group for emotional support and acceptance, it's likely that you will give in to peer pressure. If you're always looking for approval from your friends and are afraid to stand up for yourself, it's likely that you will be easily influenced by what they say.

2. **Think about what could happen.** It's difficult to think about negative consequences when a friend is raving about how much fun you're going to have. It's also hard to put up with the sarcasm and put-down that saying "no" can trigger. Other kids can be relentless when they want to goad you into going along.

That's a good time to stop and think about what could happen. Ignore all the statements like, "Hey, everybody does it. What's wrong with you?" or "There's no way we will get caught." Those aren't good reasons to go along. Think of what could happen to you or your reputation. You have to make a promise to yourself to do not only what's legally right, but also what's morally right. Your conscience can be the biggest consequence of all. Stick to your values. If you know you're not going to worry about what you did, say "no" right away. A few minutes or hours of "fun" can lead to countless days, even years, of trouble. Make a good decision and you'll feel a lot better about yourself.

3. **Decide beforehand what you're going to do or say.** You can sometimes predict when you might be pressured to do something. You know what's going on in your school. You know who is doing what. And you know the kids you shouldn't hang around with. Get out of situations in which you know you could be pressured.

Other situations are not so predictable. They happen because somebody

> ✔ **Quick Tip**
> Think ahead. Don't put yourself in an unsafe or hard situation. You are less likely to have to say no if you hang out with friends who don't smoke, drink, or do drugs, and make other good choices.
>
> Source: Excerpted from *Teen Survival Guide: Health Tips for On-the-go Girls*, GirlsHealth.gov, U.S. Department of Health and Human Services, Office on Women's Health, June 2007.

Handling Peer Pressure

comes up with a spur-of-the-moment idea, and you're expected to give an immediate answer. Even then, you can have a valid reason for not going along. Think ahead about how you can respond so that you stay out of trouble. If you don't have something in mind to say, you're likely to give in. This is one time when it's okay to think of yourself instead of others.

4. **Think of your options.** Basically, there are four things you can do.
   - Say "yes."
   - Say "no."
   - Compromise.
   - Delay.

Say "yes." This is without a doubt the easiest answer to give. But often it's also the worst. If you haven't taken the time to think things through, you could be making a big mistake.

Say "no." On the other hand, this is the hardest answer to give, but one that may be the best for you. There are some decisions that you don't even have to hesitate about. When your friends tell you there's a keg party, or that they're going to mess up some kids from another school, or that they're going to do something that's destructive, harmful, or illegal, then your answer should be automatic. "No" is the only right answer.

When you decide that "no" is the best answer, the hard part is sticking with it. You will have to be assertive whenever you refuse to go along. Let your friends know you mean what you say. If you have a good reason, give it. Usually, a good reason is one that involves some type of responsibility. For example, "I have to be home on time." "I promised Dad I'd mow the lawn." "My family's going out to eat tonight." "My parents would ground me for a year if they found out." Just because it doesn't sound like fun to most of the group, doesn't mean it isn't a good reason.

And even if you give a good reason, it doesn't mean that other kids will accept it right away. Some people will try to keep the pressure on. There are ways to turn them down without turning them off. You can thank them for asking you, tell them you appreciate their friendship, tell them you hope they have a good time, or empathize with whatever their problem is. But when you realize that a refusal is necessary, just say "no." Stick with what you know is right—calmly, firmly, and finally.

Compromise. When someone suggests doing something you're concerned about, you might be able to come up with an option that isn't as risky. You could say, for example, "Why don't we go see a movie instead?" Compromise is a "best-of-both-worlds" situation. You can still be with the group, but not join a harmful activity. It doesn't always work, but it's worth a try. Maybe you can help your friends look at situations more carefully.

Compromise requires the ability to think through and solve problems. Practice your ability to analyze problems and come up with reasonable alternatives.

Delay. Maybe you can wait until you see what unfolds. Saying things like, "I might be there later," or "I'll catch up with you in a little while," gives you a chance to sort through the others' real intentions and helps you think more clearly about what you've been asked to do.

If you haven't already faced the lure of another teenager wanting you to do something "exciting"—which usually means dangerous, harmful, or illegal—you probably will. Kids will try to get you to do something you shouldn't. And they will be very convincing. You may think you're not strong enough to resist their pressure. But you can be as strong as you want to be.

☞ Remember!!

You always have options. You shouldn't be forced to do anything that is illegal, immoral, or harmful to others in order to gain acceptance or respect. "No" is sometimes the only right answer, and it should jump out of your mouth. Other decisions require some thought. That's when you should give yourself time to think. A quick decision may be something you will regret later. Think things through before you make a decision, and you're more likely to make a good one.

Source: Excerpted from *What's Right for Me? Making Good Choices in Relationships*, by Ron Herron and Val J. Peter, published by Boys Town Press, copyright © 1998. Reprinted with permission.

Handling Peer Pressure

5. **Stick to your values and morals.** Don't compromise the good things you believe in. More important, let other people know exactly what they are. There will be times when you will be tempted to do something wrong. You might think it's worth the risk because doing it can provide immediate pleasure or popularity. But you need to think about what will happen over time. Not only are there external consequences, like getting in trouble at school, at home, or with the police, but there are internal consequences as well. In other words, there are some things you shouldn't do just because they're wrong. If you give in, you have to live with the guilt or shame of having done something you shouldn't have.

   When kids try to change the good things you believe in, you have to stand up for yourself. Hold on to the values and morals your family has passed on to you. Don't let anybody sweet-talk or pressure you out of them.

6. **Talk with close friends.** Express your feelings to your friends. Tell them how you wanted to give in to the pressure and how hard it was to resist. They can help. They probably have been in similar situations. Did they do the right thing? What did they learn from their experience?

7. **Trust your instincts.** If you feel uncomfortable, something is probably wrong. Tell whomever your with to cool it for awhile until you can figure out what you're feeling. Stick to the boundaries you have set for yourself.

8. **Be assertive.** Learn how to express your ideas and feelings without blowing up or giving in. If you are in a situation that could be harmful to you, learn how to stand your ground firmly and convincingly. Learn how to get out of negative situations (or avoid them altogether). Sometimes the answer isn't always "yes" or "no." It might be "maybe later," "Let me think about it," or "I'll wait and see."

9. **Talk to your mom or dad.** Let them know what's going on in your life. Tell them the good things that happened or the problems you encountered. Some teens are afraid of what their parents' reactions might be. And sometimes there are good reasons why they feel that way. But most parents want to know where you went and what you did because they really care.

If you have trouble talking calmly to your parents, now is the time to learn how. Learn to talk in a mature and unemotional way. Don't allow yourself to get upset when they ask questions or give you some advice. Keep your cool. That's the only mature way to proceed.

Now could be the time to change some things in their behavior, too. If they get upset when you tell them the truth, you have to train them to stay calm. Yes, that's right. It can be done. Reason with them. Set an example for them. It may not work the first time, so don't expect too much right away. But you have the power and ability to change their behavior and create a new adult relationship with them. This takes effort on your part, but it can be wonderful when it happens.

Tell them you want them to see into your world but do not want them to jump in and solve all of your problems. Let them know you will accept their advice and counsel, but you want to handle problems on your own. Assure them that if things get too tough, or if you can't handle a problem, you will come to them for help.

You may find that your parents understand and are able to help more than you think. Sharing your world with your parents can help you overcome some of the obstacles. Parents face peer pressure, too. And they have made mistakes. Their experiences can help you learn how to deal with the pressures you face.

☞ Remember!!

You should not be forced to do something you know is wrong. There will be conflict and confusion at times. Friends (or people you thought were friends) may put more pressure on you later, say sarcastic or nasty things, or try to make you feel out of it. Figure out how you're going to respond to these people and their reasoning, and then follow through. True friends will understand.

Source: Excerpted from *What's Right for Me? Making Good Choices in Relationships*, by Ron Herron and Val J. Peter, published by Boys Town Press, copyright © 1998. Reprinted with permission.

Handling Peer Pressure

10. **Talk to a trusted adult.** Maybe you don't think you know an adult you can trust. Well, they're out there. Don't be afraid to ask for help. There has to be an aunt or uncle, grandparent, cousin, counselor, teacher, coach, or someone else with whom you can build a trusting relationship. There are times when you may feel powerless and when you just want some outside advice. An adult may come up with solutions you didn't consider.

Chapter 16

Relationships Can Be Stressful

Friendships

Friendships can be tough sometimes. You may be making new friends while still trying to keep old friends. It can also be hard to know what to do when you do not agree with a friend. Keep in mind, you can have a good friendship and still fight sometimes.

Tips For Handling A Fight With A Friend

- In a healthy friendship, you should not be afraid of losing a friend because you say "no." Good friends should respect your right to say no and not give you a hard time. You should show your friends the same respect when they say no to you.

- If you and your friend fight about something, it does not mean that you have an unhealthy relationship. You will not always agree with what your friend has to say. But you should always respect one another's ideas. As long as you and your friend listen to what the other has to say, you should be able to work through a fight.

About This Chapter: Information in this chapter is from "Friendships," "Healthy Relationships," "Help! My Parents/Guardians Don't Like My Friends(s)," and "Dating," GirlsHealth.gov, sponsored by the National Women's Health Information Center, U.S. Department of Health and Human Services, May 2007.

- The relationships you have will help you learn a lot about yourself. You will learn about the kind of friends you want to have and the kind of friend you want to be.

Helping A Friend In Need

Are you worried about a friend who is not eating? A friend who is smoking or drinking? Or maybe a friend who is having trouble at home? You can listen and give advice, but your friend's problems may be more than you can handle alone. Do not be afraid to tell a trusted adult, such as a parent/guardian, teacher, or school nurse. Even though your friend may get mad at you for telling an adult, it is the only way to protect your friend's health.

Peer Pressure

Peer pressure is when people try to pressure you to do something you usually would not do or stop doing something that you normally would do. People give in to peer pressure for many reasons. They may worry about what their friends will think, not know how to say no, or fear being left out. Some friends may pressure you to do something because "everyone else does it," such as making fun of someone, using alcohol or drugs, or smoking. The best thing to do is say, "No, thanks." or "I don't want to." Keep in mind, you are always in charge of what you do and do not do, and it can help to talk with your parents/guardians about how to handle pressures that may come up.

> ✔ **Quick Tip**
>
> *Seven Ways To Know If Your Friends Really Care About You*
>
> - They want you to be happy.
> - They listen and care about what you have to say.
> - They are happy for you when you do well.
> - They say they are sorry when they make a mistake.
> - They do not expect you to be perfect.
> - They give you advice in a caring way.
> - They keep personal things between the two of you.
>
> Source: Excerpted from "Friendships," GirlsHealth.gov.

Relationships Can Be Stressful

Popularity

There are lots of things that you and your friends may do to fit in. It may be having the right clothes or being friends with the cool kids. It is normal to want to be liked by others, but it is more important to focus on what matters to you. Having lots of friends and dressing like everyone else may seem important right now, but try to focus on being yourself and having real friends who care about you.

Bullying

Friendships are very important to teens, especially when it comes to having a group of people to hang out with. Sometimes teens compete with each other for friends. When this happens, some teens may leave others out of a circle of friends or even bully them in more open ways. Being left out of a group can really hurt someone's feelings, so think about how what you do makes other people feel. You would want others to include you and treat you nicely.

Cliques

A clique is a small group of friends that is very picky about who can and cannot join the group. While it is nice to have a close group of friends, being on the outside of a clique may not be fun. Teens in cliques often leave out other teens on purpose. They may bully teens that are not "cool enough." If you are being picked on, try to make friends with new people who care about you. Keep in mind, it is the quality or value of the friendship that counts, not how many friends you have. If you are leaving someone else out, think about how you would feel if you were the one being left out.

There can be a lot of peer pressure in cliques. You may feel like you need to do things like drink or do drugs to be part of the gang. Keep in mind, you always have the right to say no. Real friends will respect that. You also have the right to make new friends.

Making New Friends

It can be really tough when you are meeting a whole bunch of new people at once if you are new at school. You may feel shy or embarrassed. You may feel like you do not have anything to say, but the other person likely feels the same way. Half the battle is feeling strong enough to talk to new people, and it will help to just be yourself.

It can also be tough to start hanging around new people at your same school. You may need to do this if you have friends who have been getting into trouble for things like ditching school or doing drugs. Even though you may care about these friends, you have to look out for yourself and make smart choices for you. If you have a hard time breaking away from old friends who may be bad news, talk to a trusted adult for help on how to do your own thing.

Sometimes, you may just want to branch out and meet new people. This is totally okay and you can still keep your old friends. It is easy to hang out with people you have known a long time or have a lot in common with, but it can also be fun to spend time with new people.

Healthy Relationships

What Makes A Relationship Healthy?

Healthy relationships are fun and make you feel good about yourself. You can have a healthy relationship with anyone in your life—family, friends, and the people you date. Relationships take time and care to make them healthy. The relationships you have as a teen are a special part of your life and will teach you good lessons about who you are.

Communication And Sharing

The most important part of any healthy relationship is communication. Communication means that you are able to share things about yourself and your feelings, and you listen to what the other person shares. This can happen by talking, e-mailing, writing, or even using body language. When you are talking to someone, look him or her in the eye to show you are listening.

When you have healthy communication, you both feel at ease. You can share your feelings with the other person. You know that he or she will be there to listen, support you, and keep personal things that you share private. In healthy relationships, people do not lie.

Respect And Trust

Fights still happen in healthy relationships, but you stay calm and talk about how you feel. Talking calmly helps you see the real reason you are not getting along. This makes it easier to figure out how to fix the problem. In healthy relationships, working through problems often makes the relationship stronger. People feel good about one another when they work through tough times rather than give up too easily.

Self-Esteem

Feeling good about yourself—having good self-esteem—and knowing that you deserve a healthy relationship is also very important.

How Do I Know That I Have A Healthy Relationship With Someone?

- You feel good about yourself when you are with that person.
- You think that both people work hard to treat the other person well.
- You feel safe around the other person.
- You like being with the other person.
- You feel that you can trust him or her with your secrets.

Keep in mind, it takes time and effort to build the trust and respect you need for a healthy relationship.

♣ It's A Fact!!

It can be common for parents/guardians and teens to run into conflict about friendships. Parents/guardians sometimes worry that their teen is hanging out with the wrong crowd.

Source: Excerpted from "Help! My Parents/Guardians Don't Like My Friend(s)," GirlsHealth.gov.

Help! My Parents/Guardians Don't Like My Friend(s)!

What Are Some Reasons Parents/Guardians Give For Not Liking Their Teen's Friends?

Parents/guardians may be concerned about things like drugs, alcohol, sex, skipping school, missing curfew, body piercings, or tattoos. Some parents/guardians may think body piercings and tattoos are signs of other behaviors, like drinking or smoking.

What Can A Teen Do If Her Parents/Guardians Don't Like Her Friend(s)?

It depends on the type of relationship the teen has with her parents/guardians.

Some parents/guardians and teens can talk to each other and work through problems. Both parties trust each other, and they know that they can work through things. In this case, the teen can sit down and talk with her parents/guardians and try to work things out.

Sometimes, the relationship is already strained. In this case, it can be helpful to bring in an outside person to help resolve things or mediate. This could be a school counselor, school social worker, clergy member, family doctor, therapist, mentor, coach, or favorite aunt.

Dating

Dating relationships can be a fun and exciting part of your life. They can also be confusing, especially if dating is new to you. Once you know that the person that you like also likes you, you may not know what to do next. You can start by learning about what makes a dating relationship healthy and safe.

When Do Teens Start Dating?

There is no best age for teens to start dating. Every person will be ready for a dating relationship at a different time. Different families may have their own rules about dating, too. When you decide to start a dating relationship, it should be because you care about someone and not because other

Relationships Can Be Stressful

people are dating. A dating relationship is a special chance to get to know someone, and it should happen only when you are really ready and your parents/guardians are okay with it.

What Is A Healthy Dating Relationship?

Healthy dating relationships should start with the same things that healthy friendships start with—good communication, honesty, and respect. Dating relationships are a little different because they may include physical ways of showing you care, like hugging, kissing, or holding hands. You may find yourself wanting to spend all of your time with your crush, but it is important to spend some time apart, too. This will let you have a healthy relationship with your crush and with your friends and family at the same time.

What If I Feel Pressure To Do Something I Do Not Want To Do?

You should never feel pressured to do something that you do not want to do. Your crush should always respect your right to say no to anything that does not feel right. Talk to your crush ahead of time about what you will and will not do.

Tips For Having Healthy And Safe Relationships

- Get to know a person by talking on the phone or at school before you go out for the first time.

- Go out with a group of friends to a public place the first few times you go out.

- Plan fun activities like going to the movies, the mall, on a picnic, or for a walk.

- Tell the other person what you feel okay doing. Also, tell the person what time your parents/guardians want you to be home.

- Tell at least one friend and your parents/guardians who you are going out with and where you are going. Also tell them how to reach you.

> **Remember!!**
> Respecting your right to say no means that your date will stop if you say "no."
>
> Source: Excerpted from "Dating," GirlsHealth.gov.

Communication, trust, and respect are key to healthy relationships. Healthy relationships make you feel good about who you are and safe with the other person. Feel good about yourself and get to know what makes you happy. The more you love yourself, the easier it will be to find healthy relationships.

Chapter 17

Dealing With Pressure To Have Sex

The pressure is on, isn't it? Pressure about grades, after-school jobs, chores at home, what your friends want you to do, and what your parents want you to do. The pressure is also on big time when it comes to having sex or doing other sexual things before you are ready. It may seem like everybody around you is having sex. The truth is, everybody may be talking about sex, but not every person your age is having sex. And what about what you see on television, in the movies, and even online? Sex may be everywhere, but they do not show you the whole story. You often do not see what can happen after sex—having a baby before being ready and getting sexually transmitted diseases (STDs) that can hurt you, such as herpes, chlamydia, and human immunodeficiency virus (HIV). Remember, it is okay not to have sex.

What You Do Not Often Hear About Sex

- Having sex before you are ready can make you feel badly about yourself.
- If someone wants to break up because you will not have sex, then that person is not good enough for you.
- Having sex at a young age can make it more likely to get a STD.

About This Chapter: Information in this chapter is from "Dealing With Pressure To Have Sex," GirlsHealth.gov, sponsored by the National Women's Health Information Center, U.S. Department of Health and Human Services, October 2007.

- Dating or hooking up with someone who is older can cause more pressure to have sex before you are ready.
- Condoms will lower your chances of getting pregnant or getting an STD such as HIV, but they do not protect you from all STDs. Birth control pills can also stop pregnancy, but they do not protect against any STDs. Neither method can stop you from getting hurt emotionally.

Things That Put The Pressure On To Have Sex

- Worry over what your friends might think about you.
- Thinking your friends are doing it.
- The person you are hooking up with wants to.
- It is easier to give in than explain why you do not want to.
- Thinking you need to have sex in order to show you care or be closer.

Ways You Can Avoid Pressure To Have Sex

- Spend time with friends who also think it is okay not to have sex.
- Date different people and hang out with different groups of friends.
- Go out with a group instead of only the person you are hanging out with.
- Have your friends over to your house and make sure they meet your parents/caregivers. You can be in control anywhere you go, but your own turf can be more comfortable.
- Carry a cell phone and money for a cab, or call a parent/caregiver or friend if you need to get away from someone.
- Practice saying "no" ahead of time, in case someone tries to pressure you.
- Do not feel like you owe someone sex in return for a night out or a gift.
- Say "no" and mean "no" if that is how you feel. People who really care about you will respect your choice.

- Stay away from alcohol and drugs, which can make it hard to think clearly.

If someone forces you to do anything sexually, tell a trusted adult, or call the National Sexual Assault Hotline at 1-800-656-4673 (HOPE).

♣ It's A Fact!!
Developing Friendships

Dating relationships can be a fun and exciting part of your life. They can also be confusing, especially if dating is new to you. Take time to develop friendships before you start dating. It is best to wait until you are at least 16 before you start going out on dates alone. Try going out with groups of friends or double dating. Always go to public places like the mall, movies, or bowling alley.

Once you know that the guy or girl you like also likes you, you may be unsure of what to do next—continue going out and having fun. Build a good friendship based on shared values and activities. Serious relationships at a young age are not good. Crushes are normal.

Dating a guy or girl two to six years older than you is not a good idea. Studies show older guys are more likely to pressure girls for sex. Girls who date older guys are much more likely—nearly four times more likely—to wind up pregnant. Other studies show that about two-thirds of babies born to teenage girls nationwide are fathered by adult men ages 20 or older.

If a girl has sex with an older guy, he may end up going to jail. Each state has its own laws governing the age of consent.

Source: Excerpted from "Developing Male Friendships," GirlsHealth.gov.

Chapter 18

Getting Over A Break-Up

If you've just had a break-up and are feeling down, you're not alone. Just about everyone experiences a break-up at sometime, and many then have to deal with heartbreak—a wave of grief, anger, confusion, low self-esteem, and maybe even jealousy all at once. Millions of poems and songs have been written about having a broken heart, and wars have even been fought because of heartbreak.

What exactly is heartbreak?

Lots of things can cause heartbreak. Some people might have had a romantic relationship that ended before they were ready. Others might have strong feelings for someone who doesn't feel the same way. Or maybe a person feels sad or angry when a close friend ends or abandons the friendship. Although the causes may be different, the feeling of loss is the same—whether it's the loss of something real or the loss of something you only hoped for. People describe heartbreak as a feeling of heaviness, emptiness, and sadness.

About This Chapter: Information in this chapter is from "Getting Over a Break-Up," November 2007, reprinted with permission from www.kidshealth.org. Copyright © 2007 The Nemours Foundation. This information was provided by KidsHealth, one of the largest resources online for medically reviewed health information written for parents, kids, and teens. For more articles like this one, visit www.KidsHealth.org, or www.TeensHealth.org.

How can I deal with how I feel?

Most people will tell you you'll get over it or you'll meet someone else, but when it's happening to you, it can feel like no one else in the world has ever felt the same way. If you're experiencing these feelings, there are things you can do to lessen the pain. Here are some tips that might help:

- **Share your feelings.** Some people find that sharing their feelings with someone they trust—someone who recognizes what they're going through—helps them feel better. That could mean talking over all the things you feel, even having a good cry on the shoulder of a comforting friend or family member. Others find they heal better if they hang out and do the things they normally enjoy, like seeing a movie or going to a concert, to take their minds off the hurt. If you feel like someone can't relate to what you're going through or is dismissive of your feelings, find someone more sympathetic to talk to. (OK, we know that sharing feelings can be tough for guys, but you don't necessarily have to tell the football team or your wrestling coach what you're going through. Talk with a friend or family member, a teacher, or counselor. It might make you more comfortable if you find a female family member or friend, like an older sister or a neighbor, to talk to).

- **Remember what's good about you.** This one is really important. Sometimes people with broken hearts start to blame themselves for what's happened. They may be really down on themselves, exaggerating their faults as though they did something to deserve the unhappiness they're experiencing. If you find this happening to you, nip it in the bud. Remind yourself of your good qualities, and if you can't think of them because your broken heart is clouding your view, get your friends to remind you.

- **Take good care of yourself.** A broken heart can be very stressful so don't let the rest of your body get broken too. Get lots of sleep, eat healthy foods, and exercise regularly to minimize stress and depression and give your self-esteem a boost.

- **Don't be afraid to cry.** Going through a break-up can be really tough, and getting some of those raw emotions out can be a big help. We

Getting Over A Break-Up

know this is another tough one for guys, but there's no shame in crying now and then. No one has to see you do it—you don't have to start blubbering in class or at soccer practice or anything. Just find a place where you can be alone, like crying into your pillow at night or in the shower when you're getting ready for the day.

- **Do the things you normally enjoy.** Whether it's seeing a movie or going to a concert, do something fun to take your mind off the negative feelings for a while.

- **Keep yourself busy.** Sometimes this is difficult when you're coping with sadness and grief, but it really helps. This is a great time to redecorate your room or try a new hobby. That doesn't mean you shouldn't think about what happened—working things through in our minds is all part of the healing process—it just means you should focus on other things too.

- **Give yourself time.** It takes time for sadness to go away. Almost everyone thinks they won't feel normal again, but the human spirit is amazing—

♣ It's A Fact!!

Some people feel that nothing will make them happy again and resort to alcohol or drugs. Others feel angry and want to hurt themselves or someone else. People who drink, do drugs, or cut themselves to escape from the reality of a loss may think they are numbing their pain, but the feeling is only temporary. They're not really dealing with the pain, only masking it, which makes all their feelings build up inside and prolongs the sadness.

Sometimes the sadness is so deep—or lasts so long—that a person may need some extra support. For someone who isn't starting to feel better after a few weeks or who continues to feel depressed, talking to a counselor or therapist can be very helpful.

So be patient with yourself, and let the healing begin.

and the heartbreak almost always heals after a while. But how long will that take? That depends on what caused your heartbreak, how you deal with loss, and how quickly you tend to bounce back from things. Getting over a break-up can take a couple of days to many weeks—and sometimes even months.

Chapter 19

Keeping Your Cool Under Prom Pressure

Gina can't believe that she almost sat out her senior prom. It's true that things started out badly. She asked Chris—her secret crush—to be her date and he said no. Then a girl she thought was her friend started telling everyone how Chris had turned Gina down. The final straw was when the store where Gina worked closed, leaving her without a job—and without the money to buy the dress she wanted. Gina decided it was all a sign she shouldn't go.

Gina's friends finally persuaded her to go with them—it was her senior prom after all, and they thought she'd regret not going. So Gina borrowed a dress from her cousin and went with her friends. She ended up spending most of the night with Chris, who turned down offers of dates because he wanted to go with his friends instead.

The prom can be one of the most important events in your high school experience—a special night to look forward to and fantasize about for months beforehand. For some teens, though, the prom can seem like just another reason to worry and feel stressed out. Here are some strategies for overcoming prom pressure.

> About This Chapter: Information in this chapter is from "Keeping Your Cool Under Prom Pressure," January 2005, reprinted with permission from www.kidshealth.org. Copyright © 2005 The Nemours Foundation. This information was provided by KidsHealth, one of the largest resources online for medically reviewed health information written for parents, kids, and teens. For more articles like this one, visit www.KidsHealth.org, or www.TeensHealth.org.

Your Money

With a little bit of planning and creativity, the prom doesn't have to cost a fortune. Here are a few less expensive options:

- Try renting dresses or tuxedos or paying for them in installments if you don't want to blow a wad of cash.
- Thrift shopping for cool finds is a great way to get style on the cheap. You may be able to find some funky vintage shoes, purses, jewelry, and other accessories.
- Think about borrowing threads from older siblings or cousins.
- If you can't afford a trip to a beauty salon, go to a drugstore with a friend and treat yourselves to some new beauty supplies. You can spend the afternoon helping one another primp to perfection.
- Instead of an expensive restaurant, opt for a romantic picnic dinner in the park or meet up at a friend's place for some home cooking.

If you're going with a date, talk openly about what's important to him or her—that way you'll have some idea of where you should spend your money. And guys shouldn't feel pressure to pay for everything—in fact, lots of girls prefer to share the expenses and have some choice in what the plans are.

Your Self-Esteem

The biggest prom worry for most people is asking and being asked. It's natural to stress out about gathering the courage to invite that special someone—and then being turned down. It's tempting to avoid the possibility of rejection by not asking, but who wants to be afraid of taking a chance? Ask. If the person says no, you can move on. That's

> ✔ **Quick Tip**
>
> If you need to ask a parent or other family member for help with your finances, offer to make up the cash by doing chores around the house like mowing the lawn, doing the dishes, or babysitting your little brother or sister. Sometimes parents are happy to help with some expenses—such as a limo. That means they won't have to worry about how you'll get home.

Keeping Your Cool Under Prom Pressure

what Gina did—and she was surprised when people told her how much they admired her for asking Chris in the first place. If you never ask, you may miss out on a dream date—someone who might be waiting for you to make the first move because he or she is too shy.

This works the other way around, of course. If you need to decline an offer, try to step back and think about the other person's feelings so you don't let him or her down too hard.

The important thing is to find a date you know you'll enjoy spending the evening with, whether it's a friend, boyfriend or girlfriend, or the object of your secret desire. Because most people want to relax and keep their options open for fun on prom night, more and more people are choosing to go with a group of friends instead of a date. Who better to spend the evening with than the people who love you for who you are?

Your Looks

Want to lose weight? As always, it's important to do what's healthy and right for you. If you are overweight and you've talked to your doctor about your need to lose weight, the prom could be a great reason to get motivated. Your best strategy is to plan ahead. Girls in particular often resort to crash dieting right before the big night—and they're usually left feeling weak, cranky, and certainly not in the mood for fun. Because the weight that's lost through crash diets is mostly water weight, most of these people gain the weight back after prom's over. What's more, studies have found that frequent "yo-yo" dieters—people who crash diet and then go back to eating normally—may end up gaining more weight over time.

To lose the weight for real—to keep it off for the rest of the summer's fun and beyond—plan to lose a pound or two (0.5 or 1 kilogram) a week through regular exercise and by eating a variety of healthy foods. Because it's almost impossible to lose more than a couple of pounds of body fat per week, set your goals early on. If you decide you'd like to lose five pounds (2.3 kilograms), for example, start your program three weeks before the big night.

Exercising and eating right will also help your skin look its best. And speaking of skin, lots of people hit the tanning bed before prom night. Most of us already know the problems tanning causes later in life. But tanning can also cause skin problems that mess with prom night good looks. Some people find they are prone to breakouts after tanning; others notice it leaves them with dull, dry, flaky skin. The best strategy is to look for alternatives to the tanning bed. Plan ahead and experiment with store-bought tanning products. Try a couple several weeks in advance to find out which one works best for you. Or visit a salon for advice on spray tanning.

Another strategy for looking prom night gorgeous? Get plenty of rest, especially on the days leading up to the prom. No matter what body type you have or how much money you spend, confidence helps you look good.

Your Health

Lots of people feel pressure from their friends to drink, do drugs, or lose their virginity on prom night. As with your other prom plans, take a minute to think in advance about how you'll avoid getting into an unwanted situation. You'll feel more confident and in control if you're prepared.

Unfortunately, drugs and alcohol impair your judgment and can hurt you. And there's also the fact that drinking and drugs are illegal—you don't want to spend prom night in the lockup.

> **Remember!!**
>
> Prom can be magical. But it's not the only time you'll have this much fun. There are plenty of other life-defining events as well. So don't let anyone use prom night to pressure you into drinking, drugs, sex, or breaking your curfew—or doing anything else you don't want to. It's your prom. Enjoy it the way you want to.

Be sure you have a safe ride home, whether it's a designated driver, parent, or that chauffeur-driven limo. It's also a good idea to have cab fare or to bring a cell phone and the number of an older sibling or parent just in case your ride gets wild.

Substances like alcohol and drugs can also play a role in teens' losing their virginity on prom night. The decision to have sex is an important personal choice that involves many factors. Don't feel pressure to have sex just because it's a special night—your night will be even more memorable if your memories are happy instead of regretful. In fact, lots of girls and guys who think about it in advance decide that there's enough excitement on prom night anyway—and that having sex is a special, personal decision that shouldn't just be a sideline to prom fun.

Chapter 20

When Your Family Has To Move

Heather didn't want to move. It had been hard enough to make the transition from junior high to high school, especially when many of her friends went to different schools. Now she liked her friends, she liked her school, and she liked her routine. She didn't want to leave the big city for a small town and felt angry with her parents and out of step with everyone else.

These feelings are common for teens who have to move. It isn't easy for anyone to pack up and leave everything that is familiar and try to fit into a new environment. But it's especially hard during a time in your life when there are already so many physical and emotional changes taking place.

Why Do I Feel Upset About Moving?

Leaving behind friends, familiar places, and activities creates anxiety for everyone involved—parents included. And it's hard work to pack and prepare for a move and then settle into a new home.

The reasons behind a move may be upsetting, too, and that can add to the stress. A parent may be forced to take a job in a new town because of

---

About This Chapter: Information in this chapter is from "The Moving Blues," October 2004, reprinted with permission from www.kidshealth.org. Copyright © 2004 The Nemours Foundation. This information was provided by KidsHealth, one of the largest resources online for medically reviewed health information written for parents, kids, and teens. For more articles like this one, visit www.KidsHealth.org, or www.TeensHealth.org.

company layoffs or staff reorganizations. Sometimes a death or divorce in the family can lead to a move, or your family may have to move to take care of a sick family member, such as a grandparent.

> ♣ **It's A Fact!!**
> Experts consider moving to be one of the major stresses in life.

During the busy, stressful time of planning, preparing, and packing for a move, your mom or dad may be too preoccupied to realize how the change is affecting you. They may not even realize you are unhappy if you don't discuss it with them. Be open with your parents and try to talk reasonably about the move and how it is affecting you. Your parents or siblings may have the same concerns or fears.

A move can lead some people to become depressed. If you find that you can't shake feelings of sadness or anxiety, talk to an adult. Don't worry that your parents are too focused on organizing their own lives and don't worry that you'll be bothering them. Most parents appreciate knowing how you feel. Or you can talk to your brother or sister or a school counselor. Not dealing with feelings now may lead to problems later (the same is true of masking emotions with alcohol or drugs).

What To Expect

Even when the reasons for a move are good (such as a promotion or better job for a parent) and you're excited about it, it's still a good idea to be prepared for unexpected changes. It's easy to get caught up in the excitement and expect everything to be perfect. Ali remembers her move to Germany. Like many military families, she'd moved many times before so it seemed like no big deal. In fact, Ali was so excited at the prospect of living abroad that she didn't think about the challenges involved in living in a place where she didn't speak the language. She was also surprised by some of the cultural differences—things she hadn't anticipated because she'd

> ☞ **Remember!!**
> It can help to remember that the problems involved in moving are always temporary. People usually feel better once they've had time to settle in.

When Your Family Has To Move

assumed that Germany would be pretty much like the United States. Today she says she makes a list of positives and negatives before she moves to help keep her expectations realistic.

One unexpected difference may be school. It's easy to assume that one school is pretty much like another, but your new school may not use the same textbooks or procedures. Some of your classes may be different, or the teacher may have already covered topics you haven't learned about yet. It can be particularly hard if you're moving in the middle of a school year, but your teachers will understand and work with you to be sure you feel comfortable.

It's common for people who move to feel like they're starting all over again. You have to learn new streets, new faces, and new ways of doing things. In your new home, the kids may dress or speak differently. The slang and accents may sound different in your new community, depending on how far you move. It's natural for people to feel out of place in a new situation where they don't know the customs and rules.

Making The Best Of It

Although there is no way to eliminate the anxiety of moving, there are many ways to make the move easier. Before you even begin packing, you can start to get to know your new home. The internet and library may contain lots of good information about your new community. Make a list of your interests and hobbies, and then find the locations and phone numbers of places where those activities take place. When you're visiting your new school, find out if there are deadlines for activities such as cheerleading, sports, and the yearbook committee and see if you can still join.

A new place seems more familiar, and it's easier to make friends, when you can participate in a common interest with people who do the things you enjoy.

Look for opportunities to try new activities as well. If you have a job, look up potential employment resources in your new city. Ask your current boss to write a reference letter for you. If you work for a food chain or a chain of stores, you might be able to arrange a transfer and have a job waiting for you.

See if you can get a city map and highlight where you will be living, where your new school is, and the location of places of worship, movie theaters, skate parks, and other places you like to go. Ask if your realtor can videotape your new house if you haven't been able to see it yet (some realtors post indoor and outdoor pictures of properties online).

It can help to learn about what makes your new city or town unique. Share the information with your friends and make them feel part of your moving experience. Soon you will feel like you already know your new community.

Packing It Up

You can pick up a copy of the United States Postal Service Mover's Guide in any post office or online; it will give you and your parents some tips. The guide includes change of address forms, a checklist of things to do, and suggestions for a survival kit that will contain items you may need to have at hand and might otherwise be packed out of reach during the move.

You can help—and feel more in control—by making a list of things that need to be done before the move. Offer to help your parents with some of their items. The more you participate and keep busy, the more it will feel like your own experience rather than something that is being done to you. For example, you can organize a yard sale to sell the stuff you don't want to take with you. You may find that friends and neighbors are interested in participating in a yard sale, too.

As soon as you know you are moving, start preparing by:

- sorting out clothes and giving away items that you aren't going to take
- packing away items you are going to take, but won't need until after you've moved
- spreading out the chores you have to do so you won't be overwhelmed during the last few days
- cleaning up your room or any other areas you are responsible for to make packing easier
- labeling your boxes so you can easily identify where things are when you get to your new home

Keeping In Touch

One of the fears of moving is losing old friends. Remember your friends when you get to your new destination by putting pictures in an album or scrapbook or in frames that you can put up around your new room. Print out copies of pictures for your friends to keep, too.

Saying goodbye is never easy, but it doesn't mean it's forever. Luckily, today it's easier than ever to stay in touch with email, instant messaging, and cell phones. Send pictures—even videos—back and forth. Share interesting information about the differences, both good and bad, between your old home and your new place. You might be able to plan summer visits to see old friends or for a friend to visit you.

Moving is hard, but you may discover that it has taught you some valuable skills—how to make new friends, be flexible, and find your way around strange places. Although learning these lessons can feel tough at the time, once you've settled in, you may find you like the new place better. And be sure to say "hi" to the next new kid in town—you may be able to teach him or her a thing or two.

Chapter 21

When Your Parents Fight

Chances are you've had an argument or twenty with your parents recently—about clothes, homework, friends, and curfew—pretty much anything. But what's going on when your parents fight with each other?

You may be a little relieved that, for once, you're not the one arguing with a parent. But most people worry when they hear their parents argue.

It's normal for parents to disagree and argue from time to time. They might disagree about important things like their careers, finances, or major family decisions. They might even disagree about little things that don't seem important at all—like what's for dinner or what time someone gets home.

Sometimes parents stay levelheaded when they disagree, and they allow each other a chance to listen and to talk. But many times when parents disagree, they argue.

About This Chapter: Information in this chapter is from "When Parents Fight," June 2006, reprinted with permission from www.kidshealth.org. Copyright © 2006 The Nemours Foundation. This information was provided by KidsHealth, one of the largest resources online for medically reviewed health information written for parents, kids, and teens. For more articles like this one, visit www.KidsHealth.org, or www.TeensHealth.org.

What Does It Mean When Parents Fight?

When your parents are fighting, thoughts might start rushing around in your head. Why are they shouting at each other? Does this mean they don't love each other anymore? Are they going to get a divorce?

It can be easy to jump to conclusions when you hear parents argue. But most of the time, arguments are just a way to let off steam when parents have a bad day, don't feel well, or are under a lot of stress—kind of like when you argue with them.

Like you, when your parents get upset with each other, they might yell, cry, or say things they don't really mean. Most people lose their cool now and then. So if your parents are fighting, don't always assume it means the worst.

It's Okay For Parents To Argue Sometimes

It's natural for people to have different opinions, feelings, or approaches to things. Talking about these differences is a first step in working toward a mutually agreeable solution. It's important for people in a family to be able to tell each other how they feel and what they think, even when they disagree.

Sometimes parents can feel so strongly about their differences that it may lead to arguments. Most of the time, these arguments are over quickly, parents apologize and make up, and the family settles back into its usual routine.

When Parents' Fighting Goes Too Far

But sometimes when parents fight, there's too much yelling and screaming, name calling, and too many harsh things said. Although some parents may do this, it's not okay to treat people in the family with disrespect, use degrading or insulting language, or yell and scream at them.

Sometimes parents' fighting really goes too far and includes pushing and shoving, throwing things, or hitting. Even if one parent is not physically injured, an argument has gone too far when one parent uses threats to try to control the other through fear. Examples include if a parent:

- threatens to injure himself or herself
- threatens to commit suicide

When Your Parents Fight 115

- threatens to leave the other parent
- threatens to report the other parent to welfare
- destroys the other's property

These things are never okay. When fights get physical or involve threats, the people fighting need to learn to get their anger under control.

What About You?

It's hard for most people to hear their parents yelling at each other. Seeing them upset and out of control can throw you off—aren't parents supposed to be the calm, composed, and mature ones in the family? How much it bothers you might depend on how often it happens, how loud or intense things get, or whether parents argue in front of other people.

You might worry more about one parent or the other during an argument. It's natural to worry that a parent may feel especially hurt by what the other parent says. Or maybe you worry that one parent could become angry enough to lose control. Should you be worried that someone might get physically hurt? With all this extra mental and emotional stress, you may get a stomachache or want to go to your room and cry. It's understandable to feel this way when there's conflict around you.

> **Remember!!**
>
> If your parents are arguing about you, this can be especially upsetting. Lots of people in this situation might mistakenly think the argument is their fault. But your parents' arguments are never your fault.

If your parents' fighting really bothers you, you might find it hard to sleep or go to school. If this is the case, try talking to one or both of your parents about their behavior. They may not even realize how upset you are until you tell them how their arguments affect you.

If you or someone you know lives in a family where the fighting goes too far, let someone else know what's going on. Talking to other relatives, a teacher, a school counselor, or any adult you trust about the fighting can be helpful.

Sometimes parents who fight can get so out of control that they hurt each other or other family members. If this happens, letting someone else know will allow the family to be helped and protected from such harmful fighting.

Family members can learn to listen to each other and talk about feelings and differences without yelling and screaming. They can get help with problem fighting from counselors and therapists. Though it may take some work, time, and practice, people in families can always learn to get along better.

Happy, Healthy Families

If your family argues from time to time, try not to sweat it. No family is perfect. Even in the happiest home, problems pop up and people argue. Usually the family members involved get what's bothering them out in the open and talk about it. Hopefully, they can reach some compromise or agreement. Everyone feels better, and life can get back to normal.

Being part of a family means everyone pitches in and tries to make life better for each other. Arguments happen and that's okay. But with love, understanding, and some work, families can solve almost any problem.

Chapter 22

When Your Parent Has A Substance Abuse Problem

Dependence on alcohol and drugs is our most serious national public health problem. It is prevalent among rich and poor, in all regions of the country, and all ethnic and social groups.

Millions of Americans misuse or are dependent on alcohol or drugs. Most of them have families who suffer the consequences, often serious, of living with this illness. If there is alcohol or drug dependence in your family, remember you are not alone.

Most individuals who abuse alcohol or drugs have jobs and are productive members of society, creating a false hope in the family that it is not that bad.

The problem is that addiction tends to worsen over time, hurting both the addicted person and all the family members. It is especially damaging to young children and adolescents.

People with this illness really may believe that they drink normally or that everyone takes drugs. These false beliefs are called denial; this denial is a part of the illness.

> About This Chapter: Information in this chapter is from "Alcohol and Drug Abuse Hurts Everyone in the Family," Center for Substance Abuse Treatment, Substance Abuse and Mental Health Services Administration; retrieved August 2007.

It Doesn't Have To Be That Way

Drug or alcohol dependence disorders are medical conditions that can be effectively treated. Millions of Americans and their families are in healthy recovery from this disease.

If someone close to you misuses alcohol or drugs, the first step is to be honest about the problem and to seek help for yourself, your family, and your loved one.

> ♣ **It's A Fact!!**
> About 11 million children in our country are growing up with at least one alcoholic parent. You are not alone.
>
> Source: Excerpted from *Teen Survival Guide: Health Tips for On-the-go Girls*, GirlsHealth.gov, U. S. Department of Health and Human Services, Office on Women's Health, June 2007.

Treatment can occur in a variety of settings, in many different forms, and for different lengths of time. Stopping the alcohol or drug use is the first step to recovery, and most people need help to stop. Often a person with alcohol or drug dependence will need treatment provided by professionals, just as with other diseases. Your doctor may be able to guide you.

Family Intervention Can Start The Healing

Getting a loved one to agree to accept help, and finding support services for all family members, are the first steps toward healing for the addicted person and the entire family.

When an addicted person is reluctant to seek help, sometimes family members, friends, and associates come together out of concern and love, to confront the problem drinker. They strongly urge the person to enter treatment and list the serious consequences of not doing so, such as family breakup or job loss.

This is called intervention. When carefully prepared and done with the guidance of a competent, trained specialist, the family, friends, and associates are usually able to convince their loved one, in a firm and loving manner, that the only choice is to accept help and begin the road to recovery.

People with alcohol or drug dependence problems can, and do, recover. Intervention is often the first step.

Children Need Help Too

Children in families experiencing alcohol or drug abuse need attention, guidance, and support. They may be growing up in homes in which the problems are either denied or covered up.

These children need to have their experiences validated. They also need safe, reliable adults in whom to confide and who will support them, reassure them, and provide them with appropriate help for their age. They need to have fun and just be kids.

Families with alcohol and drug problems usually have high levels of stress and confusion. High stress family environments are a risk factor for early and dangerous substance use, as well as mental and physical health problems.

Children living with alcohol or drug abuse in the family can benefit from participating in educational support groups in their school student assistance programs. Those age 11 and older can join Alateen groups, which meet in community settings and provide healthy connections with others coping with similar issues. Being associated with the activities of a faith community can also help.

Resources For Information And Help

There is help available in your local community. Look in the Yellow Pages under alcoholism for treatment programs and self-help groups. Call your county health department and ask for licensed treatment programs in your community. Keep trying until you find the right help for your loved one, yourself, and your family. Ask a family therapist for a referral to a trained interventionist or call the Intervention Resource Center at 1-888-421-4321.

Chapter 23

Family Violence

Amy's finger was so swollen that she couldn't get her ring off. She didn't think her finger was broken because she could still bend it. It had been a week since her dad shoved her into the wall, but her finger still hurt a lot.

Amy hated the way her dad called her names and accused her of all sorts of things she didn't do, especially after he had been drinking. It was the worst feeling, and she just kept hoping he would stop.

What Is Abuse?

Abuse can be physical, sexual, emotional, verbal, or a combination of any or all of those. Neglect—when parents or guardians don't take care of the basic needs of the children who depend on them—can also be a form of abuse.

Physical abuse is often the most easily spotted form of abuse. It may be any kind of hitting, shaking, burning, pinching, biting, choking, throwing, beating, and other actions that cause physical injury, leave marks, or produce significant physical pain.

About This Chapter: Information in this chapter is from "Abuse," November 2007, reprinted with permission from www.kidshealth.org. Copyright © 2007 The Nemours Foundation. This information was provided by KidsHealth, one of the largest resources online for medically reviewed health information written for parents, kids, and teens. For more articles like this one, visit www.KidsHealth.org, or www.TeensHealth.org.

Sexual abuse is any type of sexual contact between an adult and anyone 18 or younger, or between a significantly older child and a younger child. If a family member sexually abuses another family member, this is called incest.

Emotional abuse can be difficult to pin down because there may not be physical signs. Emotional abuse happens when yelling and anger go too far or when parents constantly criticize, threaten, or dismiss kids or teens until their self-esteem and feelings of self-worth are damaged. Emotional abuse can hurt and cause damage just as physical abuse does.

Neglect is probably the hardest type of abuse to define. Neglect occurs when a child or teen doesn't have adequate food, housing, clothes, medical care, or supervision. Emotional neglect happens when a parent doesn't provide enough emotional support or deliberately and consistently pays very little or no attention to a child. But it's not neglect if a parent doesn't give a kid something he or she wants, like a new computer or a cell phone.

Family violence can affect anyone. It can happen in any kind of family. Sometimes parents abuse each other, which can be hard for a child to witness. Some parents abuse their kids by using physical or verbal cruelty as a way of discipline.

Abuse doesn't just happen in families, of course. Bullying is a form of abusive behavior. Bullying someone through intimidation, threats, or humiliation can be just as abusive as beating someone up. People who bully others may have been abused themselves. This is also true of people who abuse someone they're dating. But being abused is no excuse for abusing someone else.

Abuse can also take the form of hate crimes directed at people just because of their race, religion, abilities, gender, or sexual orientation.

Recognizing Abuse

It may sound strange, but people sometimes have trouble recognizing that they are being abused. Recognizing abuse may be especially difficult for someone who has lived with it for many years. A person might think that it's just the way things are and that there's nothing that can be done. People who are abused might mistakenly think they bring it on themselves by not acting right or by not living up to someone's expectations.

Someone growing up in a family where there is violence or abuse may not know that there are other ways for family members to treat each other. A person who has only known an abusive relationship may mistakenly think that hitting, beating, pushing, shoving, or angry name-calling are perfectly normal ways to treat someone when you're mad. Seeing parents treat each other in abusive ways might lead a child to think that's a normal relationship. But abuse is not a normal or healthy way to treat people.

If you're not sure you are being abused, or if you suspect a friend is, it's always okay to ask a trusted adult or friend.

Why Does It Happen?

If you're one of the thousands of people living in an abusive situation, it can help to understand why some people abuse—and to realize that the violence is not your fault. Sometimes abusers manipulate the people they are abusing by telling them they did something wrong or "asked for it" in some way. But that's not true.

There is no single reason why people abuse others. But some factors seem to make it more likely that a person may become abusive.

Growing up in an abusive family is one factor. Other people become abusive because they're not able to manage their feelings properly. For example, someone who is unable to control anger or can't cope with stressful personal situations (like the loss of a job or marriage problems) may lash out at others inappropriately. Alcohol or drug use also can make it difficult for some people to control their actions.

Certain types of personality disorders or mental illness might also interfere with a person's ability to relate to others in healthy ways or cause people to have problems with aggression or self-control. Of course, not everyone with a personality disorder or mental illness becomes abusive.

Fortunately, abuse can always be corrected. Everyone can learn how to stop.

What Are The Effects Of Abuse?

When people are abused, it can affect every aspect of their lives, especially self-esteem. How much abuse harms a person depends on the situation and sometimes on how severe the abuse is. Sometimes a seemingly minor thing can trigger a big reaction. Being touched inappropriately by a family member, for example, can be very confusing and traumatic.

Every family has arguments. In fact, it's rare when a family doesn't have some rough times, disagreements, and anger. Punishments and discipline—like removing privileges, grounding, or being sent to your room—are normal. Yelling and anger are normal in parent-teen relationships too—although it can feel pretty bad to have an argument with a parent or friend. But if punishments, arguments, or yelling go too far or last too long, it can lead to stress and other serious problems.

Many people who are abused distrust others. They may feel a lot of anger toward other people and themselves, and it can be hard to make friends. Abuse is a significant cause of depression in young people. Some teens may engage in self-destructive behavior, such as cutting or abusing drugs or alcohol. They may even attempt suicide.

♣ **It's A Fact!!**
Teens who are abused (or have been in the past) often have trouble sleeping, eating, and concentrating. They may not do well at school because they are angry or frightened, or because they can't concentrate or don't care.

It's normal for people who have been abused to feel upset, angry, and confused about what happened to them. They may feel guilty and embarrassed and blame themselves. But abuse is never the fault of the person who is being abused, no matter how much the abuser tries to blame others.

Abusers may manipulate a person into keeping quiet by saying stuff like: "This is a secret between you and me," or "If you ever tell anybody, I'll hurt you or your mom," or "You're going to get in trouble if you tell. No one will believe you, and you'll go to jail for lying." This is the abuser's way of making a person feel like nothing can be done so he or she won't report the abuse.

Family Violence

People who are abused may have trouble getting help because it means they'd be reporting on someone they love—someone who may be wonderful much of the time and awful to them only some of the time. A person might be afraid of the consequences of reporting, either because they fear the abuser or the family is financially dependent on that person. For reasons like these, abuse often goes unreported.

What Should Someone Who's Being Abused Do?

People who are being abused need to get help. Keeping the abuse a secret doesn't protect anyone from being abused—it only makes it more likely that the abuse will continue.

If you or anyone you know is being abused, talk to someone you or your friend can trust—a family member, a trusted teacher, a doctor, or a school or religious youth counselor. Many teachers and counselors have training in how to recognize and report abuse.

Sometimes people who are being abused by someone in their own home need to find a safe place to live temporarily. It is never easy to have to leave home, but it's sometimes necessary to be protected from further abuse. People who need to leave home to stay safe can find local shelters listed in the phone book, or they can contact an abuse helpline. Sometimes a person can stay with a relative or friend.

People who are being abused often feel afraid, numb, or lonely. Getting help and support is an important first step toward changing the situation.

Many teens who have experienced abuse find that painful emotions may linger even after the abuse stops. Working with a therapist is one way to sort through the complicated feelings and reactions that being abused creates, and the process can help to rebuild feelings of safety, confidence, and self-esteem.

✔ Quick Tip

Telephone directories list local child abuse and family violence hotline numbers that you can call for help. There's also Childhelp USA at 800-4-A-CHILD (800-422-4453).

Chapter 24

Dealing With Divorce

For many people, their parents' divorce marks a turning point in their lives, whether the divorce happened many years ago or is taking place right now.

About half the marriages in the United States today end in divorce, so children of divorce are certainly not alone. But when it happens to you, you can feel very alone and unsure of what it all means.

Why Are My Parents Divorcing?

Parents divorce for many reasons. Usually divorce happens when couples feel they can no longer live together due to fighting and anger or because the love they had when they married has changed. Divorce can also be because one parent falls in love with someone else, and sometimes it is due to a serious problem like drinking, abuse, or gambling.

It's common for teens to think that their parents' divorce is somehow their fault, but nothing could be further from the truth. Some teens may

---

About This Chapter: Information in this chapter is from "Dealing With Divorce," August 2007, reprinted with permission from www.kidshealth.org. Copyright © 2007 The Nemours Foundation. This information was provided by KidsHealth, one of the largest resources online for medically reviewed health information written for parents, kids, and teens. For more articles like this one, visit www.KidsHealth.org, or www.TeensHealth.org.

wonder if they could have helped to prevent the split. Others may wish they had prevented arguments by cooperating more within the family, doing better with their behavior, or getting better grades. But separation and divorce are a result of a couple's problems with each other, not with their kids. The decisions adults make about divorce are their own.

If your parents are divorcing, you may experience a lot of feelings. Your emotions may change frequently, too. You may feel angry, frustrated, upset, or sad. You might feel protective of one parent or blame one for the situation. You may feel abandoned, afraid, worried, or guilty. You may also feel relieved, especially if there has been a lot of tension at home. These feelings are normal and talking about them with a friend, family member, or trusted adult can really help.

> **Remember!!**
> It may seem hard, but it is possible to cope with divorce—and have a good family life in spite of some changes divorce may bring.

How Will Divorce Change My Life?

Depending on what happens in your family, you may have to adjust to many changes. These could include things like moving, changing schools, spending time with both parents separately, and perhaps dealing with parents' unpleasant feelings toward one another.

Your parents may go to court to determine custody arrangements. You may end up living with one parent most of the time and visiting the other, or your parents may split their time with you evenly.

Some teens have to travel between parents, and that may create challenges both socially and practically. But with time you can create a new routine that works. Often, it takes a while for custody arrangements to be finalized. This can give people time to adapt to these big changes and let families figure out what works best.

Dealing With Divorce

Money matters may change for your parents, too. A parent who didn't work during the marriage may need to find a job to pay for rent or a mortgage. This might be something a parent is excited about, but he or she may also feel nervous or pressured about finances. There are also expenses associated with divorce, from lawyers' fees to the cost of moving to a new place to live.

Your family may not be able to afford all the things you were used to before the divorce. This is one of the difficult changes often associated with divorce. There can be good changes too—but how you cope with the stressful changes depends on your situation, your personality, and your support network.

What Parents And Teens Can Do To Make Divorce Easier

Keep the peace. Dealing with divorce is easiest when parents get along. Teens find it especially hard when their parents fight and argue or act with bitterness toward each other. You can't do much to influence how your parents behave during a divorce, but you can ask them to do their best to call a truce to any bickering or unkind things they might be saying about each other. No matter what problems a couple may face, as parents they need to handle visiting arrangements peacefully to minimize the stress their kids may feel.

Be fair. Most teens say it's important that parents don't try to get them to "take sides." You need to feel free to relate to one parent without the other parent acting jealous, hurt, or mad. It's unfair for anyone to feel that relating to one parent is being disloyal to the other or that the burden of one parent's happiness is on your shoulders.

When parents find it hard to let go of bitterness or anger, or if they are depressed about the changes brought on by divorce, they can find help from a counselor or therapist. This can help parents get past the pain divorce may have created, to find personal happiness, and to lift any burdens from their kids. Kids and teens can also benefit from seeing a family therapist or someone who specializes in helping them get through the stress of a family breakup.

Keep in touch. Going back and forth between two homes can be tough, especially if parents live far apart. It can be a good idea to keep in touch with a parent you see less often because of distance. Even a quick email saying

"I'm thinking of you" helps ease the feelings of missing each other. Making an effort to stay in touch when you're apart can keep both of you up to date on everyday activities and ideas.

Work it out. You may want both parents to come to special events, like games, meets, plays, or recitals. But sometimes a parent may find it awkward to attend if the other is present. It helps if parents can figure out a way to make this work, especially because you may need to feel the support and presence of both parents even more during divorce. You might be able to come up with an idea for a compromise or solution to this problem and suggest it to both parents.

Talk about the future. Lots of teens whose parents divorce worry that their own plans for the future could be affected. Some are concerned that the costs of divorce (like legal fees and expenses of two households) might mean there will be less money for college or other things.

Pick a good time to tell your parents about your concerns—when there's enough time to sit down with one or both parents to discuss how the divorce will affect you. Don't worry about putting added stress on your parents. It's better to bring your concerns into the open than to keep them to yourself and let worries or resentment build. There are solutions for most problems, and counselors who can help teens and their parents find those solutions.

Figure out your strengths. How do you deal with stress? Do you get angry and take it out on siblings, friends, or yourself? Or are you someone who is more of a pleaser who puts others first? Do you tend to avoid conflict altogether and just hope that problems will magically disappear? A life-changing event like a divorce can put people through some tough times, but it can also help them learn about their strengths and put in place some new coping skills. For example, how do you cope if one parent bad-mouths another? Sometimes staying quiet until the anger has subsided and then discussing it calmly with your mom or dad can help. You may want to tell them you have a right to love both your parents, no matter what they are doing to each other.

If you need help figuring out your strengths or how to cope—like from a favorite aunt or from your school counselor—ask for it. And if you find it hard to confront your parents, try writing them a letter. Figure out what works for you.

Live your life. Sometimes during a divorce, parents may be so caught up in their own changes, it can feel like your own life is on hold. In addition to staying focused on your own plans and dreams, make sure you participate in as many of your normal activities as possible. When things are changing at home, it can really help to keep some things, such as school activities and friends, the same. If things get too hard at home, see if you can stay with a friend or relative until things calm down. Take care of yourself by eating right and getting regular exercise—two great stress busters.

Let others support you. Talk about your feelings and reactions to the divorce with someone you trust. If you're feeling down or upset, let your friends and family members support you. These feelings usually pass. If they don't, and if you're feeling depressed or stressed out, or if it's hard to concentrate on your normal activities, let a counselor or therapist help you. Your parents, school counselor, or a doctor or other health professional can help you find one.

> ✔ **Quick Tip**
>
> Many communities and schools have support groups for kids and teens whose parents have divorced. It can really help to talk with other people your age who are going through similar experiences.

Bringing Out The Positive

There will be ups and downs in the process, but teens can cope successfully with their parents' divorce and the changes it brings. You may even discover some unexpected positives. Many teens find their parents are actually happier after the divorce, or they may develop new and better ways of relating to both parents when they have separate time with each one.

Some teens learn compassion and caring skills when a younger brother or sister needs their support and care. Siblings who are closer in age may form tighter bonds, learning to count on each other more because they're facing the challenges of their parents' divorce together. Coping well with divorce also can bring out strength and maturity. Some become more responsible, better problem solvers, better listeners, or better friends. Looking back on the experience, lots of people say that they learned coping skills they never knew they had and feel stronger and more resilient as a result of what they went through.

Many movies have been made about divorce and stepfamilies—some with happy endings, some not. That's how it is in real life too. But most teens who go through a divorce learn (sometimes to their surprise) that they can make it through this difficult situation successfully. Giving it time, letting others support you along the way, and keeping an eye on the good things in your life can make all the difference.

Chapter 25

Stepfamilies: Adjusting To Change

Sometimes when parents break up or someone passes away, mom or dad may eventually start a new relationship. This is how people come to have stepfamilies. All relationships have their ups and downs, and stepfamilies are no exception.

Benefits Of Stepfamilies

There are many good things about living in a stepfamily.

- Some young people have said they like the idea of being a family again.

- Others say that they feel more safe and secure.

- Some young people have said they have two sets of parents to look up to, to get support from, to help with homework, to talk with about other problems, and to help with major decisions, for example, education and career.

- You have another adult to do things with.

- You may have stepbrothers and sisters to do things with and have fun.

- Some may enjoy the differences between two homes.

About This Chapter: Information in this chapter is from "Step-families," reprinted with permission, © 2007 Children, Youth and Women's Health Service, Government of South Australia.

- Some say it's nice to see their parent so happy being with a new partner.
- Some young people recognize that their standard of living is better because there is more money coming into the household.
- Having more relatives can be positive.
- There may be a new baby brother or sister to love.
- Some have said that one benefit is getting more presents.
- Others enjoy having a bigger family.

> ♣ **It's A Fact!!**
> When one or more people join your family, it can create a lot of change, and this can be hard to accept at first, but being in a stepfamily can be really cool too.

The Not So Good Stuff

Being in a stepfamily may not always be fun. There can be some difficult issues to deal with.

The following sections cover some of the potential problems and how they can be worked through.

Loss

Young people in new stepfamilies will have experienced important losses.

- You may have been through the trauma of your parents breaking up and experienced all the feelings of loss this brings.
- When one parent moves into another relationship, this can mean the loss of all your dreams and wishes that your parents will reunite.
- If a parent has died, there is grief and mourning of the loss of your parent.
- There may be the loss of time and attention from your parent as he or she spends time in the new relationship.

Stepfamilies: Adjusting To Change

- There is a loss of the old familiar ways of how your family used to be and the ways that the family used to do things.
- If stepbrothers and sisters move in, it may mean having to give up or share your bedroom.
- If you're moving to a new house, it may mean the loss of a familiar neighborhood, friends, and school.

Just one of these losses alone can be difficult to deal with, yet sometimes young people will have to face several losses at one time.

When this happens, support and love from parents is really comforting. Sometimes parents can be caught up in what is happening for themselves with the break-up, death, or the new relationship, and need time for themselves also.

- Try talking to your parents about how you are feeling, ask for help, and share the new experiences together.
- Try working out solutions together, for example, if you are moving, can arrangements be made for you to stay at your old school?
- If it's too hard to talk to your parents, is there a relative or adult family friend you trust and can talk to?
- How about your student counselor, teacher, or youth health service?

Change

In a new stepfamily, young people have to get used to different ways of doing things and get used to living with new people.

- Apart from the new stepparent, there may be new stepbrothers and stepsisters to get used to. For example, you might not be the oldest or the youngest in the family anymore.
- Change can also be a source of stress, and even simple changes such as day-to-day chores around the house can take time

> ♣ **It's A Fact!!**
> Change can also be a source of stress, and even simple changes such as day-to-day chores around the house can take time to get used to.

to get used to. For example:

- Do you do the dishes after each meal of the day or do you do them once a day?
- What meal times and routines are people used to?
- Do you eat meals at the table or in front of the television?
- How do you divide up household tasks?

Change can also be a good thing. You might learn new and better ways of doing things in a stepfamily, or you might be able to teach other members of the stepfamily some new ideas.

Feeling Torn

- Some young people feel like they're divided between their two natural parents. You may love both parents but feel bad because there is still some conflict between them. It can be really upsetting to hear awful things about the other parent.

- You could notice one parent is still really upset about the break-up. The break-up probably happened for many reasons, not just one thing, and neither person can be entirely to blame. All you can do is let the hurting parent know that you love him or her and that you care and maybe do something nice for that parent.

- As hard as it is for you, these things are for your parents to work out. It is their problem. If you're angry about the break up, it can be best to find other ways to get the anger out, perhaps by talking to a school counselor.

- Some parents continually ask young people questions about the other parent. It's best not to get involved. You may have to even tell your parent, "I don't want to get involved in telling you things about Mom. It is too hard for me to be pulled in the middle. If you want to know things about her, please ask her." Say it as respectfully, yet as assertively, as you can manage.

Discipline

It can be difficult to get used to the idea of discipline coming from a stepparent.

Stepfamilies: Adjusting To Change

- Your new stepparent may have different ideas about discipline from your parent.
- If the issue becomes a problem, it's best to get things out into the open and let your parent know how you are feeling.
  - The most effective way to discuss any conflict is to make a time to talk together when you won't be interrupted.
  - Be respectful and try and stay calm (yes, it is difficult when you're upset about something, but it works better this way).
- If you can't talk to your parent, is there a family friend or relative who can help? Is there a school counselor who can help?

Moving Between Houses

Sometimes young people can have two houses to stay at. If things aren't going well at one, then it's handy to have somewhere else to go to. But if this becomes a way to avoid solving problems, then house hopping can become a problem in itself.

An alternative to constantly moving between houses might be:

- Tell your parent/s you want to discuss something that is really important to you and ask that they make a time when you can sit down together quietly.
  - Tell them how you're feeling—in a respectful way, without blaming.
  - Ask if there is any way you can work this out together, for example, set new rules that give you a little more freedom so that you all know exactly where you stand.
- If this is just too hard, is there a relative you could talk to who could speak to your parents for you?
- Would you consider going to counseling or mediation with your parents? Mediation is when a trained person helps both parties to come to an agreement together. The mediator should not take sides.

Getting Kicked Out

- Sometimes it happens that there is so much conflict between a young person and parent or stepparent that the parents ask or demand that the young person leave the home.
- If this happens, it is a good idea to check out where you stand by talking to someone at your local government body responsible for children's welfare.
- In most places, parents do have some responsibility for their children, depending on their age.
- There are counseling services that can help to mediate the situation.
- If the conflict can't be resolved, can you live with another family member? Can you stay with a family member for a while so that you and your parents can have a break from each other?

Contact

Contact refers to the time young people and parents agree to share with one another.

Contact can have its ups and downs. Some of the good things are having fun with your other parent, going out with him or her, seeing other relatives or stepbrothers and stepsisters, and talking with and getting support from your parent.

Some of the tougher things can be living out of a suitcase and feeling like it's not really your home. See if you can make it more like home for yourself. Here are some ideas:

- Ask if you can put up a poster or two.
- Keep some of your "things" there, like a trophy or something you made at school.
- Ask if you can have a cupboard or even a drawer you can keep things in.
- Keep a toothbrush and a few spare clothes there.
- Can you invite a friend over?

Stepfamilies: Adjusting To Change

- Can you give the phone number to your friends so they can call you there?
- Try and keep up with your usual weekend sports. If your parent or stepparent can't take you, can you arrange something else?

Stepparents

You don't have to like your stepparent—although it would be nicer for you both if you do like each other. It can be difficult living in the same house with an adult you don't like. The best way to ensure that things run smoothly in the home is if everyone tries to treat everyone else with respect.

Many stepparents feel unsure of themselves and their place in the family; they can feel like outsiders.

- You could try doing some nice things for your stepparent to include him or her in the family. Little things like saying thanks for a lift or a meal can be helpful, so can saying hello and goodbye as you would with your parent.
- Inviting a stepparent to your sports event or another function can be helpful in including them in your family life.

Stepparents seem to take on different roles.

- Some are like friends, some are like another parent, and others seem like a distant stranger.
- There's no real right or wrong; it's what works best for your family and the different people who are in your family.

Some stepparents get really bossy and try to take control of everything. It is hard to get along well with someone who is bossy all the time. In this situation, it may be best to get counseling or mediation to live together in a more positive way.

Sometimes it can be so tough young people start using drugs and alcohol as a way to try and forget painful feelings.

- This may work for a short time while the person is affected by a drug, but doesn't always block the bad feelings out (think about people who get drunk and cry about their problems).

- When the person straightens up, the problems and painful feelings are still there because the feelings haven't really been dealt with.
- What's worse, you may have spent a ton of money, have a hangover, or have taken other health, legal, and safety risks in using drugs.

It's best to get some support about ways to handle the feelings. That way you'll find solutions that last. Talk to a counselor or another supportive friend or relative.

> ♣ **It's A Fact!!**
> ### If A Stepparent Is Abusive
> If you are in a situation of real abuse from a stepparent or a parent, this is very different from the normal (but still difficult) conflicts that arise in a family. It is important to get some outside help.

Stepsiblings

Sometimes stepbrothers and sisters get along really well and become close friends. Sometimes they become friends for life.

Sometimes stepbrothers and sisters become sexually attracted to each other. It is normal to become attracted to someone you like. But in a stepfamily it can become a problem for several reasons:

- Having a relationship with someone in the same household can cause all kinds of upset to relationships in the house.
- Parents may suspect young people of sneaking into each other's bedrooms, and arguments begin between parents and the young people.
- The couple may argue or break up (which is highly likely at a young age), and this can cause major dramas in the household.
- One may eventually want to go out with another person. Can you

Stepfamilies: Adjusting To Change

imagine how uncomfortable that other person would feel coming over to the house?

What is the answer? It can be difficult to handle this attraction. It may be best to bring the situation out into the open by talking about it to your parents or to speak to a counselor at school, a youth service, or a community health center.

Other problems arise because there are jealousies or feelings of not being treated fairly, or because one person in the family feels left out.

One sex can be outnumbered by the other.

Chapter 26

Living With A Chronic Illness Or Disability

Illness And Disability

What Is An Illness?

An illness is a sickness. An illness can be acute, which means it comes on quickly and is over quickly (like a cold or the flu) or it can be chronic, which means it lasts a long time (like asthma or diabetes).

What Is A Disability?

A disability is a physical or mental problem that makes it harder to do normal daily activities.

Millions Of Young People Have An Illness Or Disability

There are a lot of different kinds of illnesses and disabilities and each one affects teens in a different way.

If you have an illness or disability, it can be hard to take care of your needs, but you are not alone. Your friends and family are there to support

---

About This Chapter: Information in this chapter is from "Welcome!," "Learning You Have an Illness or Disability," "Going to the Hospital," "When Kids Tease," "Talking about Your Illness or Disability," "Becoming Independent," and "Things You Can Do to Become More Independent," GirlsHealth.gov, sponsored by the National Women's Health Information Center, U.S. Department of Health and Human Services, June 2007.

you. And remember, there are many young people out there who have to take extra care of their health just like you.

Learning You Have An Illness Or Disability

Being a teen is not easy, but it can be even harder when you learn you have an illness or disability. If you have just learned you have an illness or disability, you may be scared because you do not know exactly what it means or what to expect. You may be overwhelmed by the changes you will need to make to manage your condition. You may be asking yourself, "How will this change my life?" or "How will I make it through this?" These feelings are normal.

Finding out you have an illness or disability is tough. There are some things you can do that may help you feel better. Research your illness or disability. What is it? What causes it? How do you manage it? Talk to teens that have an illness or disability. Ask them how they felt when they first found out and how they live with their conditions.

Going To The Hospital

If you are very sick, you might have to stay in the hospital for a long time. Sometimes it can even be months or longer. This can make it hard to see your friends and do the things you like to do, but it is important that you get the care you need.

Keeping Up With School

You may be in a hospital that can bring school to you. This type of program will bring teachers, books, and computers to the hospital so that you can learn and get treatment at the same time. This program will also help you get ready to go back to your school when you leave the hospital. Talk with your parents about asking your hospital and school if a program like this can be put together for you.

Even with the help of programs like this, going in and out of the hospital can be tough. It is sad to miss out on fun things at school and time with your friends, but try to have a good attitude and focus on feeling better.

Living With A Chronic Illness Or Disability

> ✔ **Quick Tip**
>
> ### When You Are In The Hospital
>
> - Keep in touch by phone and e-mail as much as you can.
>
> - Invite your friends to come visit you, if you are able to have visitors. Hospitals might be scary for people who have never been to one, but tell your friends not to worry, and that their visits will help you feel better.
>
> - Make friends with other young people who know how you feel—both in the hospital and in cyberspace. You can also visit the room for teens or kids at your hospital. You will find fun things to do, and it is a good way to make friends who know how you feel.
>
> - Find an activity you like to do that helps you feel less worried or sad, such as writing in a journal.
>
> Source: Excerpted from "Going to the Hospital," GirlsHealth.gov.

When Kids Tease

Kids often make fun of things they do not understand, which is one reason why they might make fun of someone with an illness or disability. This is not a good excuse for people who tease. It is just important to know that the problem is with the person who teases, not the person who is getting teased.

Why Do People Tease?

- To make people pay attention to them.
- They do not have good role models.
- It makes them feel better about themselves to put others down.
- They think it is cool.
- They make fun of things they do not understand, such as a learning disability.

It may sound funny, but not all teasing is bad. Teasing can be fun if it makes the person being teased laugh, too, but mean and hurtful teasing that is only meant to make someone feel badly can cause sadness and anger. It is important to know the difference: playful teasing can help you have a sense of humor and make it easier to get along with others, and harmful bullying can cause low or poor self-esteem.

What Can You Do?

If you are being teased, talk to your parents or guardians about what is going on. You may not be able to stop others from picking on you, but you can do something about the way it makes you feel. Here are some things you can do:

- When someone teases you, remind yourself that it does not matter what this person is saying.
- Know that you can handle it, even if you do not like it.
- Ignore the person who is teasing you, but remember to talk to your parents or guardians, especially if the teasing keeps happening.
- Picture the mean words bouncing right off of you.
- If you are around others, such as in a classroom, ask the teacher to tell them to stop.
- Use a calm voice when talking to people who pick on you to show you are not afraid and that you are a much more polite person.

Talking About Your Illness Or Disability

Talking about your illness or disability with your friends and others at school can be very tough. It is hard not knowing how people might feel about it, but being unsure sometimes is just a part of life. If you need a hand getting started, use these tips to make it easier to talk about your health.

- **You can decide who to tell.** You may choose to tell all of your friends or only a few close ones. Some illnesses or disabilities are easier to see than others. If you have an illness like cancer and the treatment causes you to lose your hair, it may be easier to tell all of your classmates or anyone else you see all the time. If your illness or disability cannot be seen as easily on the outside, you may decide you only want to tell a few people.
- **Tell people in a way that feels okay to you.** Whether you plan to tell just one friend or your whole class, it can help to practice. Try writing

down what you would like to say and practice in front of a mirror or a friend who already knows.

- **You can choose how much to tell.** Classmates may need only a little bit of information, such as how your illness or disability affects you at school. Beyond this, it is up to you how much to tell people. It can help to take your time to get a feel for how people are taking in what you are saying. If they seem open and you would like to tell them more, go ahead. They might also want to think about what you have said and ask you questions later. Either way, you can choose to share more details only with close friends.

- **Your real friends will still like you.** If someone decides they do not want to be friends with you because of your health problem, that person is not a good friend to have anyway.

The more you talk about your health and answer questions, the easier it will get. As more of your friends learn from you, you will find more support from them in return.

Becoming Independent

The truth is, any change is hard. Whether you are moving from special education to mainstream classes, planning to go to college, or preparing for life on your own someday, getting started can seem scary, but there are ways to make these transitions (changes) smoother.

The first important step is to write down what you would like your goals to be, meaning, what you would like to do when you get older. If you are not sure about your goals, write down the things you like to do. This will help you when you talk to your "team," which includes your counselor, teacher, doctor, parents/guardian, and most importantly, you. This team will help you put a plan into action, and it is not too early to start planning now for when you are older.

Things You Can Do To Become More Independent

There are lots of ways to show your independence. It may mean the following:

- Taking the bus or train by yourself

- Helping your parents with your health care at home
- Joining a support group (It may not sound very independent, but being around others who share your disability or illness can help you feel stronger.)

Everyone is different in what they can do, whether or not they have a disability or illness. Be proud of everything you do and never be afraid to ask for help. Asking for help will not make you any less independent.

> ✔ **Quick Tip**
>
> **Moving From Special Education To Mainstream Classes**
>
> If you are moving into a mainstream classroom, it is because you really belong there. Even so, there may be things you need help with. Never be afraid to ask someone for a hand. If something is out of your reach, or you have a question about the assignment, that does not mean you do not belong there. Everyone needs help sometimes, so do not be afraid to ask for it. You just may make a new friend.
>
> Source: "Moving From Special Education to Mainstream Classes," GirlsHealth.gov.

Helping Out At Home

Helping out at home is a great way to learn about responsibility and gain more independence. Our Skills Checklist will help you see which skills you know well and which ones you need to practice.

Being A Part Of The Community

There are many things you can do in your neighborhood to get to know others, help out, and show your independence. Talk to your parents about trying out some of these ideas:

- Use public transportation such as the bus or train.

Living With A Chronic Illness Or Disability

- Open a bank account.
- Spend time at the library.
- Send your mail at the post office.
- Volunteer to help out at a community event.
- Find a bathroom in an unfamiliar building by learning how to feel comfortable asking where it is.
- Join a group for people with your chronic illness or disability.
- Be a role model for younger people who share the same disability or illness as you.

Chapter 27

Chronic Pain And Psychological Stress Go Hand In Hand

Sources Of Stress

Chronic pain and psychological stress go hand in hand. Three sources of stress can be identified for chronic pain sufferers. First, the pain experience is in itself inherently stressful. Unless you happen to be a masochist, pain sensations are perceived as unwanted and undesirable. You tend to automatically fight and resist pain. Pain creates tension, both physical and mental/emotional. Physical tension typically manifests as elevated muscle tension in areas where the pain seems to originate. Of course other body systems react to tension as well (for example, cardiovascular, gastrointestinal, and immune systems). Mental and emotional tension can take different forms such as increased frustration and anger, anxiety and worry, sadness and discouragement, etc. Unfortunately, the physical and mental/emotional tension created by pain tends to worsen the pain.

The second source of stress refers to all of the negative consequences that the chronic pain condition has had on your life. Chronic pain can have adverse consequences on your employment, financial security, family activities,

---

About This Chapter: Information in this chapter is from "Pain and Stress," by Richard W. Hanson, Ph.D., *Self-Management of Chronic Pain: Patient Handbook,* April 2003, Chronic Pain Management Program, Long Beach VA Healthcare System. Reprinted with permission.

social life, hobbies and recreational activities, etc. Many find that dealing with doctors, medical clinics, and disability systems are stressful. Chronic pain and disability can also adversely affect your self-esteem and feelings of self-worth. All of these adverse consequences can be viewed as stressful.

The third general source of stress refers to all of the stressful life events and hassles that you encounter, probably nearly every day, that have nothing to do with the pain itself or the consequences of the pain on your life. We refer to this as the stress of everyday living. Unfortunately, when these everyday stressors get added on top of your pain-related stressors, the problem becomes much worse. As a result, you not only have chronic pain, but also chronic stress.

Effect Of Stress On Pain

Some people respond to chronic stress with excessive or prolonged activation of body systems. This in turn can create additional stress-related physical problems including headaches, muscle aches and pains, elevated blood pressure, upset stomach, bowel problems, etc.

♣ **It's A Fact!!**
Whatever the source of stress, the effect on pain is usually to intensify it.

Chronic anger and irritability, or anxiety and worry can make you feel constantly on edge. Others respond to chronic stress with physical deactivation and loss of energy. They become depressed and listless, with little motivation or interest. Whether you respond to stress with excessive physical and emotional activation or deactivation and depression, the result in most cases is increased pain and suffering.

As a result of this important connection between pain and stress, we place a lot of emphasis on learning how to either minimize or cope better with stress and tension. Although you may not be able to completely rid yourself of pain, you can have a significant influence on your pain by learning how to better manage stress in your life.

Stress Management

The issue of stress management can be approached from two directions. One direction is to identify and change maladaptive ways of coping with stress. The word maladaptive refers to ways of coping with stress, which may

Chronic Pain And Psychological Stress 153

seem to work in the short run, but ultimately do not work and in many cases create additional problems in the long run. Examples of some common maladaptive ways of coping with stress include:

- Denying to yourself and/or others that you are experiencing any stress in the first place

- Inhibiting or suppressing the outward expression of feelings arising from the stress

- Taking out your feelings on innocent people or other targets in a destructive manner

- Using alcohol or other drugs to change the way you feel in response to stress; drugs include not only illicit drugs, but also prescription and non-prescription drugs, and even common drugs such as nicotine and caffeine

- Filling your time with busy activities while avoiding the real sources of your stress

- Withdrawal, isolation, procrastination, and other forms of avoidance

In addition to changing maladaptive ways of coping with stress, the other direction is to find and make use of more healthy ways of managing stress.

Healthy Stress Management Procedures

It is important to understand that there is no single right way or best way to cope with stress. Your response to a particular stressful situation will depend upon several factors including the nature of the situation itself, how you perceive that situation, the degree of emotional distress that you are experiencing, and the specific coping options and resources which are available to you.

Following are examples of some healthier strategies for managing stress and tension:

- Constructive problem solving

- Establishing priorities and organizing your time more effectively

- Changing unhealthy, irrational, and distorted thoughts and attitudes and replacing them with more healthy ways of thinking

- Physical exercise and other healthy physical outlets
- Talking things over with a friend
- Getting professional counseling
- In some cases, prescribed medications may by beneficial
- Religious or spiritual practices (for example, attending church or synagogue, prayer, reading the Bible or other religious literature)
- Relaxation and meditation techniques

Chapter 28

Dealing With Grief

What Is Grief?

Grief is the normal response of sorrow, emotion, and confusion that comes from losing someone or something important to you. It is a natural part of life. Grief is a typical reaction to death, divorce, job loss, a move away from family and friends, or loss of good health due to illness.

How does grief feel?

Just after a death or loss, you may feel empty and numb, as if you are in shock. You may notice physical changes such as trembling, nausea, trouble breathing, muscle weakness, dry mouth, or trouble sleeping and eating.

You may become angry—at a situation, a particular person, or just angry in general. Almost everyone in grief also experiences guilt. Guilt is often expressed as "I could have, I should have, and I wish I would have" statements.

About This Chapter: Information under the heading "What Is Grief?" is from "How to Deal With Grief," National Mental Health Information Center, Substance Abuse and Mental Health Services Administration, United States Department of Health and Human Services, cited August 2007. Text under the heading "When A Friend Dies By Suicide" is from "When a Friend Dies by Suicide," © 2006 Maine Youth Suicide Prevention Program. Reprinted with permission. For additional information, visit http://www.main.gov/suicide/youth/index.htm.

People in grief may have strange dreams or nightmares, be absent-minded, withdraw socially, or lack the desire to return to work. While these feelings and behaviors are normal during grief, they will pass.

How long does grief last?

Grief lasts as long as it takes you to accept and learn to live with your loss. For some people, grief lasts a few months. For others, grieving may take years.

The length of time spent grieving is different for each person. There are many reasons for the differences, including personality, health, coping style, culture, family background, and life experiences. The time spent grieving also depends on your relationship with the person lost and how prepared you were for the loss.

How will I know when I am done grieving?

Every person who experiences a death or other loss must complete a four-step grieving process as follows:

1. Accept the loss.
2. Work through and feel the physical and emotional pain of grief.
3. Adjust to living in a world without the person or item lost.
4. Move on with life.

The grieving process is over only when a person completes the four steps.

How does grief differ from depression?

Depression is more than a feeling of grief after losing someone or something you love. Clinical depression is a whole body disorder. It can take over the way you think and feel. Symptoms of depression include the following:

- A sad, anxious, or "empty" mood that will not go away
- Loss of interest in what you used to enjoy
- Low energy, fatigue, feeling "slowed down"

Dealing With Grief

- Changes in sleep patterns
- Loss of appetite, weight loss, or weight gain
- Trouble concentrating, remembering, or making decisions
- Feeling hopeless or gloomy
- Feeling guilty, worthless, or helpless
- Thoughts of death or suicide or a suicide attempt
- Recurring aches and pains that do not respond to treatment

If you recently experienced a death or other loss, these feelings may be part of a normal grief reaction, but if these feelings persist with no lifting mood, ask for help.

When A Friend Dies By Suicide

- First and most important of all understand that it was not your fault. The only person responsible for the decision to kill him/herself is that person.
- Expect to feel lots of emotions including shock, denial, sadness, anger, guilt, and shame. Don't be afraid to talk to people about your feelings, write in a journal, etc.
- Doing something positive to remember the person can be very comforting (for example, writing a poem, song, or letter; attending the funeral service; making a scrapbook; etc.)
- Grieving is hard work, and the grief associated with suicide lasts longer than other kinds of grief. Seek out people who will support you during this difficult time.
- Some days may be more difficult (for example, the person's birthday, anniversary of their death, holidays, etc.) Be gentle with yourself on those days.
- It's okay to have and share good memories of the person, and it's okay to laugh. These are signs of healing.

✔ **Quick Tip**

Grieving The Loss Of Your Pet

A common aspect of owning a companion animal—a part many rarely discuss—is the loss of a pet. When you lose your best friend—the one you could always count on when you were down, the one who warmed you, played with you, and made you laugh no matter how bad you felt—it can be a devastating experience. It's important to grieve this loss and work through the emotions.

Feelings Are Feelings

Remember, it's okay to cry. Many of your friends may not understand how painful it is to lose a pet, but only you know the strength of the bond between you and the animal. No one else has the right to judge your sorrow.

Turning Sorrow Into Joy

- Talk to friends about your pet—the good times, the bad times, and the way it ended. Talking about your loss will help you feel better.

- Make a memorial donation in your pet's honor to an animal shelter and care agency.

- Have a memorial service in the woods or by your pet's favorite creek or pond. Bring a cherished photograph to symbolize your pet. Say a prayer or read a poem that expresses your feelings. Leave flowers, dog biscuits, or kitty treats as a parting gift of remembrance.

- Let yourself feel the pain and loss and appreciate all the years you had together.

Seek Support

Many humane societies offer grief counseling services. Check with your local agency for information about hotlines and support groups.

Source: "Grieving the Loss of Your Pet," Copyright © 2007 American Humane Association. All rights reserved. Additional information is available at www.americanhumane.org.

Part Three
How Stress Affects Your Body And Mind

Chapter 29

Stress And Disease: What's The Connection?

Whether from a charging lion, or a pending deadline, the body's response to stress can be both helpful and harmful. The stress response gives us the strength and speed to ward off or flee from an impending threat; but when it persists, stress can put us at risk for obesity, heart disease, cancer, and a variety of other illnesses.

Perhaps the greatest understanding of stress and its effects has resulted from a theory by George Chrousos, M.D., Chief of the Pediatric and Reproductive Endocrinology Branch at the National Institute of Child Health and Human Development (NICHD), and Philip Gold, M.D., of the Clinical Neuroendocrinology Branch at the National Institute of Mental Health (NIMH).

Introduction

A threat to your life or safety triggers a primal physical response from the body, leaving you breathless, heart pounding, and mind racing. From deep within your brain, a chemical signal speeds stress hormones through the

> About This Chapter: Information in this chapter is from "Stress System Malfunction Could Lead to Serious, Life Threatening Disease," NIH Backgrounder, National Institutes of Health, September 2002. Reviewed February 22, 2008 by David A. Cooke, M.D., Diplomate, American Board of Internal Medicine.

bloodstream, priming your body to be alert and ready to escape danger. Concentration becomes more focused, reaction time faster, and strength and agility increase. When the stressful situation ends, hormonal signals switch off the stress response, and the body returns to normal.

In our modern society, stress does not always let up. Many of us now harbor anxiety and worry about daily events and relationships. Stress hormones continue to wash through the system in high levels, never leaving the blood and tissues, so the stress response that once gave ancient people the speed and endurance to escape life-threatening dangers runs constantly in many modern people and never shuts down.

Research now shows that such long-term activation of the stress system can have a hazardous, even lethal effect on the body, increasing risk of obesity, heart disease, depression, and a variety of other illnesses.

Much of the current understanding of stress and its effects has resulted from the theory by Drs. Chrousos and Gold. Their theory explains the complex interplay between the nervous system and stress hormones—the hormonal system known as the hypothalamic-pituitary-adrenal (HPA) axis. Over the past 20 years, Dr. Chrousos and his colleagues have employed the theory to understand a variety of stress-related conditions, including depression, Cushing syndrome, anorexia nervosa, and chronic fatigue syndrome.

♣ It's A Fact!!

Emotions And Asthma

Emotions do not cause asthma but can make asthma worse. Strong feelings can lead to changes in breathing patterns. Times of "good" stress and "bad" stress can cause problems for people with asthma. However, it is important to express your emotions, and good asthma management can minimize the effect of stress.

Source: Excerpted from "What makes asthma worse?" © Copyright 2007 National Jewish Medical and Research Center. All rights reserved. For additional information, visit http://www.nationaljewish.org or call 1-800-222 LUNG.

The Stress Circuit

The HPA axis is a feedback loop by which signals from the brain trigger the release of hormones needed to respond to stress. Because of its function, the HPA axis is also sometimes called the "stress circuit."

Briefly, in response to a stress, the brain region known as the hypothalamus, releases corticotropin-releasing hormone (CRH). In turn, CRH acts on the pituitary gland, just beneath the brain, triggering the release of another hormone, adrenocorticotropin (ACTH) into the bloodstream. Next, ACTH signals the adrenal glands, which sit atop the kidneys, to release a number of hormonal compounds.

These compounds include epinephrine (formerly known as adrenaline), norepinephrine (formerly known as noradrenaline), and cortisol. All three hormones enable the body to respond to a threat. Epinephrine increases blood pressure and heart rate, diverts blood to the muscles, and speeds reaction time. Cortisol, also known as glucocorticoid, releases sugar (in the form of glucose) from the body reserves so that this essential fuel can be used to power the muscles and the brain.

Normally, cortisol also exerts a feedback effect to shut down the stress response after the threat has passed, acting upon the hypothalamus and causing it to stop producing CRH.

This stress circuit affects systems throughout the body. The hormones of the HPA axis exert their effect on the autonomic nervous system, which controls such vital functions as heart rate, blood pressure, and digestion.

The HPA axis also communicates with several regions of the brain, including the limbic system, which controls motivation and mood, with the amygdala, which generates fear in response to danger, and with the hippocampus, which plays an important part in memory formation as well as in mood and motivation. In addition, the HPA axis is also connected with brain regions that control body temperature, suppress appetite, and control pain.

Similarly, the HPA axis also interacts with various other glandular systems, among them those producing reproductive hormones, growth hormones, and thyroid hormones. Once activated, the stress response switches off the hormonal systems regulating growth, reproduction, metabolism, and immunity. Short term, the response is helpful, allowing us to divert biochemical resources to dealing with the threat.

Stress, Heredity, And The Environment

According to Dr. Chrousos, this stress response varies from person to person. Presumably, it is partially influenced by heredity. For example, in most people the HPA axis probably functions appropriately enough, allowing the body to respond to a threat and switching off when the threat has passed. Due to differences in the genes that control the HPA axis, however, other people may fail to have a strong enough response to a threat, while still others may over respond to even minor threats.

Beyond biological differences, the HPA axis also can alter its functioning in response to environmental influences. The HPA axis may permanently be altered as a result of extreme stress at any time during the life cycle—during adulthood, adolescence, early childhood, or even in the womb.

If there are major stresses in early childhood, the HPA feedback loop becomes stronger and stronger with each new stressful experience. This results in an individual who, by adulthood, has an extremely sensitive stress circuit in place. In life-threatening situations, such as life in an area torn by war, this exaggerated response would help an individual to survive. In contemporary society, however, it usually causes the individual to overreact hormonally to comparatively minor situations.

Effects On The Body

Stress And The Reproductive System

Stress suppresses the reproductive system at various levels, says Dr. Chrousos. First, CRH prevents the release of gonadotropin-releasing hormone (GnRH), the "master" hormone that signals a cascade of hormones that direct reproduction and sexual behavior. Similarly, cortisol and related glucocorticoid hormones not only inhibit the release of GnRH, but also the release of luteinizing hormone, which prompts ovulation and sperm release. Glucocorticoids also inhibit the testes and ovaries directly, hindering production of the male and female sex hormones testosterone, estrogen, and progesterone.

Stress And Disease: What's The Connection?

The HPA over activity that results from chronic stress has been shown to inhibit reproductive functioning in anorexia nervosa and in starvation, as well as in highly trained ballet dancers and runners. For example, in one study, Chrousos found that men who ran more than 45 miles per week produced high levels of ACTH and cortisol in response to the stress of extreme exercise. These male runners had low luteinizing hormone (LH) and testosterone levels. Other studies have shown that women undertaking extreme exercise regimens had ceased ovulating and menstruating.

However, the interaction between the HPA axis and the reproductive system is also a two-way street. The female hormone estrogen exerts partial control of the gene that stimulates CRH production. This may explain why, on average, women have slightly elevated cortisol levels. In turn, higher cortisol levels in combination with other as yet unknown factors, may be the reason why women are more vulnerable than men to depression, anorexia nervosa, panic disorder, obsessive compulsive disorder, and autoimmune diseases like lupus and rheumatoid arthritis.

Growth And Stress

The hormones of the HPA axis also influence hormones needed for growth. Prolonged HPA activation will hinder the release of growth hormone and insulin-like growth factor 1 (IGF-1), both of which are essential for normal growth. Glucocorticoids released during prolonged stress also cause tissues to be less likely to respond to IGF-1. Children with Cushing syndrome, which results in high glucocorticoid levels, lose about 7.5 to 8.0 centimeters from their adult height.

Similarly, premature infants are at an increased risk for growth retardation. The stress of surviving in an environment for which they are not yet suited, combined with the prolonged stress of hospitalization in the intensive care unit, presumably activates the HPA axis. Growth retarded fetuses also have higher levels of CRH, ACTH, and cortisol, probably resulting from stress in the womb or exposure to maternal stress hormones.

Old research has also shown that the stress from emotional deprivation or psychological harassment may result in the short stature and delayed physical maturity of the condition known as psychosocial short stature (PSS).

PSS was first discovered in orphanages in infants who failed to thrive and grow. When these children were placed in caring environments in which they received sufficient attention, their growth resumed. The children's cortisol levels were abnormally low, a seeming contradiction, which Chrousos investigated by studying a small, non-human primate, the common marmoset. These monkeys live in small family groups in which infants are cared for by both parents. As in human society, the infants are sometimes well cared for, but sometimes abused. Like humans, the abused monkeys showed evidence of PSS.

The researchers determined that the stressed and abused monkeys appeared to respond normally to stress but seemed unable to "switch off" the stress response by secreting appropriate cortisol levels, thereby remaining in a state of prolonged stress arousal as compared to their peers.

The Gastrointestinal Tract And Stress

As many of us know, stress can also result in digestive problems. The stress circuit influences the stomach and intestines in several ways. First, CRH directly hinders the release of stomach acid and emptying of the stomach. Moreover, CRH also directly stimulates the colon, speeding up the emptying of its contents. In addition to the effects of CRH alone on the stomach, the entire HPA axis, through the autonomic nervous system, also hinders stomach acid secretion and emptying, as well as increasing the movement of the colon.

Also, continual high levels of cortisol, as occur in some forms of depression or during chronic psychological stress, can increase appetite and lead to weight gain. Rats given high doses of cortisol for long periods had increased appetites and had larger stores of abdominal fat. The rats also ate heavily when they would normally have been inactive. Overeating at night is also common among people who are under stress.

The Immune System And Stress

The HPA axis also interacts with the immune system, making you more vulnerable to colds and flu, fatigue, and infections.

In response to an infection or an inflammatory disorder like rheumatoid arthritis, cells of the immune system produce three substances that cause

Stress And Disease: What's The Connection?

inflammation: interleukin 1 (IL-1), interleukin 6 (IL-6), and tumor necrosis factor (TNF). These substances, working either singly or in combination with each other, cause the release of CRH. IL-6 also promotes the release of ACTH and cortisol. Cortisol and other compounds then suppress the release of IL-1, IL-6, and TNF, in the process switching off the inflammatory response.

Ideally, stress hormones damp down an immune response that has run its course. When the HPA axis is continually running at a high level, however, that damping down can have a down side, leading to decreased ability to release the interleukins and fight infection.

In addition, the high cortisol levels resulting from prolonged stress could serve to make the body more susceptible to disease by switching off disease-fighting white blood cells. Although the necessary studies have not yet been conducted, Dr. Chrousos considers it possible that this same deactivation of white blood cells might also increase the risk for certain types of cancer.

Conversely, there is evidence that a depressed HPA axis, resulting in too little corticosteroid, can lead to a hyperactive immune system and increased risk of developing autoimmune diseases—diseases in which the immune system attacks the body's own cells. Over-activation of the antibody-producing B cells may aggravate conditions like lupus, which result from an antibody attack on the body's own tissues.

Stress-Related Disorders

One of the major disorders characteristic of an overactive HPA axis is melancholic depression. Chrousos' research has shown that people with depression have a blunted ability to "counter regulate," or adapt to the negative feedback of increases in cortisol. The body turns on the "fight or flight" response but is prevented from turning it off again. This produces constant anxiety and over-reaction to stimulation followed by the paradoxical response called "learned helplessness," in which victims apparently lose all motivation.

Hallmarks of this form of depression are anxiety, loss of appetite, loss of sex drive, rapid heart beat, high blood pressure, and high cholesterol and triglyceride levels. People with this condition tend to produce higher-than-normal levels of

> ♣ **It's A Fact!!**
>
> **Psychological Stress And Cancer**
>
> The complex relationship between physical and psychological health is not well understood. Scientists know that many types of stress activate the body's endocrine (hormone) system, which in turn can cause changes in the immune system, the body's defense against infection and disease (including cancer). However, the immune system is a highly specialized network whose activity is affected not only by stress, but also by a number of other factors. It has not been shown that stress-induced changes in the immune system directly cause cancer.
>
> Some studies have indicated an increased incidence of early death, including cancer death, among people who have experienced the recent loss of a spouse or other loved one. However, most cancers have been developing for many years and are diagnosed only after they have been growing in the body for a long time (from 2 to 30 years). This fact argues against an association between the death of a loved one and the triggering of cancer.
>
> The relationship between breast cancer and stress has received particular attention. Some studies of women with breast cancer have shown significantly higher rates of this disease among those women who experienced traumatic life events and losses within several years before their diagnosis. Although studies have shown that stress factors (such as death of a spouse, social isolation, and medical

CRH. The high levels of CRH are probably due to a combination of environmental and hereditary causes, depending on the person affected.

However, rather than producing higher amounts of ACTH in response to CRH, depressed people produce smaller amounts of this substance, presumably because their hippocampuses have become less sensitive to the higher amounts of CRH. In an apparent attempt to switch off excess CRH production, the systems of people with melancholic depression also produce high levels of cortisol. However, by-products of cortisol, produced in response to high levels of the substance, also depress brain cell activity. These by-products serve as sedatives and perhaps contribute to the overall feeling of depression.

Other conditions are also associated with high levels of CRH and cortisol. These include anorexia nervosa, malnutrition, obsessive-compulsive disorder,

> school examinations) alter the way the immune system functions, they have not provided scientific evidence of a direct cause-and-effect relationship between these immune system changes and the development of cancer. One National Cancer Institute (NCI)-sponsored study suggests that there is no important association between stressful life events, such as the death of a loved one or divorce, and breast cancer risk. However, more research to find if there is a relationship between psychological stress and the transformation of normal cells into cancerous cells is needed.
>
> One area that is currently being studied is the effect of stress on women already diagnosed with breast cancer. These studies are looking at whether stress reduction can improve the immune response and possibly slow cancer progression. Researchers are doing this by determining whether women with breast cancer who are in support groups have better survival rates than those not in support groups.
>
> Many factors come into play when determining the relationship between stress and cancer. At present, the relationship between psychological stress and cancer occurrence, or progression, has not been scientifically proven. However, stress reduction is of benefit for many other health reasons.
>
> Source: National Cancer Institute Fact Sheet, National Cancer Institute, U.S. National Institutes of Health, March 1998. Reviewed February 22, 2008 by David A. Cooke, M.D., Diplomate, American Board of Internal Medicine.

anxiety disorder, alcoholism, alcohol and narcotic withdrawal, poorly controlled diabetes, childhood sexual abuse, and hyperthyroidism.

The excessive amount of the stress hormone cortisol produced in patients with any of these conditions is responsible for many of the observed symptoms. Most of these patients share psychological symptoms including sleep disturbances, loss of libido, and loss of appetite, as well as physical problems such as an increased risk for accumulating abdominal fat and hardening of the arteries and other forms of cardiovascular disease. These patients may also experience suppression of thyroid hormones and of the immune system. Because they are at higher risk for these health problems, such patients are likely to have their life spans shortened by 15 to 20 years if they remain untreated.

Although many disorders result from an overactive stress system, some result from an under active stress system. For example, in the case of Addison disease, lack of cortisol causes an increase of pigment in the skin, making the patient appear to have a tan. Other symptoms include fatigue, loss of appetite, weight loss, weakness, loss of body hair, nausea, vomiting, and an intense craving for salt. Lack of the hormone CRH also results in the feelings of extreme tiredness common to people suffering from chronic fatigue syndrome. Lack of CRH is also central to seasonal affective disorder (SAD), the feelings of fatigue and depression that plague some patients during winter months.

Chrousos and his team showed that sudden cessation of CRH production may also result in the depressive symptoms of postpartum depression. In response to CRH produced by the placenta, the mother's system stops manufacturing its own CRH. When the baby is born, the sudden loss of CRH may result in feelings of sadness or even severe depression for some women.

Recently, Dr. Chrousos and his co-workers uncovered evidence that frequent insomnia is more than just having difficulty falling asleep. The researchers found that when compared to a group of people who did not have difficulty falling asleep, the insomniacs had higher ACTH and cortisol levels, both in the evening and in the first half of the night. Moreover, the insomniacs with the highest cortisol levels tended to have the greatest difficulty falling asleep.

The researchers theorized that, in many cases, persistent insomnia may be a disorder of the stress system. From their ACTH and cortisol levels, it appears that the insomniacs have nervous systems that are on overdrive, alert and ready to deal with a threat, when they should otherwise be quieting down. Rather than prescribing drugs known as hypnotics to regulate the sleep system, the researchers suggested that physicians might have more success prescribing antidepressants to help calm an overactive stress system. Behavior therapy, to help insomniacs relax in the evening, might also be useful.

After conducting many years of research into the functioning of the HPA axis, Dr. Chrousos concluded that chronic stress should not be taken lightly or accepted as a fact of life.

"Persistent, unremitting stress leads to a variety of serious health problems," Dr. Chrousos said. "Anyone who suffers from chronic stress needs to take steps to alleviate it, either by learning simple techniques to relax and calm down, or with the help of qualified therapists.

Chapter 30
Stress And The Immune System

For thousands of years, people believed that stress made you sick. Up until the nineteenth century, the idea that the passions and emotions were intimately linked to disease held sway, and people were told by their doctors to go to spas or seaside resorts when they were ill. Gradually these ideas lost favor as more concrete causes and cures were found for illness after illness. In the last decade, scientists like Dr. Esther Sternberg, director of the Integrative Neural Immune Program at National Institutes of Health's National Institute of Mental Health (NIMH), have been rediscovering the links between the brain and the immune system.

The Immune System And The Brain

When you have an infection or something else that causes inflammation such as a burn or injury, many different kinds of cells from the immune system stream to the site. Dr. Sternberg likens them to soldiers moving into battle, each kind with its own specialized function. Some are like garbage collectors, ingesting invaders. Some make antibodies, the "bullets" to fight the infectious agents; others kill invaders directly. All these types of immune cells must coordinate

---

About This Chapter: Information in this chapter is from "Stress and Disease: New Perspectives," by Harrison Wein, Ph.D., *The NIH on Word Health*, NIH Office of Communications and Public Liaison, National Institutes of Health, October 2000. Reviewed February 22, 2008 by David A. Cooke, M.D., Diplomate, American Board of Internal Medicine.

their actions, and the way they do that is by sending each other signals in the form of molecules that they make in factories inside the cell.

"It turns out that these molecules have many more effects than just being the walkie-talkie communicators between different kinds of immune cells," Dr. Sternberg says. "They can also go through the bloodstream to signal the brain or activate nerves nearby that signal the brain."

These immune molecules, Dr. Sternberg explains, cause the brain to change its functions. "They can induce a whole set of behaviors that we call sickness behavior...You lose the desire or the ability to move, you lose your appetite, you lose interest in sex." Scientists can only speculate about the purpose of these sickness behaviors, but Dr. Sternberg suggests that they might help us conserve energy when we are sick so we can better use our energy to fight disease.

These signaling molecules from the immune system can also activate the part of the brain that controls the stress response, the hypothalamus. Through a cascade of hormones released from the pituitary and adrenal glands, the hypothalamus causes blood levels of the hormone cortisol to rise. Cortisol is the major steroid hormone produced by our bodies to help us get through stressful situations. The related compound known as cortisone is widely used as an anti-inflammatory drug in creams to treat rashes and in nasal sprays to treat sinusitis and asthma. It was not until very recently that scientists realized the brain also uses cortisol to suppress the immune system and tone down inflammation within the body.

Stress And The Immune System

This complete communications cycle from the immune system to the brain and back again allows the immune system to talk to the brain and the brain to then talk back and shut down the immune response when it is no longer needed.

"When you think about this cross-talk, this two-way street," Dr. Sternberg explains, "you can begin to understand the kinds of illnesses that might result if there is either too much or too little communication in either direction."

> ♣ **It's A Fact!!**
>
> There is considerable evidence that emotional traits, both negative and positive, influence people's susceptibility to infection. Following systematic exposure to a respiratory virus in the laboratory, individuals who report higher levels of stress or negative moods have been shown to develop more severe illness than those who report less stress or more positive moods. Recent studies suggest that the tendency to report positive, as opposed to negative, emotions may be associated with greater resistance to objectively verified colds. These laboratory studies are supported by longitudinal studies pointing to associations between psychological or emotional traits and the incidence of respiratory infections.
>
> Source: Excerpted from "Mind-Body Medicine: An Overview," National Center for Complementary and Alternative Medicine, National Institutes of Health, July 2007.

According to Dr. Sternberg, if you are chronically stressed, the part of the brain that controls the stress response is going to be constantly pumping out a lot of stress hormones. The immune cells are being bathed in molecules, which are essentially telling them to stop fighting. In situations of chronic stress, your immune cells are less able to respond to an invader like a bacteria or a virus.

This theory holds up in studies looking at high levels of shorter term stress or chronic stress—in caregivers like those taking care of relatives with Alzheimer disease, medical students undergoing exam stress, Army rangers undergoing extremely grueling physical stress, and couples with marital stress. People in these situations, Dr. Sternberg says, show a prolonged healing time, a decreased ability of their immune systems to respond to vaccination, and an increased susceptibility to viral infections like the common cold.

Some Stress Is Good

People tend to talk about stress as if it is all bad. It is not.

"Some stress is good for you," Dr. Sternberg says. "I have to get my stress response to a certain optimal level, so I can perform in front of an audience when I give a talk." Otherwise, she may come across as lethargic and listless.

While some stress is good, too much is not good. "If you're too stressed, your performance falls off," Dr. Sternberg says. "The objective should be not to get rid of stress completely because you can't get rid of stress—stress is life, life is stress. Rather, you need to be able to use your stress response optimally."

The key is to learn to move yourself to that optimal peak point so that you are not underperforming, but you are also not so stressed that you are unable to perform. How much we are able to do that is the challenge, Dr. Sternberg admits. This may not be possible in all situations, or for all people, because just as with the animals Dr. Sternberg studies, some people may have a more sensitive stress response than others.

"But your goal should be to try to learn to control your stress to make it work for you," Dr. Sternberg says. "Don't just think of getting rid of your stress; think of turning it to your advantage."

Controlling The Immune Response

Problems between the brain and the immune system can go the other way, too. If for some reason you are unable to make enough of these brain stress hormones, you will not be able to turn off the immune cells once they are no longer needed.

"There has to be an exit strategy for these battles that are being fought by the immune system, and the brain provides the exit strategy through stress hormones," Dr. Sternberg says. "If your brain can't make enough of these hormones to turn the immune system off when it doesn't have to be active anymore, then it could go on unchecked and result in autoimmune diseases like rheumatoid arthritis, lupus, or other autoimmune diseases that people recognize as inflammation."

Dr. Sternberg says that there are several factors involved in these autoimmune conditions. There are many different effects that the brain and its nervous system can have on the immune system, depending on the kinds of nerve chemicals that are being made, where they are being made, what kind of nerves they come from, and whether they are in the bloodstream or not. Still, at least part of the problem in these diseases seems to involve the brain's hormonal stress response.

"So if you have too much stress hormone shutting down the immune response, you can't fight off infection and you're more susceptible to infection," Dr. Sternberg concludes. "Too little stress hormones and the immune response goes on unchecked and you could get an inflammatory disease."

Pinpointing The Problems

Why these miscommunications between the brain and the immune system come about is still largely unknown and involves many genes and environmental factors; but by studying animals, scientists have finally been able to start understanding how the miscommunications occur.

Dr. Sternberg first started publishing work on the links between the brain and the immune system back in 1989, studying rats with immune problems. "In many of these cases, it's very hard to show the mechanism in humans," Dr. Sternberg explains, "but you can show the mechanism in animals because you can manipulate all the different parts of the system, and you can begin to understand which parts affect which other parts." It has taken "a good ten years" to gather enough evidence in human studies to show that the principles her lab uncovered in rats were also relevant to human beings.

Drugs that have been tested in rats to correct brain/immune system problems have had unpredictable effects. That is because nothing happens in isolation when it comes to the brain and the immune system. Dr. Sternberg points out that our bodies are amazing machines, which at every moment of the day are constantly responding to a myriad of different kinds of stimuli—chemical, psychological, and physical. "These molecules act in many different ways in different parts of the system," she says. Understanding how the brain and the immune system work together in these different diseases should help scientists develop new kinds of drugs to treat them that would never have occurred to them before.

> ✔ **Quick Tip**
>
> **Stress Control**
>
> First try to identify the things in your life that cause you stress. Once you identify and understand how these stressors affect you, you can begin to figure out ways to change your environment and manage them.
>
> If there is a problem that can be solved, set about taking control and solving it.
>
> Some chronic stressors cannot be changed. For those, support groups, relaxation, meditation, and exercise are all tools you can use to manage your stress. If nothing you do seems to work for you, seek a health professional who can help. Also seek professional help if you find that you worry excessively about the small things in life.
>
> Keep in mind that chronic stress can be associated with mental conditions like depression and anxiety disorders as well as physical problems. Seek professional help if you have the following:
>
> - difficulty sleeping
> - changes in appetite
> - panic attacks
> - muscle tenseness and soreness
> - frequent headaches
> - gastrointestinal problems
> - prolonged feelings of sadness or worthlessness
>
> Source: Excerpted from "Stress and Disease: New Perspectives," by Harrison Wein, Ph.D., *The NIH on Word Health*.

Taking Control Now

Dr. Sternberg thinks that one of the most hopeful aspects of this science is that it tells us it is not all in our genes. A growing number of studies show that, to some degree, you can use your mind to help treat your body. Support groups, stress relief, and meditation may, by altering stress hormone levels, all help the

Stress And The Immune System

immune system. For example, women in support groups for their breast cancer have longer life spans than women without such psychological support.

There are several components of stress to think about, including its duration, how strong it is, and how long it lasts. Every stress has some effect on the body, and you have to take into account the total additive effect on the body of all stressors when considering how to reduce stress.

Perhaps the most productive way to think about stress is in terms of control. Dr. Sternberg shows a slide of an F-14 jet flying sideways by the deck of an aircraft carrier, its wings completely vertical. "The Navy commander who flew that jet told me that he was the only one in the photo who was not stressed, and that's because he was the one in control. The officer sitting in the seat ten feet behind him was in the exact same physical situation but was not in control. Control is a very important part of whether or not we feel stressed.

So if you can learn to feel that you're in control, or actually take control of certain aspects of the situation that you're in, you can reduce your stress response." Studies show that gaining a sense of control can help patients cope with their illness, if not help the illness itself.

Until science has more solid answers, it cannot hurt to participate in support groups and seek ways to relieve stress, Dr. Sternberg says. What you need to remember is if you do these things and you are not successful in correcting whatever the underlying problem is, it is not your fault because there is a biology to the system. "You need to know the benefits of the system," she says, "but its limitations as well." In other words, try not to get too stressed about being stressed.

Chapter 31

Stress And Insomnia

I have a lot of stress, and I also have periodic bouts of insomnia. Could there be a connection between the two?

In a word, yes. Not all insomnia is due to stress, but people who are under considerable stress can have insomnia. In the case of insomnia related to stress, alleviating the stress should alleviate the insomnia. Stress causes insomnia by making it difficult to fall asleep and to stay asleep, and by affecting the quality of your sleep. Stress causes hyper-arousal, which can upset the balance between sleep and wakefulness. Nevertheless, many people under stress do not have insomnia.

How can I know if my insomnia is the result of stress or something else?

As with any symptom, an important question to ask is "when did it start?" Does the sleep problem come and go with the occurrence and disappearance of stress or does it persist through all the permutations of one's life? That is, is it situational? Also it is helpful to clarify what one means by stress.

About This Chapter: Information in this chapter is from "Stress and Insomnia," by Neil B. Kavey, MD. © 2001 National Sleep Foundation (www.sleepfoundation.org). All rights reserved. Reprinted with permission. This article originally appeared in the Spring 2001 issue of sleepmatters. Despite the older date of this document, the information presented is still appropriate for readers seeking to understand this issue.

For example, are you frequently anxious whether or not you are under unusual stress? Is it hard for you to "wind down" at the end of the day? Are you frequently infuriated? Or do you feel depressed? If you feel "blue" much of the time, your problem may be a mood disorder, more than a problem with stress.

What then should I do to help my insomnia?

No matter what the cause of your insomnia, it's important to get on a good behavior program—one that pays attention to periods of relaxation. These three steps are suggested:

- First, set your bedtime and your wake-up time according to the number of hours of sleep you are getting currently. For example, if you are sleeping only five hours a night (even though you usually plan to spend eight hours in bed), set your sleep time for that amount. Then gradually increase the amount of time allotted for sleep by 15 minutes or so every few nights. The idea is to "squeeze out" the middle of the nighttime awakening and gradually increase the amount of sleep you will get during the night.

- Spend some time "winding down." A person with insomnia needs a "buffer zone," a period of time to allow the activating processes in the brain to wind down to allow the alerting mechanisms to decrease their activity so that the sleep systems can take over. Start winding down two hours before bedtime. Stop all work and end phone calls to family and friends, as often they are activating.

- Finally, focus on conditioning yourself for different sleep behavior. Insomnia is painful for people—it can takecontrol of their lives. When someone suffering from insomnia walks into their bedroom, they often feel anxious, uncomfortable, and tense, as they know from their experience that they might spend the night tossing and turning. They need to set up a situation so that they like going to their bedroom. The bedroom should be

> ✔ **Quick Tip**
> Watching television is all right in the evening. However, reading or listening to music an hour before bed is recommended.

visually pleasing and very comfortable. One should use the bedroom only for sleep, changing clothes, and pleasant activities, and if awake in the night, should leave the bed and bedroom and spend "unpleasant" times awake in another room. "Waking" activities such as working on the computer, talking with one's partner, talking on the phone, and watching television should take place out of the bedroom.

What about over-the-counter medications? Do they help?

Over-the-counter (OTC) medications, in combination with a good behavior program, can be helpful for a few days; but the problem with OTC medications is that they tend to have limited effectiveness over the long term and can have a high incidence of "hangovers." Many people taking OTC medications still feel tired the next day and attribute it to their insomnia, but it can be a lingering effect of the medication. Be wary of OTC medications—use them only as you would aspirin for a headache, only so much for so long.

At what point should I seek professional help?

It's important to recognize that transient insomnias are very common. A night or two of insomnia may not be much of a problem for most people. But if insomnia persists for days and has an impact on the way you feel during the day, you should think about speaking to your doctor. Most doctors will turn to prescription medications for short-term insomnia. When judiciously used, medications can be very safe and highly effective in combination with the kind of behavioral program described. If the problem persists, you might need to turn to a board certified sleep expert.

What's the most important thing to know about insomnia?

A lot of people suffer from insomnia, and they say to themselves, "I know what this is, but I can't do anything about it." However, consider the toll insomnia takes on your life, the effect it has on your family, your ability to work at a high level, and to socialize with others. The consequences are so enormous that it's important to do something about it. It can be addressed through proper diagnosis and treatment. And if your physician can't help you, seek out an expert in sleep medicine. By all means, don't accept it as a necessary part of your life.

Chapter 32

Chronic Fatigue Syndrome

What is chronic fatigue syndrome (CFS)?

A person with CFS feels completely worn out and overtired. This extreme tiredness makes it hard to do the daily tasks that most of us do without thinking, like dressing, bathing, or eating. Sleep or rest does not make the tiredness go away. It can be made worse by moving, exercising, or even thinking.

CFS can happen over time or come on suddenly. People who get CFS over time get more and more tired over weeks or months. People who get CFS suddenly feel fine one day and then feel extremely tired the next. A person with CFS may have muscle pain, trouble focusing, or insomnia (not being able to sleep). The extreme tiredness may come and go. In some cases, the extreme tiredness never goes away. The extreme tiredness must go on for at least six months before a diagnosis of CFS can be made.

What causes CFS?

No one knows for sure what causes CFS. Many people with CFS say it started after an infection, such as a cold or stomach bug. It also can follow a bout of infectious mononucleosis (mono), the "kissing disease" that drains your energy.

> About This Chapter: Information in this chapter is from "Chronic Fatigue Syndrome," National Women's Health Information Center, U.S. Department of Health and Human Services, June 2006.

It can be hard to figure out if a person has CFS because extreme tiredness is a common symptom of many illnesses. Also, some medical treatments, such as chemotherapy, can cause extreme tiredness.

What are the signs of CFS?

The signs of CFS can come and go, or they can stay with a person. At first, you may feel like you have the flu. As well as extreme tiredness and weakness, CFS symptoms include the following:

> ♣ **It's A Fact!!**
> Some people with CFS say it started after a time of great stress, such as the loss of a loved one or major surgery.

- forgetting things or having a hard time focusing
- feeling tired even after sleeping
- muscle pain or aches
- pain or aches in joints without swelling or redness
- feeling discomfort or "out-of-sorts" for more than 24 hours after being active
- headaches of a new type, pattern, or strength
- tender lymph nodes in the neck or under the arm
- sore throat

Many people with CFS report other symptoms too, ranging from a constant cough to feelings of depression. If you think you may have CFS, talk to your doctor.

How common is CFS? Who gets it?

Experts think as many as half a million Americans have a CFS-like condition. The exact number of people with CFS is not known. CFS can affect people of all ages, racial/ethnic backgrounds, and economic statuses.

More women than men are diagnosed with CFS, but it is not known for sure that this illness affects more women than men. It may be that women talk to their doctors more often about things like tiredness and pain.

Chronic Fatigue Syndrome

How would my doctor know if I have CFS?

It can be hard for your doctor to diagnose CFS because there is no lab test for it, and many signs of CFS are also signs of other illnesses or medical treatments.

If you think you may have CFS, see your doctor. Your doctor will do the following:

- ask you about your physical and mental health
- do a physical exam
- order urine and blood tests, which will tell your doctor if something other than CFS might be causing your symptoms
- order more tests, if your urine and blood tests do not show a cause for your symptoms
- classify you as having CFS if you have been extremely tired for six months or more and tests do not show a cause for your symptoms and you have four or more of the symptoms listed in the section "What are the signs of CFS?" in this chapter.

This process can take a long time (even years), so try to be patient with your doctor. While these tests are being done, talk to your doctor about ways to help ease your symptoms.

How is CFS treated?

Right now, there is no cure for CFS, but there are things you can do to feel better. Talk to your doctor about ways to ease your symptoms and deal with your tiredness. You might also try lifestyle changes or medications.

Lifestyle Changes

- **Try to stop or do less of the things that seem to trigger your tiredness.** For a week or two, write down what you do each day and note when you feel really tired. Then, look over this list to find out which activities tend to tire you out. An occupational therapist can help you by looking at your daily habits and suggesting changes to help you save energy. Your doctor can help you find an occupational therapist near where you live.

- **Regular exercise** can lessen body aches and joint and muscle pain and increase your energy level. Be sure to talk to your doctor before starting an exercise plan. Your doctor can help you create a plan that is right for you. Do not exercise too much. Too much exercise can cause more tiredness.

Medications

- **Over-the-counter pain relievers** such as Advil, Motrin, or Aleve can help with body aches, headaches, and muscle and joint pain.
- **Non-drowsy antihistamines** can help with allergy symptoms, such as runny nose and itchy eyes.
- **Antidepressants** can help improve sleep and ease pain.

Some people say their CFS symptoms get better with complementary or alternative treatments, such as massage, acupuncture, chiropractic care, yoga, stretching, or self-hypnosis. Keep in mind that many alternative treatments, dietary supplements, and herbal remedies claim to cure CFS, but they might do more harm than good. Talk to your doctor before seeing someone else for treatment or before trying alternative therapies.

Also, keep in mind that your doctor may need to learn more about CFS to better help you. If you feel your doctor does not know a lot about CFS or has doubts about it being a real illness, see another doctor for a second opinion. Contact a local university medical school or research center for help finding a doctor who treats people with CFS.

What can I do to cope with CFS?

It is normal to feel cranky, sad, angry, or upset when you have an illness like CFS. Here are some things you can do that may help you to feel better:

- **Talk therapy** can help you learn how to deal with your feelings.
- **Join a CFS support group.** Sometimes it helps to talk with people who are going through the same thing.

What is the latest research on CFS?

Both the National Institutes of Health (NIH) and the Centers for Disease Control and Prevention (CDC) fund CFS studies. Today, they have a much better understanding of CFS, but researchers are still searching for the cause(s). They also are looking for ways to prevent CFS and for the best ways to ease CFS symptoms. In time, research findings will be used to develop a cure for CFS.

Chapter 33

Fibromyalgia

What is fibromyalgia?

Fibromyalgia syndrome is a common and chronic disorder characterized by widespread muscle pain, fatigue, and multiple tender points. The word fibromyalgia comes from the Latin term for fibrous tissue (fibro) and the Greek ones for muscle (myo) and pain (algia). Tender points are specific places on the body—on the neck, shoulders, back, hips, and upper and lower extremities—where people with fibromyalgia feel pain in response to slight pressure.

Although fibromyalgia is often considered an arthritis-related condition, it is not truly a form of arthritis (a disease of the joints) because it does not cause inflammation or damage to the joints, muscles, or other tissues. Like arthritis, however, fibromyalgia can cause significant pain and fatigue, and it can interfere with a person's ability to carry on daily activities. Also like arthritis, fibromyalgia is considered a rheumatic condition.

You may wonder what exactly rheumatic means. Even physicians do not always agree on whether a disease is considered rheumatic. If you look up the word in the dictionary, you will find it comes from the Greek word rheum,

---

About This Chapter: Information in this chapter is excerpted from "Questions and Answers About Fibromyalgia," National Institute of Arthritis and Musculoskeletal and Skin Diseases, National Institutes of Health, U.S. Department of Health and Human Services, June 2004.

which means flux—not an explanation that gives you a better understanding. In medicine, however, the term rheumatic means a medical condition that impairs the joints and/or soft tissues and causes chronic pain.

In addition to pain and fatigue, people who have fibromyalgia may experience the following:

- sleep disturbances
- morning stiffness
- headaches
- irritable bowel syndrome
- painful menstrual periods
- numbness or tingling of the extremities
- restless legs syndrome
- temperature sensitivity
- cognitive and memory problems (sometimes referred to as "fibro fog")
- a variety of other symptoms

> ♣ **It's A Fact!!**
> Fibromyalgia is a syndrome rather than a disease. Unlike a disease, which is a medical condition with a specific cause or causes and recognizable signs and symptoms, a syndrome is a collection of signs, symptoms, and medical problems that tend to occur together but are not related to a specific, identifiable cause.

Who gets fibromyalgia?

According to a paper published by the American College of Rheumatology (ACR), fibromyalgia affects 3 to 6 million, or as many as 1 in 50, Americans. For unknown reasons, between 80 and 90 percent of those diagnosed with fibromyalgia are women; however, men and children also can be affected. Most people are diagnosed during middle age, although the symptoms often become present earlier in life.

People with certain rheumatic diseases, such as rheumatoid arthritis, systemic lupus erythematosus (commonly called lupus), or ankylosing spondylitis (spinal arthritis) may be more likely to have fibromyalgia, too.

Several studies indicate that women who have a family member with fibromyalgia are more likely to have fibromyalgia themselves, but the exact reason for this, whether it be hereditary or caused by environmental factors

Fibromyalgia

or both, is unknown. One study supported by the National Institute of Arthritis and Musculoskeletal and Skin Diseases (NIAMS) is trying to identify if certain genes predispose some people to fibromyalgia.

What causes fibromyalgia?

The causes of fibromyalgia are unknown, but there are probably a number of factors involved. Many people associate the development of fibromyalgia with a physically or emotionally stressful or traumatic event, such as an automobile accident. Some connect it to repetitive injuries. Others link it to an illness. People with rheumatoid arthritis and other autoimmune diseases, such as lupus, are particularly likely to develop fibromyalgia. For others, fibromyalgia seems to occur spontaneously.

Many researchers are examining other causes, including problems with how the central nervous system (the brain and spinal cord) processes pain.

Some scientists speculate that a person's genes may regulate the way his or her body processes painful stimuli. According to this theory, people with fibromyalgia may have a gene or genes that cause them to react strongly to stimuli that most people would not perceive as painful. However, those genes, if they, in fact, exist, have not been identified.

How is fibromyalgia diagnosed?

Research shows that people with fibromyalgia typically see many doctors before receiving the diagnosis. One reason for this may be that pain and fatigue, the main symptoms of fibromyalgia, overlap with many other conditions. Therefore, doctors often have to rule out other potential causes of these symptoms before making a diagnosis of fibromyalgia. Another reason is that there are currently no diagnostic laboratory tests for fibromyalgia; standard laboratory tests fail to reveal a physiologic reason for pain. Because there is no generally accepted objective test for fibromyalgia, some doctors unfortunately may conclude a patient's pain is not real, or they may tell the patient there is little they can do.

> ♣ **It's A Fact!!**
> Many people associate the development of fibromyalgia with a physically or emotionally stressful or traumatic event, such as an automobile accident.

A doctor familiar with fibromyalgia, however, can make a diagnosis based on two criteria established by the ACR: a history of widespread pain lasting more than three months and the presence of tender points. Pain is considered to be widespread when it affects all four quadrants of the body; that is, you must have pain in both your right and left sides as well as above and below the waist to be diagnosed with fibromyalgia. The ACR also has designated 18 sites on the body as possible tender points. For a fibromyalgia diagnosis, a person must have 11 or more tender points. One of these pre-designated sites is considered a true tender point only if the person feels pain upon the application of 4 kilograms of pressure to the site. People who have fibromyalgia certainly may feel pain at other sites, too, but those 18 standard possible sites on the body are the criteria used for classification.

How is fibromyalgia treated?

Fibromyalgia can be difficult to treat. Not all doctors are familiar with fibromyalgia and its treatment, so it is important to find a doctor who is. Many family physicians, general internists, or rheumatologists (doctors who specialize in arthritis and other conditions that affect the joints or soft tissues) can treat fibromyalgia.

Fibromyalgia treatment often requires a team approach, with your doctor, a physical therapist, possibly other health professionals, and most importantly, yourself, all playing an active role. It can be hard to assemble this team, and you may struggle to find the right professionals to treat you. When you do, however, the combined expertise of these various professionals can help you improve your quality of life.

You may find several members of the treatment team you need at a clinic. There are pain clinics that specialize in pain and rheumatology clinics that specialize in arthritis and other rheumatic diseases, including fibromyalgia.

Following are some of the most commonly used categories of drugs for fibromyalgia.

Analgesics

Analgesics are painkillers. They range from over-the-counter acetaminophen (Tylenol) to prescription medicines, such as tramadol (Ultram), and even stronger narcotic preparations. For a subset of people with fibromyalgia, narcotic medications are prescribed for severe muscle pain. However, there is no solid evidence showing that narcotics actually work to treat the chronic pain of fibromyalgia, and most doctors hesitate to prescribe them for long-term use because of the potential that the person taking them will become physically or psychologically dependent on them.

Non-steroidal Anti-Inflammatory Drugs (NSAIDs)

As their name implies, non-steroidal anti-inflammatory drugs, including aspirin, ibuprofen (Advil, Motrin), and naproxen sodium (Anaprox, Aleve), are used to treat inflammation. Although inflammation is not a symptom of fibromyalgia, NSAIDs also relieve pain. The drugs work by inhibiting substances in the body called prostaglandins, which play a role in pain and inflammation. These medications, some of which are available without a prescription, may help ease the muscle aches of fibromyalgia. They may also relieve menstrual cramps and the headaches often associated with fibromyalgia.

Antidepressants

Perhaps the most useful medications for fibromyalgia are several in the antidepressant class. Antidepressants elevate the levels of certain chemicals in the brain, including serotonin and norepinephrine (which was formerly called adrenaline). Low levels of these chemicals are associated not only with depression, but also with pain and fatigue. Increasing the levels of these chemicals can reduce pain in people who have fibromyalgia. Doctors prescribe several types of antidepressants for people with fibromyalgia.

Benzodiazepines

Benzodiazepines help some people with fibromyalgia by relaxing tense, painful muscles and stabilizing the erratic brain waves that can interfere with deep sleep. Benzodiazepines also can relieve the symptoms of restless legs syndrome, which is common among people with fibromyalgia. Restless legs syndrome is characterized by unpleasant sensations in the legs as well as twitching, particularly at night. Because of the potential for addiction, doctors usually prescribe benzodiazepines only for people who have not responded to other therapies. Benzodiazepines include clonazepam (Klonopin) and diazepam (Valium).

Other Medications

In addition to the previously described general categories of drugs, doctors may prescribe others, depending on a person's specific symptoms or fibromyalgia-related conditions. In recent years, the Food and Drug Administration (FDA) have approved two medications, tegaserod (Zelnorm) and alosetron (Lotronex), for the treatment of irritable bowel syndrome. Gabapentin (Neurontin) currently is being studied as a treatment for fibromyalgia. Other symptom-specific medications include sleep medications, muscle relaxants, and headache remedies.

People with fibromyalgia also may benefit from a combination of physical and occupational therapy, from learning pain management and coping techniques, and from properly balancing rest and activity.

Complementary And Alternative Therapies

Many people with fibromyalgia also report varying degrees of success with complementary and alternative therapies, including massage, movement therapies (such as Pilates and the Feldenkrais method), chiropractic treatments, acupuncture, and various herbs and dietary supplements for different fibromyalgia symptoms.

Though some of these supplements are being studied for fibromyalgia, there is little, if any, scientific proof that they help. The FDA does not regulate the sale of dietary supplements, so information about side effects, the proper dosage, and the amount of a preparation's active ingredient may not be well known. If you are using, or would like to try a complementary or alternative therapy, you should first speak with your doctor, who may know more about the therapy's effectiveness, as well as whether it is safe to try in combination with your medications.

Will fibromyalgia get better with time?

Fibromyalgia is a chronic condition, meaning it lasts a long time—possibly a lifetime. However, it may comfort you to know that fibromyalgia is not a progressive disease. It is never fatal, and it will not cause damage to your joints, muscles, or internal organs. In many people, the condition does improve over time.

Fibromyalgia

> ### ❧ What's It Mean?
>
> Arthritis: Literally means joint inflammation, but is often used to indicate a group of more than 100 rheumatic diseases. These diseases affect not only the joints, but also other connective tissues of the body, including important supporting structures, such as muscles, tendons, and ligaments, as well as the protective covering of internal organs.
>
> Chronic Disease: An illness that lasts for a long time, often a lifetime.
>
> Fibromyalgia: A chronic syndrome that causes pain and stiffness throughout the connective tissues that support and move the bones and joints. Pain and localized tender points occur in the muscles, particularly those that support the neck, spine, shoulders, and hip. The disorder includes widespread pain, fatigue, and sleep disturbances.
>
> Inflammation: A characteristic reaction of tissues to injury or disease. It is marked by four signs: swelling, redness, heat, and pain. Inflammation is not a symptom of fibromyalgia.
>
> Joint: A junction where two bones meet. Most joints are composed of cartilage, joint space, fibrous capsule, synovium, and ligaments.
>
> Muscle: A structure composed of bundles of specialized cells that, when stimulated by nerve impulses, contract and produce movement.
>
> Tender Points: Specific places on the body where a person with fibromyalgia feels pain in response to slight pressure.

What can I do to try to feel better?

Besides taking medicine prescribed by your doctor, there are many things you can do to minimize the impact of fibromyalgia on your life. These include the following:

- **Getting Enough Sleep:** Getting enough sleep, and the right kind of sleep, can help ease the pain and fatigue of fibromyalgia. Even so, many people with fibromyalgia have problems such as pain, restless legs syndrome, or brain wave irregularities that interfere with restful sleep.

- **Exercising:** Though pain and fatigue may make exercise and daily activities difficult, it is crucial to be as physically active as possible. Research has repeatedly shown that regular exercise is one of the most effective treatments for fibromyalgia. People who have too much pain or fatigue to do vigorous exercise should begin with walking or other gentle exercise and build their endurance and intensity slowly. Although research has focused largely on the benefits of aerobic and flexibility exercises, one study is examining the effects of adding strength training to the traditionally prescribed aerobic and flexibility exercises.

- **Eating Well:** Although some people with fibromyalgia report feeling better when they eat or avoid certain foods, no specific diet has been proven to influence fibromyalgia. Of course, it is important to have a healthy, balanced diet. Not only will proper nutrition give you more energy and make you generally feel better, it will also help you avoid other health problems.

Chapter 34

Irritable Bowel Syndrome

What is irritable bowel syndrome (IBS)?

Irritable bowel syndrome is a disorder characterized most commonly by cramping, abdominal pain, bloating, constipation, and diarrhea. IBS causes a great deal of discomfort and distress, but it does not permanently harm the intestines and does not lead to a serious disease, such as cancer. Most people can control their symptoms with diet, stress management, and prescribed medications. For some people, however, IBS can be disabling. They may be unable to work, attend social events, or even travel short distances.

As many as 20 percent of the adult population, or one in five Americans, has symptoms of IBS, making it one of the most common disorders diagnosed by doctors. It occurs more often in women than in men, and it begins before the age of 35 in about 50 percent of people.

What are the symptoms of IBS?

Abdominal pain, bloating, and discomfort are the main symptoms of IBS. However, symptoms can vary from person to person. Some people have constipation, which means hard, difficult-to-pass, or infrequent bowel movements.

About This Chapter: Information in this chapter is from "Irritable Bowel Syndrome," NIH Publication No. 07-693, National Digestive Diseases Information Clearinghouse, a service of the National Institute of Diabetes and Digestive and Kidney Diseases, National Institutes of Health, July 2007.

Often these people report straining and cramping when trying to have a bowel movement but cannot eliminate any stool, or they are able to eliminate only a small amount. If they are able to have a bowel movement, there may be mucus in it, which is a fluid that moistens and protect passages in the digestive system. Some people with IBS experience diarrhea, which is frequent, loose, watery, stools. People with diarrhea frequently feel an urgent and uncontrollable need to have a bowel movement. Other people with IBS alternate between constipation and diarrhea. Sometimes people find that their symptoms subside for a few months and then return, while others report a constant worsening of symptoms over time.

What causes IBS?

Researchers have yet to discover any specific cause for IBS. One theory is that people who suffer from IBS have a colon, or large intestine, that is particularly sensitive and reactive to certain foods and stress. The immune system, which fights infection, may also be involved.

Normal motility, or movement, may not be present in the colon of a person who has IBS. It can be spasmodic or can even stop working temporarily. Spasms are sudden strong muscle contractions that come and go.

The lining of the colon called the epithelium, which is affected by the immune and nervous systems, regulates the flow of fluids in and out of the colon. In IBS, the epithelium appears to work properly. However, when the contents inside the colon move too quickly, the colon loses its ability to absorb fluids. The result is too much fluid in the stool. In other people, the movement inside the colon is too slow, which causes extra fluid to be absorbed. As a result, a person develops constipation.

A person's colon may respond strongly to stimuli, such as certain foods or stress that would not bother most people.

Recent research has reported that serotonin is linked with normal gastrointestinal (GI) functioning. Serotonin is a neurotransmitter, or chemical, that delivers messages from one part of your body to another. Ninety-five percent of the serotonin in your body is located in the GI tract, and the other five percent is found in the brain. Cells that line the inside of the bowel work

Irritable Bowel Syndrome

as transporters and carry the serotonin out of the GI tract. People with IBS, however, have diminished receptor activity, causing abnormal levels of serotonin to exist in the GI tract. As a result, they experience problems with bowel movement, motility, and sensation—having more sensitive pain receptors in their GI tract.

Researchers have reported that IBS may be caused by a bacterial infection in the gastrointestinal tract. Studies show that people who have had gastroenteritis sometimes develop IBS, otherwise called post-infectious IBS.

Researchers have also found very mild celiac disease in some people with symptoms similar to IBS. People with celiac disease cannot digest gluten, a substance found in wheat, rye, and barley. People with celiac disease cannot eat these foods without becoming very sick because their immune system responds by damaging the small intestine. A blood test can determine whether celiac disease may be present.

How is IBS diagnosed?

If you think you have IBS, seeing your doctor is the first step. IBS is generally diagnosed on the basis of a complete medical history that includes a careful description of symptoms and a physical examination.

> ♣ **It's A Fact!!**
>
> People with IBS have colons that are more sensitive and reactive to things that might not bother other people, such as stress, large meals, gas, medicines, certain foods, caffeine, or alcohol.

There is no specific test for IBS, although diagnostic tests may be performed to rule out other problems. These tests may include stool sample testing, blood tests, and x rays. Typically, a doctor will perform a sigmoidoscopy, or colonoscopy, which allows the doctor to look inside the colon. This is done by inserting a small, flexible tube with a camera on the end of it through the anus. The camera then transfers the images of your colon onto a large screen for the doctor to see.

If your test results are negative, the doctor may diagnose IBS based on your symptoms, including how often you have had abdominal pain or discomfort during the past year, when the pain starts and stops in relation to bowel function, and how your bowel frequency and stool consistency have changed. Many doctors refer to a list of specific symptoms that must be present to make a diagnosis of IBS.

Symptoms include the following:

- Abdominal pain or discomfort for at least 12 weeks out of the previous 12 months. These 12 weeks do not have to be consecutive.
- The abdominal pain or discomfort has two of the following three features:
    - It is relieved by having a bowel movement.
    - When it starts, there is a change in how often you have a bowel movement.
    - When it starts, there is a change in the form of the stool or the way it looks.
- Certain symptoms must also be present, such as the following:
    - A change in frequency of bowel movements
    - A change in appearance of bowel movements
    - Feelings of uncontrollable urgency to have a bowel movement
    - Difficulty or inability to pass stool
    - Mucus in the stool
    - Bloating
- Bleeding, fever, weight loss, and persistent severe pain are not symptoms of IBS and may indicate other problems such as inflammation, or rarely, cancer.

The following have been associated with a worsening of IBS symptoms:

- Large meals
- Bloating from gas in the colon
- Medicines
- Wheat, rye, barley, chocolate, milk products, or alcohol

Irritable Bowel Syndrome

- Drinks with caffeine, such as coffee, tea, or colas
- Stress, conflict, or emotional upsets

Researchers have found that women with IBS may have more symptoms during their menstrual periods, suggesting that reproductive hormones can worsen IBS problems.

In addition, people with IBS frequently suffer from depression and anxiety, which can worsen symptoms. Similarly, the symptoms associated with IBS can cause a person to feel depressed and anxious.

What is the treatment for IBS?

Unfortunately, many people suffer from IBS for a long time before seeking medical treatment. Up to 70 percent of people suffering from IBS are not receiving medical care for their symptoms. No cure has been found for IBS, but many options are available to treat the symptoms. Your doctor will give you the best treatments for your particular symptoms and encourage you to manage stress and make changes to your diet.

> ♣ **It's A Fact!!**
> Most people can control their symptoms by taking medicines such as laxatives, antidiarrhea medicines, antispasmodics, or antidepressants; reducing stress; and changing their diet.

Medications are an important part of relieving symptoms. Your doctor may suggest fiber supplements or laxatives for constipation or medicines to decrease diarrhea, such as Lomotil or loperamide (Imodium). An antispasmodic is commonly prescribed, which helps to control colon muscle spasms and reduce abdominal pain. Antidepressants may relieve some symptoms. However, both antispasmodics and antidepressants can worsen constipation, so some doctors will also prescribe medications that relax muscles in the bladder and intestines, such as Donnapine and Librax. These medications contain a mild sedative, which can be habit forming, so they need to be used under the guidance of a physician.

A medication available specifically to treat IBS is alosetron hydrochloride (Lotronex). Lotronex has been reapproved with significant restrictions by the U.S. Food and Drug Administration (FDA) for women with severe IBS who have not responded to conventional therapy and whose primary symptom is diarrhea. However, even in these patients, Lotronex should be used with great caution because it can have serious side effects such as severe constipation or decreased blood flow to the colon.

With any medication, even over-the-counter medications such as laxatives and fiber supplements, it is important to follow your doctor's instructions. Some people report a worsening in abdominal bloating and gas from increased fiber intake, and laxatives can be habit forming if they are used too frequently.

Medications affect people differently, and no one medication or combination of medications will work for everyone with IBS. You will need to work with your doctor to find the best combination of medicine, diet, counseling, and support to control your symptoms.

♣ **It's A Fact!!**
Some evidence suggests that IBS is affected by the immune system, which fights infection in the body. The immune system is affected by stress. For all these reasons, stress management is an important part of treatment for IBS.

How does stress affect IBS?

Stress—feeling mentally or emotionally tense, troubled, angry, or overwhelmed—can stimulate colon spasms in people with IBS. The colon has many nerves that connect it to the brain. Like the heart and the lungs, the colon is partly controlled by the autonomic nervous system, which responds to stress. These nerves control the normal contractions of the colon and cause abdominal discomfort at stressful times. People often experience cramps or "butterflies" when they are nervous or upset. In people with IBS, the colon can be overly responsive to even slight conflict or stress. Stress makes the mind more aware of the sensations that arise in the colon, making the person perceive these sensations as unpleasant.

Stress management options include the following:

- Stress reduction (relaxation) training and relaxation therapies such as meditation

Irritable Bowel Syndrome

- Counseling and support
- Regular exercise such as walking or yoga
- Changes to the stressful situations in your life
- Adequate sleep

What does the colon do?

The colon, which is about five feet long, connects the small intestine to the rectum and anus. The major function of the colon is to absorb water, nutrients, and salts from the partially digested food that enters from the small intestine. Two pints of liquid matter enter the colon from the small intestine each day. Stool volume is a third of a pint. The difference between the amount of fluid entering the colon from the small intestine and the amount of stool in the colon is what the colon absorbs each day.

Nerves, hormones, and impulses in the colon muscles control colon motility—the contraction of the colon muscles and the movement of its contents. These contractions move the contents inside the colon toward the rectum. During this passage, water and nutrients are absorbed into the body, and what is left over is stool. A few times each day contractions push the stool down the colon, resulting in a bowel movement. However, if the muscles of the colon, sphincters, and pelvis do not contract in the right way, the contents inside the colon do not move correctly, resulting in abdominal pain, cramps, constipation, a sense of incomplete stool movement, or diarrhea.

Can changes in diet help IBS?

For many people, careful eating reduces IBS symptoms. Before changing your diet, keep a journal noting the foods that seem to cause distress. Then discuss your findings with your doctor. You may want to consult a registered dietitian who can help you make changes to your diet. For instance, if dairy products cause your symptoms to flare up, you can try eating less of those foods. You might be able to tolerate yogurt better than other dairy products because it contains bacteria that supply the enzyme needed to digest lactose, the sugar found in milk products. Dairy products are an important source of calcium and other nutrients. If you need to avoid dairy products, be sure to get adequate nutrients in the foods you substitute, or take supplements.

In many cases, dietary fiber may lessen IBS symptoms, particularly constipation. However, it may not help with lowering pain or decreasing diarrhea. Whole grain breads and cereals, fruits, and vegetables are good sources of fiber. High-fiber diets keep the colon mildly distended, which may help prevent spasms. Some forms of fiber keep water in the stool, thereby preventing hard stools that are difficult to pass. Doctors usually recommend a diet with enough fiber to produce soft, painless bowel movements. High-fiber diets may cause gas and bloating, although some people report that these symptoms go away within a few weeks.

Drinking six to eight glasses of plain water a day is important, especially if you have diarrhea. Drinking carbonated beverages, such as sodas, may result in gas and cause discomfort. Chewing gum and eating too quickly can lead to swallowing air, which also leads to gas.

Large meals can cause cramping and diarrhea, so eating smaller meals more often, or eating smaller portions, may help IBS symptoms. Eating meals that are low in fat and high in carbohydrates such as pasta, rice, whole grain breads and cereals (unless you have celiac disease), fruits, and vegetables may help.

Is IBS linked to other health problems?

As its name indicates, IBS is a syndrome—a combination of signs and symptoms. IBS has not been shown to lead to a serious disease, including cancer. Through the years, IBS has been called by many names, among them colitis, mucous colitis, spastic colon, or spastic bowel. However, no link has been established between IBS and inflammatory bowel diseases such as Crohn disease or ulcerative colitis.

Chapter 35

Stress And Weight Gain: Is There A Link?

Some people quickly gain weight when they are stressed. A new study has uncovered a molecular connection between stress and weight gain. The discovery may lead to ways of helping people who are chronically stressed control their weight.

Dr. Zofia Zukowska of Georgetown University Medical Center leads a team of researchers that previously showed a molecule called neuropeptide Y (NPY) is involved in angiogenesis, the growth of the blood vessels necessary to support new tissue growth. NPY is released from certain nerve cells during stress. Other research had shown that NPY and its receptors seem to play a role in appetite and obesity. Putting these results together, the researchers thought that NPY might be involved in new fat growth during stressful situations.

Funded in part by National Institutes of Health's National Heart, Lung, and Blood Institute (NHLBI) and National Institute of Dental and Craniofacial Research (NIDCR), the researchers tested the effects of chronic stress on fat growth in mice. They compared the effects of stress when the mice were fed a normal diet and one high in fat and sugar to reflect the comfort foods many people eat when they are stressed.

About This Chapter: Information in this chapter is from "Stress, Obesity Link Found," by Harrison Wein, Ph.D., National Institutes of Health, U.S. Department of Health and Human Services, July 2007.

> ♣ **It's A Fact!!**
>
> The Federal Trade Commission (FTC) has charged marketers of two dietary supplements with claiming, falsely and without substantiation, that their products can cause weight loss and reduce the risk of, or prevent, serious health conditions. According to the FTC's complaint, Los Angeles area marketers Window Rock Enterprises, Inc. and Infinity Advertising, Inc., their principals, Stephen Cheng and Gregory Cynaumon, and business partner and product formulator Shawn Talbott have sold "CortiSlim" and "CortiStress" through a number of widely aired infomercials and short television commercials, as well as radio and print advertisements and internet websites.
>
> The FTC alleges that the defendants promoted cortisol control as "the answer" for anyone who wants to lose weight, especially abdominal weight. According to the FTC's complaint, the defendants' broadcast ads, print ads, and websites claimed that persistently elevated levels of cortisol, the "stress hormone," are the underlying cause of weight gain and weight retention and also claimed that CortiSlim effectively reduces and controls cortisol levels and thereby causes substantial weight loss. The FTC alleges that the defendants claimed that CortiSlim: (1) causes weight loss of 10 to 50 pounds for virtually all users; (2) causes users to lose as much as 4 to 10 pounds per week over multiple weeks; (3)

The researchers found that making the mice stand in cold water or exposing them to an aggressive mouse for ten minutes a day led to the release of NPY from nerves. For the mice eating the normal diet, stress had little effect on body fat. For those mice eating the high fat and sugar diet, however, stress led to a significant increase in belly fat over a two-week period.

In the presence of the high fat and sugar diet, the researchers found abdominal fat produced more NPY along with its receptor, NPY2R. This stimulated angiogenesis in fat tissue and the proliferation of fat cells, resulting in more belly fat. Eventually, after three months of stress and a high fat and sugar diet, the mice developed a metabolic syndrome-like condition. Metabolic syndrome in people is linked to abdominal obesity and increases your chance for heart disease, diabetes, and other health problems.

The researchers then tested whether they could use NPY to manipulate fat levels. They put a pellet under the animals' skin that releases NPY over a

> causes users to lose weight specifically from the abdomen, stomach, and thighs; (4) causes rapid and substantial weight loss; (5) causes long-term or permanent weight loss; and (6) causes weight loss. The FTC also alleges that the defendants claimed that the effectiveness of CortiSlim and its ingredients is demonstrated by over 15 years of scientific research. According to the FTC's complaint, these claims are false or unsubstantiated.
>
> The FTC alleges that the defendants promoted cortisol control as "perhaps the most important aspect" of reducing health and disease risks. According to the FTC's complaint, the defendants' infomercial claimed that persistently elevated levels of cortisol are the underlying cause of "every modern lifestyle disease that is associated with this fast-paced 21st century lifestyle" and also claimed that CortiStress controls cortisol and thus should be taken "for as long as you want to have good health." The FTC alleges that the defendants claimed that CortiStress reduces the risk of, or prevents, conditions such as osteoporosis, obesity, diabetes, Alzheimer disease, cancer, and cardiovascular disease. According to the FTC's complaint, these claims are false or unsubstantiated.
>
> Source: Excerpted from "FTC Targets Products Claiming to Affect the Stress Hormone Cortisol," Federal Trade Commission, June 2007.

period of 14 days. The pellet increased the amount of fat tissue in both genetically obese and lean mice by 50%. By contrast, injections with a molecule that blocks NPY2R decreased the amount of fat tissue in both obese and lean mice by 50%. The NPY2R-blocking molecule, the researchers found, decreased the number of blood vessels and fat cells in abdominal fat pads. NPY, then, acting through NPY2R, stimulates angiogenesis and fat tissue growth.

The researchers showed that NPY and its receptor also play a role in the growth of human fat cells. Other studies have found genetic evidence linking NPY and NPY2R to the regulation of obesity in people. Zukowska said, "We are hopeful that these findings might eventually lead to the control of metabolic syndrome, which is a huge health issue for many Americans."

Chapter 36

Stress And Your Skin

Link Found Between Teens' Stress Levels And Acne Severity

The largest study ever conducted on acne and stress reveals that teenagers who were under high levels of stress were 23 percent more likely to have increased acne severity, according to researchers from Wake Forest University School of Medicine and colleagues.

"Acne significantly affects physical and psychosocial well-being, so it is important to understand the interplay between the factors that exacerbate acne," said Gil Yosipovitch, M.D., lead author and a professor of dermatology. "Our study suggests a significant association between stress and severity of acne."

The results of the study, which involved 94 adolescents from Singapore, are reported in *Acta Derm Venereol*, a Swedish medical journal.

While psychological stress had been identified among many factors that can worsen acne, there has been little research to understand the mechanisms

---

About This Chapter: Information under the heading "Link Found Between Teens' Stress Levels And Acne Severity" is from "Link Found Between Teens' Stress Levels and Acne Severity," March 6, 2007, © Wake Forest University Baptist Medical Center. Reprinted with permission. Text under the heading "Cold Sores" is from "What Are Cold Sores?" © 2006 Academy of General Dentistry (www.agd.org). Reprinted with permission.

behind this relationship. The current study looked at whether levels of sebum, the oily substance that coats the skin and protects the hair, increase in times of stress and are related to acne severity. Hormone levels, sebum production, and bacteria are all known to play major roles in acne.

The study involved secondary school students in Singapore with a mean age of 14.9 years. The students' self-reported stress levels and acne severity were measured at two different times—just before mid-year exams and during summer break. Students' long-term career prospects are influenced by the results of the examinations, and they are known to induce psychological stress.

Stress levels were measured using the Perceived Stress Scale, a 14-item, self-questionnaire that is widely used in stress research. Acne severity was measured using a system that classifies acne based on type and number of lesions. Ninety-two percent of the girls and 95 percent of the boys reported having acne.

Acne is an inflammatory disease of the skin caused by changes in the hair follicle and the sebaceous glands of the skin that produce sebum. The oily substance plugs the pores, resulting in whiteheads or blackheads (acne comedonica) and pimples (acne papulopustulosa).

The researchers suspected that stress increases the quantity of sebum, which leads to increased acne severity. However, the results showed that sebum production didn't differ significantly between the high-stress and low-stress conditions.

The researchers did find that students reporting high stress were 23 percent more likely to have increased severity of acne papulopustulosa. Levels of stress were not linked to severity of acne comedonica.

"Our research suggests that acne severity associated with stress may result from factors others than sebum quantity," said Yosipovitch. "It's possible that inflammation may be involved."

Singapore was selected as the study location because sebum production is known to fluctuate with variations in temperature and humidity. In Singapore's tropical climate, temperature and humidity are consistent throughout the year.

The research was funded by the National Medical Research Council of Singapore.

Cold Sores

What are cold sores?

Cold sores, also known as fever blisters, are tiny, clear, fluid-filled blisters that form around the mouth and are caused by the herpes simplex virus (usually type 1, or HSV-1) living inside your nerve tissue. Cold sores usually do not last longer than two weeks. However, the sores are highly contagious and tend to recur when the virus is reactivated by a trigger such as stress, sunlight, fever, or illness.

What is the difference between a cold sore and a canker sore?

> ♣ **It's A Fact!!**
> *Does Eating Chocolate Cause Pimples?*
>
> No way—and neither do dirt, fried foods, or sexual activity. Changes in your skin during puberty trigger acne. Stress, your period, picking at or popping your pimples, scrubbing your skin too hard, getting too much sun, and using oil-based lotions, makeup, or hair gels can cause breakouts to get worse.
>
> Source: Excerpted from *Teen Survival Guide: Health Tips for On-the-go Girls*, GirlsHealth.gov, U.S. Department of Health and Human Services, Office on Women's Health, June 2007.

Like cold sores, canker sores, also known as aphthous ulcers, can be quite painful and often recur. While cold sores are caused by a virus, the formation of a canker sore may be triggered by multiple factors such as stress, food allergies, or a weakened immune system. A canker sore forms in the soft tissues of your mouth and is not contagious, whereas a cold sore usually appears around the lip area outside the mouth and is highly contagious. If a cold sore appears inside the mouth, usually it appears on the non-movable parts such as the roof, rather than the tongue or soft palate.

What happens when you are first exposed to HSV-1?

Most people get HSV-1 infections during infancy or childhood and usually catch the virus from an infected family member or friend. Only an

> ♣ **It's A Fact!!**
>
> ## What is blushing?
>
> Blushing is a sudden reddening of the face, neck, and occasionally, upper chest. Blushing is the result of neurological flushing. It occurs most often after a high level of anxiety, for example it may occur in a person during a presentation, meeting, or social situation where they are anxious of being judged, criticized, and evaluated by other people. However, blushing also occurs without stress or anxiety. Some individuals are born to blush excessively without any apparent emotional stimuli. Blushing can cause severe embarrassment and frustration to anyone who experiences it regularly, and it can often lead to social phobia or other anxiety disorders. Erythrophobia is the name given to the compulsive state related to the fear of blushing.
>
> ## What causes blushing?
>
> As part of the "fight or flight" response when we are exposed to environmental or emotional stimuli, the body responds via the sympathetic nervous system. This causes the widening of small blood vessels (capillaries) just beneath the surface of the skin, hence blushing occurs.
>
> ## What treatment is available?
>
> In most people, facial blushing takes a minute or two for the blush to disappear, hence causing slight embarrassment. However, in some people severe and frequent blushing can become a real hindrance and affect both personal and professional life. Several treatments are available for severe facial blushing.
>
> *Psychological Treatments*
>
> Cognitive behavior therapy is a form of psychotherapy that helps you to weaken the connections between troublesome situations and how you react to them, for

estimated 30 percent of those infected actually develop the characteristic blisters. If sores do develop, they can appear anywhere from 2 to 12 days after exposure to an infected person. Other persons with a primary infection may have flu-like symptoms such as a high fever, sore throat, swollen neck glands, and mouth soreness.

example, blushing (behavior therapy), and teaches you awareness of how certain thinking patterns cause you to blush (cognitive therapy).

Drug Treatments

Several medications are available to help treat facial blushing. See your doctor for suitability of medical treatments.

- **Anxiety Medications:** Used to help calm the person and reduce frequency and/or severity of blushing

- **Clonidine:** Used to treat uncontrollable facial blushing by reducing the widening of blood vessels that results in blushing

- **Beta-Blockers:** Manage the symptoms of anxiety such as blushing and heart palpitations

Surgical Treatments

Often blushing occurs alongside hyperhidrosis (excessive sweating). Endoscopic thoracic sympathectomy (ETS) is a surgical treatment considered an effective way to treat severe facial blushing and hyperhidrosis. The operation is performed under general anesthesia and involves clamping off parts of the overactive sympathetic nerves that causes these symptoms. Because of the risks associated with surgery under general anesthesia, this procedure should only be performed if other more conventional therapies have failed.

Source: This information is reprinted with the permission from DermNet, the website of the New Zealand Dermatological Society. Visit www.dermnet.org.nz for patient information on numerous skin conditions and their treatment. © 2006 New Zealand Dermatological Society.

What are the stages of a cold sore?

Day 1—Prodrome (Tingle) Stage: Before a cold sore has formed, you may feel a tingling, itching, or burning sensation beneath the skin, usually around the mouth or the base of the nose. Applying antiviral medications during this stage can help alleviate cold sore symptoms.

Days 2 to 3—Blister Stage: An outbreak of fluid-filled blisters is the first visible sign of cold sore formation.

Day 4—Ulcer or Weeping Stage: Typically, the most contagious and painful stage of cold sores is when blisters rupture, leaving a shallow, reddish, open sore.

Days 5 to 8—Crusting Stage: After a few days, the blisters dry up and form a yellow or brownish crust, which eventually falls off. During this stage, it is important to care for the scab, which can crack or break.

Days 9 to 12—Healing Stage: Usually a series of scabs will form on the lesion, which eventually flake off. Each new scab will be smaller than the previous one, until the cold sore heals completely, usually without scarring.

What triggers a cold sore outbreak?

There may be long periods when the herpes virus remains inactive. The following factors can trigger cold sores:

- Illness, such as cold or flu
- Dental treatment
- Physical stress or fatigue
- Menstruation or pregnancy
- Mouth trauma
- An immune system deficiency
- Sunlight exposure or ultraviolet lamps
- Food allergies

How are cold sores treated?

Most cold sores are mild and do not require treatment. Antiviral medications can reduce the frequency, duration, and severity of outbreaks. Medications with a numbing agent, such as benzyl alcohol, can help alleviate a cold sore's burning, itching, and pain. Emollients can reduce cracking and soften scabs. Applying aloe vera balm three times a day to the cold sore also can help fight the infection and enhance healing.

If over-the-counter remedies don't help, ask your dentist for a prescription. A dentist also can accurately diagnose cold sores and base treatment on important factors such as your age, overall health, medical history, and tolerance for specific medications.

What precautions should be taken?

To prevent transmission of the virus to another person, avoid:

- Intimate physical contact with others
- Sharing eating utensils, toothbrushes, towels, and razors
- Touching the blisters (always wash your hands after applying medication)

What can I do to minimize recurrent outbreaks?

- Eat foods high in lysine (an amino acid found in red meats, fish, and dairy products) or take supplements
- Apply sunscreen to the face and lips before going outdoors
- Shave with a disposable razor during an outbreak
- Replace your toothbrush
- Engage in relaxing activities to reduce stress

Chapter 37

Stress And Hair Loss

It is normal to lose up to about 100 hairs a day on one's comb, brush, in the sink, or on the pillow. This is the result of the normal hair growth cycle. Hairs will grow for a few years, then rest for a few months, shed, and regrow. Telogen is the name for the resting stage of the hair growth cycle. A telogen effluvium is when some stress causes hair roots to be pushed prematurely into the resting state. Telogen effluvium can be acute or chronic.

If there is some "shock to the system," as many as 70% of the scalp hairs are then shed in large numbers about two months after the "shock." This sudden increase in hair loss, usually described as the hair coming out in handfuls, is acute telogen effluvium. This is a different problem than gradual genetic hair thinning. However, this can be seen in the less common chronic telogen effluvium, only after a significant amount of hair has already been lost.

A considerable number of different causes for telogen effluvium exist. Among the common causes are high fevers, childbirth, severe infections, severe chronic illness, severe psychological stress, major surgery or illnesses, over or under active thyroid gland, crash diets with inadequate protein, and a variety of medications. Most hair loss from medications is this type, and causes

---

About This Chapter: Information in this chapter is from "Telogen Effluvium Hair Loss," © American Osteopathic College of Dermatology (www.aocd.org). Reprinted with permission; cited September 2007.

> ### ✎ What's It Mean?
> Telogen Effluvium: Telogen is the name for the resting stage of the hair growth cycle. A telogen effluvium is when some stress causes hair roots to be pushed prematurely into the resting state.

include retinoids, beta-blockers, calcium channel blockers, antidepressants, and non-steroidal anti-inflammatory drugs (NSAIDs), including ibuprofen.

Typically, abrupt diffuse hair loss is noticed several weeks to several months after the incident has initiated the biologic program for hair loss. While the most often noticed hair loss occurs on the scalp, some individuals may also notice hair loss elsewhere on the body. Significant hair shedding usually occurs when shampooing, combing, or even when gently manipulating the hair. Shedding usually slowly decreases over six to eight months once the cause for the hair loss is no longer present. As some of the causes represent ongoing problems, it is important to determine the likely cause when possible and take appropriate measures to prevent continued hair loss.

These shed or loose hairs all have club-shaped "roots" typical of resting, telogen hairs and may be easily identified under the microscope. After shampooing, the bulk of existing loose hair has often been shed, and loose hair may not again appear until additional hairs enter this resting phase. When there is any doubt about the presence of this condition, a small piece of skin may be taken from the scalp as a biopsy to be examined under the microscope. In this way, the condition of the hair follicles, the tissues that produce the hair, may be determined.

No treatment is needed for most cases of telogen effluvium. Remember that the hairs fall out when a new hair growing beneath it pushes it out. Thus with this type of hair loss, hair falling out is a sign of hair regrowth. As the new hair first comes up through the scalp and pushes out the dead hair, a fine fringe of new hair is often evident along the forehead hairline.

The most important issue in telogen effluvium is to determine if an underlying cause for the problem is present. Blood tests may need to be done if

Stress And Hair Loss

the cause is not obvious, such as mild iron deficiency. If the telogen effluvium is caused by a medication, the medication needs to be stopped. When the cause of the hair loss is something like giving birth, a transient illness, or other self-limited problem, the induced telogen effluvium is also usually self-limited and requires no treatment.

Chronic telogen effluvium is recently recognized and not uncommon. It often occurs in women who previously had very thick hair in their teens and twenties and still have an apparently normal head of hair to a casual observer. It affects the entire scalp with no obvious cause apparent. It usually affects women of 30 to 60 years of age, starts suddenly, and has a tendency to fluctuate for a period of years. The degree of shedding is usually severe in the early stages, and the hair may come out in handfuls. It does not cause complete baldness and does appear to be self-limiting in the long run.

Chapter 38

Headaches And Facial Tics

Headaches And Stress

Stress is the most commonly recognized trigger of headaches. Stress can be physical or emotional. It can be good or bad. It is an unavoidable part of modern life.

Events causing emotional stress can trigger a migraine headache. Migraine sufferers are thought to be highly responsive emotionally, reacting quickly to stress. In times of emotional stress, certain chemicals are released that provoke the vascular changes that cause a migraine headache. The attacks become more frequent in periods of increased stress. Factors related to stress include anxiety, worry, shock, depression, excitement, and mental fatigue. Repressed emotions can also precipitate migraine headaches, and the muscle tension often brought on by stressful situations can add to the severity of the headache. After a stressful period there may be a letdown, which can, in itself, trigger a migraine headache. This may be one reason for weekend headaches.

Stress is also an important factor in tension-type headaches. Episodic tension-type headaches can be related to specific instances of increased worry, concern, or stress and usually are helped by eliminating the stressful situation

About This Chapter: Information under the heading "Headaches And Stress," is from "Stress," and text under the heading "Tension-Type Headache" is from "Tension-Type Headache," reprinted with permission from the National Headache Foundation (www.headaches.org), © 2005. All rights reserved.

Facial Tics

♣ **It's A Fact!!**

Definition

A facial tic is a repetitive, spasmodic movement often involving the eyes and facial muscles.

Causes, Incidence, And Risk Factors

Tics most often occur in children, but may persist into adulthood in some cases. Tics occur three to four times as often in boys as girls. Tics may affect as many as one-fourth of all children at some time. The cause of tics is unknown, but stress appears to increase the severity of already established tics.

Short-lived or transient tics are common in childhood and may appear and disappear within a matter of weeks or months (transient tic disorder). These tics often involve the eyes or facial muscles. The most commonly seen facial tics are repetitive eye blinking, squinting, wrinkling of the nose, and twitches around the mouth. Repetitive throat clearing or deep, throaty sounds or grunts may also be considered tics.

Certain medications, such as methylphenidate (used to treat hyperactivity in children), were previously thought to precipitate tics in children already prone to the disorder. However, recent studies published do not support this notion and suggest that these medications can be used in children with tics who also have attention deficit disorder, which commonly occurs in the same population.

A chronic motor tic disorder also exists. It may last for years. This form is extremely rare compared to the common short-lived childhood tic. Gilles de la Tourette syndrome is a separate condition in which tics are a predominant symptom.

Symptoms

- Repetitive, involuntary spasmodic muscle movements, such as:
    - Eye blinking
    - Squinting
    - Nose wrinkling
    - Mouth twitches

- Facial grimacing
- Repetitive throat clearing or grunting

Signs And Tests

A tic is generally diagnosed during a physical examination. No special tests are necessary. Rarely, an individual may require an electroencephalogram (EEG) to rule out seizures or seizure-type activity.

Treatment

Transient childhood tics are not treated. Calling the child's attention to a tic may increase its severity or prolong its disappearance. A non-stressful environment is helpful in both decreasing the frequency of a tic and hastening its disappearance.

If tics are disabling, medications such as risperidone (as well as others) may be effective in controlling the tics.

Expectations (Prognosis)

Simple childhood tics can be expected to disappear spontaneously over a period of months. Chronic tics may last indefinitely.

Complications

In most cases, there are no complications.

Calling Your Health Care Provider

Call for an appointment with your health care provider if tics are severe, affect multiple muscle groups, or are persistent.

Prevention

Many cases are not preventable. Reducing stress may be helpful, and sometimes counseling is advised to help the child learn how to cope with stress.

Source: © 2007 A.D.A.M., Inc. Reprinted with permission.

or by over-the-counter analgesics. Chronic and repeated stress will cause daily, or almost daily, tension-type headaches. The headache is generalized (typically in a "hat-band" distribution) and is often accompanied by a sleep disturbance. Help is provided by lowering stress, psychotherapy, biofeedback, behavioral modification, and the use of antidepressant drugs under the watchful eye of a physician.

Stress cannot be completely avoided, but learning to better deal with stress can help reduce headaches.

Tension-Type Headache

Tension-type headache is a nonspecific headache, which is not vascular or migrainous, and is not related to organic disease. The most common form of headache, it may be related to muscle tightening in the back of the neck and/or scalp. There are two general classifications of tension-type headache: episodic and chronic, differentiated by frequency and severity of symptoms. Both are characterized as dull, aching, and non-pulsating pain, and affect both sides of the head.

Symptoms for both types are similar and may include:

- Muscles between head and neck contract.
- A tightening band-like sensation around the neck and/or head, which is a "vice-like" ache
- Pain primarily occurs in the forehead, temples, or the back on head and/or neck.

Episodic

Episodic tension-type headache occurs randomly and is usually triggered by temporary stress, anxiety, fatigue, or anger. They are what most of us consider "stress headaches." It may disappear with the use of over-the-counter analgesics, withdrawal from the source of stress, or a relatively brief period of relaxation.

For this type of headache, over-the-counter drugs of choice are aspirin, acetaminophen, ibuprofen, or naproxen sodium. Combination products with caffeine can enhance the action of the analgesics.

Chronic

Chronic tension-type headache is a daily or continuous headache, which may have some variability in the intensity of the pain during a 24-hour cycle. It is always present. If a sufferer is taking medication daily, or almost daily, and is receiving little or no relief from the pain, then a physician should be seen for diagnosis and treatment.

The primary drug of choice for chronic tension-type headache is amitriptyline or some of the other antidepressants. Antidepressant drugs have analgesic actions, which can provide relief for headache sufferers. Although a patient may not be depressed, these drugs may be beneficial. Selecting an antidepressant is based on the presence of a sleep disturbance. For the patient with chronic tension-type headaches, habituating analgesics must be strictly avoided. Biofeedback techniques can also be helpful in treating tension-type headaches.

Chronic tension-type headache can also be the result of either anxiety or depression. Changes in sleep patterns or insomnia, early morning or late day occurrence of headache, feelings of guilt, weight loss, dizziness, poor concentration, ongoing fatigue, and nausea commonly occur. One should seek professional diagnosis for proper treatment if these symptoms exist.

Chapter 39

Does Stress Really Cause Heart Disease?

For years it has been "common knowledge" that people who are under a lot of stress have an increased risk of heart disease. But is this common knowledge correct? And if so, what kind of stress increases the risk of heart disease, how does it increase risk, and what can be done about it?

Sorting out the effect of stress on the heart is made complicated by three factors: 1) people mean different things by "stress"; 2) the kind of stress people think causes heart disease may not be the worst kind; 3) scientific evidence that stress causes heart disease has been sparse.

What Kind Of Stress Are We Talking About?

Physical Stress: Physical stress, exercise or other forms of physical exertion, places measurable and reproducible demands on the heart. This physical stress is generally acknowledged to be good. In fact, the lack of physical stress (that is, a sedentary lifestyle) constitutes a major risk factor for coronary artery disease. So this kind of "stress" is usually considered to be good for the heart—as long as the heart is normal.

About This Chapter: © 2007 by Richard N. Fogoros, M.D., "Does Stress Really Cause Heart Disease," http://heartdisease.about.com/cs/riskfactors/a/stresshtdisease.htm. Used with permission of About, Inc., which can be found online at www.about.com. All rights reserved.

If there is underlying heart disease, however, too much physical stress can be dangerous. In a person who has coronary artery disease, for instance, exercise can place demands on the heart muscle that the diseased coronary arteries cannot meet, and the heart becomes ischemic (that is, starved for oxygen.) The ischemic heart muscle can cause either angina (chest pain), or a heart attack (actual death of cardiac muscle).

In summary, physical stress is generally good for you, and is to be encouraged, as long as you have a normal heart. On the other hand, with certain kinds of heart disease, too much or the wrong kind of physical exertion may be harmful.

But either way, physical stress does not cause heart disease.

Emotional Stress: Emotional stress is generally the kind of stress people are talking about when they refer to stress causing heart disease. "It's no wonder she died," you'll hear people say, "with all the mess he put her through." But is it true? Did Ed really kill Elsie with all his gambling and drinking and staying out all hours of the night?

Everyone, even doctors, have the notion that emotional stress, if it is severe enough or chronic enough, is bad for you. Most even believe that this kind of stress can cause heart disease. But scientific evidence that it actually does so has been hard to come by.

♣ **It's A Fact!!**

When people refer to "stress," they may be talking about two different things: physical stress or emotional stress. Most of the medical literature on stress and heart disease refers to physical stress. But most people are referring to the emotional variety when they talk about stress.

Source: © 2007 by Richard N. Fogoros, M.D., "Does Stress Really Cause Heart Disease," http://heartdisease.about.com/cs/riskfactors/a/stresshtdisease.htm. Used with permission of About, Inc., which can be found online at www.about.com. All rights reserved.

Emotional Stress And Heart Disease

There is a fair amount of circumstantial evidence that chronic emotional stress can be associated with heart disease and early death.

Several studies have documented that people without spouses die earlier than married people. (While some might claim this constitutes evidence that emotional stress is actually good for you, most authorities agree that having a spouse actually provides a significant degree of emotional support and stability.) Other studies have shown fairly conclusively that people who have had recent major life changes (loss of a spouse or other close relative, loss of a job, moving to a new location) have a higher incidence of death. People who are quick to anger or who display frequent hostility have an increased risk of heart disease.

So emotional stress is bad, right? It didn't start out bad. Evolutionarily speaking, emotional stress is a protective mechanism. When our ancestors walked over a rise and suddenly saw a saber-toothed tiger 40 yards away, a surge of adrenaline prepared them for either fight or flight as they considered their options.

But in modern times, now that saber tooth tigers are few and far between, most often neither fight nor flight is the appropriate reaction to a stressful situation. (Neither fleeing from nor punching your annoying boss, for instance, is generally considered proper.) So today, the adrenaline surge that accompanies a stressful situation is not channeled to its rightful conclusion. Instead of being released in a burst of physical exertion, it is internalized into a clenched-teeth smile and a "Sure, Mr. Smithers, I'll be happy to fly to Toledo tomorrow and see about the Henderson account."

It appears that the unrequited fight-or-flight reaction, if it occurs often enough and chronically enough, may be harmful.

How Does Emotional Stress Cause Heart Problems?

From a scientific standpoint, we really don't know for sure that it does. But we do know that people who live in a chronically stressed-out condition are more likely to take up smoking and overeating, and are far less likely to exercise.

We also know that the surge in adrenaline caused by severe emotional stress causes the blood to clot more readily, increasing the risk of heart attacks. British investigators have shown that chronic work stress can produce chronic increases in adrenaline levels, and have related those changes to an increased risk of heart disease. A study at Duke University showed that the stress of performing difficult arithmetic problems can constrict the coronary arteries in such a way that blood flow to the heart muscle is reduced. So while it has not been proven scientifically that emotional stress causes coronary artery disease, a) it is associated with behaviors that do produce coronary artery disease, and b) there is suggestive evidence that it may even have a direct effect in producing coronary disease.

Is All Emotional Stress Bad?

No. It has been observed for years, for instance, that many executives with high-pressure jobs seem to remain quite healthy until old age—they seem to flourish in their pressure-cooker jobs. Recent studies have shed light on this phenomenon.

It turns out that the type of emotional stress one experiences is important. In comparing the outcomes of individuals with different types of job-related stress, it was found that people with relatively little control over their own workplace destiny (clerks and secretaries for instance) fared far worse than their bosses. (Bosses, of course, tend to have more control over their own lives—and the lives of others. As someone once said, it's good to be king.) A sense of loss of control, therefore, appears to be a particularly important form of emotional stress. Furthermore, this evidence seems to confirm that if some sense of control over one's destiny is maintained, job related stress can be exhilarating rather than debilitating.

What Can Be Done About Emotional Stress?

Actually, quite a bit of evidence suggests that it may be the individual, and not the stress itself that is the problem. People with Type A personalities (time-sensitive, impatient, chronic sense of urgency, tendency toward hostility, competitive) are at higher risk for coronary artery disease than people with Type B personalities (patient, low-key, non-competitive). In other words, given the same stressful situation, some will respond with frustration and anger, the rush of adrenaline and the fight-or-flight mode, and some will react serenely.

This is why the common advice to "avoid stress" is so useless. Nobody can avoid all stress without completely dropping out of society and becoming a monk. Besides, people of the Type A persuasion will create their own stressful situations. A simple trip to the grocery store will be filled with episodes of bad drivers, poorly-timed traffic lights, crowded aisles, indifferent checkout clerks, and thin plastic grocery bags that rip too easily. "The world is filled with half-brained incompetents whose only purpose is to get in my way," they will conclude. "It's a wonder any of them survived to adulthood."

With this sort of mind-set, retiring, changing jobs, or moving to Tucson are not likely to significantly reduce stress levels—the stress will be there whether it is imposed externally, or whether you have to manufacture it. Reducing stress levels in these cases, then, requires not an elimination of stressful situations (which is impossible), but a change in the way stress is handled. Type As have to learn to become more B-like.

Essentially, new responses need to be learned, so that the fight-or-flight adrenaline surge is not automatically engaged at the first sign of trouble.

♣ **It's A Fact!!**

Over the past 20 years, mind-body medicine has provided considerable evidence that psychological factors can play a substantive role in the development and progression of coronary artery disease. There is evidence that mind-body interventions can be effective in the treatment of coronary artery disease, enhancing the effect of standard cardiac rehabilitation in reducing all-cause mortality and cardiac event recurrences for up to two years.

Source: Excerpted from "Mind-Body Medicine: An Overview," National Center for Complimentary and Alternative Medicine, National Institutes of Health, July 2007.

Stress management programs have begun to demonstrate some success in accomplishing this end.

Stress management programs often consist of breathing exercises, stretching exercises, yoga, meditation, and/or massage. There are probably several useful approaches, but they all aim toward the same goal—to blunt the adrenaline response to minor stress.

A recent study from Duke University reported a significant reduction in heart attacks among patients with coronary artery disease who underwent a formal stress management program, which was used in conjunction with a smoking cessation program, a weight loss program, and control of lipids.

Recommendations

Stress management techniques may be quite helpful in reducing the risk of coronary events, and have the added benefit of being risk-free. Thus, there seems to be little reason not to recommend some form of stress management in people with heart disease, or with risk factors for heart disease. And finally, it should be pointed out that exercise is a great way of reducing chronic stress, and in addition has the advantage of directly lessening the risk of coronary artery disease and helping to control obesity.

Chapter 40
Adolescent Stress And Depression

Adults commonly tell young people that the teenage years are the "best years of your life." The rosy remembrance highlights happy groups of high school students energetically involved at a dance or sporting event, and a bright-eyed couple holding hands or sipping sodas at a local restaurant. This is only part of the picture. Life for many young people is a painful tug of war filled with mixed messages and conflicting demands from parents, teachers, coaches, employers, friends, and oneself. Growing up—negotiating a path between independence and reliance on others—is a tough business. It creates stress, and it can create serious depression for young people ill equipped to cope, communicate, and solve problems.

A study and a survey conducted in Minnesota provide information about the prevalence of adolescent stress and depression. The study and survey point out some of the stressful events young people experience, describe how young people deal with stress, and indicate the risk factors for young people most vulnerable to stress, depression, and self destructive behavior. This major research project provides data on adolescent stress, depression, and suicide collected from nearly 4,300 high school students in 52 rural Minnesota counties.

> About This Chapter: Information in this chapter is from "Adolescent Stress and Depression," by Joyce Walker, © 2005 University of Minnesota Extension. Reprinted with permission.

Stress And Depression Are Real

Stress and depression are serious problems for many teenagers, as the study of Minnesota high school students reveals. Although 61 percent of the students are not depressed and seem to handle their problems in constructive ways, 39 percent suffer from mild to severe depression. These young people often rely on passive or negative behaviors in their attempts to deal with problems.

Stress is characterized by feelings of tension, frustration, worry, sadness, and withdrawal that commonly last from a few hours to a few days. Depression is both more severe and longer lasting. Depression is characterized by more extreme feelings of hopelessness, sadness, isolation, worry, withdrawal, and worthlessness that last for two weeks or more. The finding that nine percent of high school students are severely depressed is important since depression is the most important risk factor for suicide. The Minnesota study found that 88 percent of the youth who reported making suicide attempts were depressed. Approximately six percent of the students reported suicide attempts in the previous six months.

> ✔ **Quick Tip**
> On a piece of paper, write down the things you are grateful for. List the people who care about you. Write about your hopes for the future. Keep what you have written in a safe place. Whenever you are hurting or feeling mixed up, read what you have written to remind yourself that your life is important.
>
> Source: Excerpted from *Teen Survival Guide: Health Tips for On-the-go Girls*, GirlsHealth.gov, U.S. Department of Health and Human Services, Office on Women's Health, June 2007.

Common Causes And Responses To Stress

Young people become stressed for many reasons. The Minnesota study presented students with a list of 47 common life events and asked them to identify those they had experienced in the last six months that they

Adolescent Stress And Depression

considered to be "bad." The responses indicated that they had experienced an average of two negative life events in the last six months. The most common of these were:

- Break up with boyfriend or girlfriend
- Increased arguments with parents
- Trouble with brother or sister
- Increased arguments between parents
- Change in parents' financial status
- Serious illness or injury of family member
- Trouble with classmates
- Trouble with parents

These events are centered in the two most important domains of a teenager's life: home and school. They relate to issues of conflict and loss. Loss can reflect the real or perceived loss of something concrete such as a friend or money, and it can mean the loss of such intrinsic things as self-worth, respect, friendship, or love.

In a more informal survey of 60 young people, the primary sources of tension and trouble for teens and their friends were: relationships with friends and family; the pressure of expectations from self and others; pressure at school from teachers, coaches, grades, and homework; financial pressures; and tragedy in the lives of family and friends (described as death, divorce, cancer).

Most teenagers respond to stressful events in their lives by doing something relaxing, trying positive and self-reliant problem solving, or seeking friendship and support from others. Common examples include listening to music, trying to make their own decisions, daydreaming, trying to figure out solutions, keeping up friendships, watching television, and being close to people they care about. These behaviors are appropriate for adolescents who are trying to become independent, take responsibility for themselves, and draw on friends and family for support.

Troubled Youth Respond Differently

The majority of young people face the stress of negative life events, find internal or external resources to cope, and move on. But for others, the events pile up and the stressors are too great. In the Minnesota study, teens who reported that they had made a suicide attempt had five additional "bad" events on their list: parents' divorce, loss of a close friend, change to a new school, failing grades, and personal illness or injury. It is significant that the young people who showed high degrees of depression, and who had made suicide attempts, reported over five of these "bad" events in the past six months, more than twice as many as the rest of the group.

The actions in response to stress were also different for those who reported serious depression or a suicide attempt. Young people who are depressed are at a much greater risk of attempting suicide than non-depressed youth—although not all youth who attempt suicide are depressed. These young people report exhibiting much more anger and ventilation; avoidance and passivity; and aggressive, antisocial behavior. They describe yelling, fighting, and complaining; drinking, smoking, and using doctor-prescribed drugs more frequently; and sleeping, riding around in cars, and crying more often.

✔ Quick Tip

Try these pick-me-ups when you are feeling down:

Relax. Take a shower, watch a funny movie, or listen to some feel-good music.

Talk. Your friends, parents, teachers, or other trusted adult can help you sort through your feelings.

Work out. Your body makes mood-boosting chemicals called endorphins when you exercise.

Get a good night's sleep. It's hard to cope with strong feelings when you are tired.

Source: Excerpted from *Teen Survival Guide: Health Tips for On-the-go Girls*, GirlsHealth.gov, U.S. Department of Health and Human Services, Office on Women's Health, June 2007.

Adolescent Stress And Depression

They are less inclined to do things with their family or to go along with parents' rules and requests.

A Closer Look At High Risk Youth

It is important not to overreact to isolated incidents. Young people will have problems and will learn, at their own rate, to struggle and deal with them. A good starting point for identifying and intervening with highly troubled and depressed young people is the careful study of suicidal adolescents.

Family history and biology can create a predisposition for dealing poorly with stress. These factors make a person susceptible to depression and self-destructive behavior.

- History of depression and/or suicide in the family
- Alcoholism or drug use in the family
- Sexual or physical abuse patterns in the family
- Chronic illness in oneself or family
- Family or individual history of psychiatric disorders such as eating disorders, schizophrenia, manic-depressive disorder, conduct disorders, delinquency
- Death or serious loss in the family
- Learning disabilities or mental/physical disabilities
- Absent or divorced parents; inadequate bonding in adoptive families
- Family conflict; poor parent/child relationships

Personality traits, especially when they change dramatically, can signal serious trouble. These traits include:

- Impulsive behaviors, obsessions, and unreal fears
- Aggressive and antisocial behavior
- Withdrawal and isolation; detachment
- Poor social skills resulting in feelings of humiliation, poor self-worth, blame, and feeling ugly

- Over-achieving and extreme pressure to perform
- Problems with sleeping and/or eating

Psychological and social events contribute to the accumulation of problems and stressors.

- Loss experience such as a death or suicide of a friend or family member; broken romance, loss of a close friendship, or a family move
- Unmet personal or parental expectation such as failure to achieve a goal, poor grades, social rejection
- Unresolved conflict with family members, peers, teachers, coaches that results in anger, frustration, rejection
- Humiliating experience resulting in loss of self-esteem or rejection
- Unexpected events such as pregnancy or financial problems

Predispositions, stressors, and behaviors weave together to form a composite picture of a youth at high risk for depression and self-destructive behavior. Symptoms such as personal drug and alcohol use, running away from home, prolonged sadness and crying, unusual impulsivity or recklessness, or dramatic changes in personal habits are intertwined with the family and personal history, the individual personality, and the emotional/social events taking place in a person's life.

It is not always easy for one person to see the "whole picture." That's why it is essential that people who have "hunches" that something is wrong take the lead to gather perspectives from other friends, family members, and professionals who know the young person. It is all too often true that the survivors of an adolescent suicide only "put the pieces together" after the fact, when they sit together and try to figure out what happened. How fortunate a troubled young person is to have a caring adult take the initiative to look more closely before something serious happens.

Young people must learn and practice coping skills to get them through an immediate conflict or problem. Coping strategies must emphasize self-responsibility to find positive, non-destructive ways to find relief. Second, communication skills are important. This involves being able to talk and selecting a good listener. It is important to express feelings, vent emotions,

Adolescent Stress And Depression

and talk about the problems and issues. Peers are good sympathizers, but it often takes an adult perspective to begin to plan how to make changes for the better. Third, young people need help to learn problem-solving skills. Sorting out the issues, setting goals, and making plans to move forward are skills that can be taught and practiced.

Chapter 41

Stress, Depression, And Suicide: Helping A Friend In Trouble

We all have bad days, or weeks, or even months. We all feel overwhelmed at times. Things usually get better. Sometimes that's hard to remember when you're down. But stress, depression, and even suicide happen in the lives of people young and old.

Problems get people down. We feel tense, fearful, or angry because things are changing—they seem out of control. It's hard to manage. More than 2,000 Minnesota junior and senior high school students were asked how they handle serious problems in their lives. Can you guess what they said? They either try to handle the problem themselves or talk to their friends. It's important to think about how to help yourself as well as a friend who comes to you.

How People React To Stress And Problems

Failure on a test, a fight with a friend, an argument with a parent, or a put-down by a teacher can be upsetting. Many things that cause problems are beyond our control: parents divorcing, a family moving away, the death

> About This Chapter: Information in this chapter is from "Helping Friends in Trouble: Stress, Depression, and Suicide," by Joyce Walker, © 2005 University of Minnesota Extension. Reprinted with permission.

of someone close to us, or family financial problems. We all know someone who has broken up with a boyfriend or girlfriend, feared pregnancy, gotten in trouble with the law, or felt utterly deserted and alone.

There are three basic ways of reacting to the problem:

1. You can get angry—scream, shout, throw things, start a fight, or go on a rampage.

2. You can withdraw—take a drink, shut up in a room, take a pill, daydream, stop talking to everyone.

3. You can take charge—think out the problem, try to find a solution, ask for help, or work for change.

Unhealthy Ways To React To Problems

Aggression and anger get attention. Striking out at whomever seems responsible for the problem brings temporary relief. But aggressive actions, like drinking too much, driving recklessly, swearing at people, and breaking up things, can cause trouble in the long run. They don't usually solve the problem.

Withdrawal can also be destructive. It's normal to react, "Just leave me alone!" But if it goes on for a long time, we are without what we need most—sharing, understanding, and help. Alone with a problem, we feel like no one cares. The depression and anger become worse, and we begin to make bad choices instead of healthy ones.

Healthy Ways To React To Problems

When your stomach churns, your head aches, and fear creeps through your insides, your mind and body are reacting to stress. There are a number of things you can do, such as:

- Talk to someone you trust.
- Share what is bothering you.
- Listen to music and relax.
- Get some physical exercise.

Stress, Depression, Suicide: Helping A Friend In Trouble

- Do something that normally gives you pleasure.
- Give yourself a chance to think.

These are first-aid actions. They don't solve the problem, but you can blow off some steam. Once that's done, it's a good idea to get in touch with someone you trust and respect. This could be a friend, a friend's parent, a coach, or someone you work with. Go have a good talk. Lay out the problem and try to figure out some ways to solve it.

Warning Signs Of Trouble

Be aware of real trouble signs. Any one of these alone, lasting only a short time, is normal. But if you know a friend with several of these problems lasting more than a couple of weeks, they may be nearing a crisis. They need help. The warning signs can include:

- Avoiding friends, activities, school, social events
- Totally unable to think of anything but the problem
- Unexpected outbursts of anger or crying
- Unable to sleep; always feeling exhausted, irritated
- Unable to eat; or eating and vomiting
- Escaping by sleeping or daydreaming all the time
- Severe behavior change—quiet person becoming wild or active
- Person becoming withdrawn
- Excessive use of drugs or alcohol

There are four other signals that should be taken particularly seriously because they are suicide danger signals.

Suicide Danger Signals

- Threats or talk of killing themselves
- Preparing for death—giving away prized possessions, making a will, writing farewell letters, gathering pills, or saying good-bye

- Talking like there is no hope even in the future
- Acting or talking like not a single person cares; completely giving up on themselves and others

Support You Can Offer To Friends

Take the problem seriously. Even if the problem doesn't seem real important to you, it may be important to them. Things may be piling up. Show them you understand.

Don't put them down. It doesn't help to say, "Things will be better tomorrow" or "Keep your chin up." Their problem is real to them.

Encourage them to talk to other people as well as to you. Offer to go along with them to talk with some adult friend they can trust.

Offer to join the person in some activity they normally enjoy. They need a chance to have some fun and get their mind cleared.

☞ Remember!!
CLUES—Five Action Steps
To Help A Troubled Person

C *Connect:* Make contact, reach out, and talk to them. Notice their pain.

L *Listen:* Take the time and really pay attention. You don't have to have all the answers. Just listen.

U *Understand:* Nod, pay attention, and let them know you appreciate what they are going through.

E *Express concern:* Say that you care, you are worried, and you want to be helpful.

S *Seek help:* Tell them you want to go with them to talk to a third person, preferably an adult with experience and the ability to help. Don't agree to be secretive. Enlarge the circle of support.

Let them know you care. They may try to put you off. Stay in touch. Reach out. Invite them to do things with you. Don't force them to be cheerful. Stick with them.

Dos And Don'ts If A Person Threatens Suicide

Take the threat seriously. Insist on getting help. If they don't agree to help themselves, then you need to go to someone who can help.

Do not agree to keep suicide thoughts or threats a secret. Keeping the secret won't help the person. And you cannot bear the responsibility if they do hurt or kill themselves.

Don't try to call their bluff. It may not be one. Reinforce the fact that you care about them and insist they get help.

Let them know you care they are alive.

Being A Helping Friend

It is important to remember that you cannot be responsible for another person's actions when they are stressed, depressed, or suicidal. Whether they are crying out for help or suffering silently in despair, only they can help themselves. What you can do is be the most caring and responsible friend possible during the hard times. This means listening to their concerns, supporting them, and helping them get skilled help from a trusted and capable adult friend.

Chapter 42

Anxiety Disorders

Introduction

Unlike the relatively mild, brief anxiety caused by a stressful event (such as speaking in public or a first date), anxiety disorders last at least six months and can get worse if they are not treated. Anxiety disorders commonly occur along with other mental or physical illnesses, including alcohol or substance abuse, which may mask anxiety symptoms or make them worse. In some cases, these other illnesses need to be treated before a person will respond to treatment for the anxiety disorder. Effective therapies for anxiety disorders are available, and research is uncovering new treatments that can help most people with anxiety disorders lead productive, fulfilling lives. If you think you have an anxiety disorder, you should seek information and treatment right away.

Panic Disorder

Panic disorder is a real illness that can be successfully treated. It is characterized by sudden attacks of terror, usually accompanied by a pounding heart, sweatiness, weakness, faintness, or dizziness. During these attacks, people with panic disorder may flush or feel chilled; their hands may tingle or feel

---

About This Chapter: Information in this chapter is excerpted from "Anxiety Disorders," National Institute of Mental Health, National Institutes of Health, September 2007.

numb; and they may experience nausea, chest pain, or smothering sensations. Panic attacks usually produce a sense of unreality, a fear of impending doom, or a fear of losing control.

A fear of one's own unexplained physical symptoms is also a symptom of panic disorder. People having panic attacks sometimes believe they are having heart attacks, losing their minds, or on the verge of death. They cannot predict when or where an attack will occur, and between episodes many worry intensely and dread the next attack.

Panic attacks can occur at any time, even during sleep. An attack usually peaks within ten minutes, but some symptoms may last much longer. Panic disorder affects about six million Americans and is twice as common in women as men. Panic attacks often begin in late adolescence or early adulthood, but not everyone who experiences panic attacks will develop panic disorder. Many people have just one attack and never have another. The tendency to develop panic attacks appears to be inherited.

♣ **It's A Fact!!**
Anxiety disorders affect about 40 million Americans in a given year, causing them to be filled with fearfulness and uncertainty.

People who have full-blown, repeated panic attacks can become very disabled by their condition and should seek treatment before they start to avoid places or situations where panic attacks have occurred. For example, if a panic attack happened in an elevator, someone with panic disorder may develop a fear of elevators that could affect the choice of a job or an apartment and restrict where that person can seek medical attention or enjoy entertainment.

Some people's lives become so restricted that they avoid normal activities, such as grocery shopping or driving. About one-third become housebound or are able to confront a feared situation only when accompanied by a spouse or other trusted person. When the condition progresses this far, it is called agoraphobia, or fear of open spaces.

Early treatment can often prevent agoraphobia, but people with panic disorder may sometimes go from doctor to doctor for years and visit the emergency room repeatedly before someone correctly diagnoses their condition.

Anxiety Disorders

This is unfortunate, because panic disorder is one of the most treatable of all the anxiety disorders, responding in most cases to certain kinds of medication or certain kinds of cognitive psychotherapy, which help change thinking patterns that lead to fear and anxiety.

Panic disorder is often accompanied by other serious problems, such as depression, drug abuse, or alcoholism. These conditions need to be treated separately. Symptoms of depression include feelings of sadness or hopelessness, changes in appetite or sleep patterns, low energy, and difficulty concentrating. Most people with depression can be effectively treated with antidepressant medications, certain types of psychotherapy, or a combination of the two.

Obsessive-Compulsive Disorder

People with obsessive-compulsive disorder (OCD) have persistent, upsetting thoughts (obsessions) and use rituals (compulsions) to control the anxiety these thoughts produce. Most of the time, the rituals end up controlling them.

For example, if people are obsessed with germs or dirt, they may develop a compulsion to wash their hands over and over again. If they develop an obsession with intruders, they may lock and relock their doors many times before going to bed. Being afraid of social embarrassment may prompt people with OCD to comb their hair compulsively in front of a mirror; sometimes they get "caught" in the mirror and cannot move away from it. Performing such rituals is not pleasurable. At best, it produces temporary relief from the anxiety created by obsessive thoughts.

Other common rituals are a need to repeatedly check things, touch things (especially in a particular sequence), or count things. Some common obsessions include having frequent thoughts of violence and harming loved ones, persistently thinking about performing sexual acts the person dislikes, or having thoughts that are prohibited by religious beliefs. People with OCD may also be preoccupied with order and symmetry, have difficulty throwing things out (so they accumulate), or hoard unneeded items.

Healthy people also have rituals, such as checking to see if the stove is off several times before leaving the house. The difference is that people with OCD perform their rituals even though doing so interferes with daily life, and they find the repetition distressing. Although most people with OCD recognize that what they are doing is senseless, some adults and most children may not realize that their behavior is out of the ordinary.

OCD affects about 2.2 million Americans and the problem can be accompanied by eating disorders, other anxiety disorders, or depression. It strikes men and women in roughly equal numbers and usually appears in childhood, adolescence, or early adulthood. One-third of adults with OCD develop symptoms as children, and research indicates that OCD might run in families.

The course of the disease is quite varied. Symptoms may come and go, ease over time, or get worse. If OCD becomes severe, it can keep a person from working or carrying out normal responsibilities at home. People with OCD may try to help themselves by avoiding situations that trigger their obsessions, or they may use alcohol or drugs to calm themselves.

OCD usually responds well to treatment with certain medications and/ or exposure-based psychotherapy, in which people face situations that cause fear or anxiety and become less sensitive (desensitized) to them.

Social Phobia (Social Anxiety Disorder)

Social phobia, also called social anxiety disorder, is diagnosed when people become overwhelmingly anxious and excessively self-conscious in everyday social situations. People with social phobia have an intense, persistent, and chronic fear of being watched and judged by others and of doing things that will embarrass them. They can worry for days or weeks before a dreaded situation. This fear may become so severe that it interferes with work, school, and other ordinary activities, and can make it hard to make and keep friends.

While many people with social phobia realize that their fears about being with people are excessive or unreasonable, they are unable to overcome them. Even if they manage to confront their fears and be around others, they are usually very anxious beforehand, are intensely uncomfortable throughout the encounter, and worry about how they were judged for hours afterward.

Social phobia can be limited to one situation (such as talking to people, eating or drinking, or writing on a blackboard in front of others) or may be

Anxiety Disorders

so broad (such as in generalized social phobia) that the person experiences anxiety around almost anyone other than the family.

Physical symptoms that often accompany social phobia include blushing, profuse sweating, trembling, nausea, and difficulty talking. When these symptoms occur, people feel as though all eyes are focused on them.

Social phobia affects about 15 million Americans. There is some evidence that genetic factors are involved. Social phobia is often accompanied by other anxiety disorders or depression, and substance abuse may develop if people try to self-medicate their anxiety.

Social phobia can be successfully treated with certain kinds of psychotherapy or medications.

> ♣ **It's A Fact!!**
> Women and men are equally likely to develop social phobia, which usually begins in childhood or early adolescence.

Specific Phobias

A specific phobia is an intense fear of something that poses little or no actual danger. Some of the more common specific phobias are centered on closed-in places, heights, escalators, tunnels, highway driving, water, flying, dogs, and injuries involving blood. Such phobias are not just extreme fear; they are irrational fear of a particular thing. You may be able to ski the world's tallest mountains with ease but be unable to go above the fifth floor of an office building. While people with phobias realize that these fears are irrational, they often find that facing, or even thinking about facing, the feared object or situation brings on a panic attack or severe anxiety.

Specific phobias affect an estimated 19.2 million Americans and are twice as common in women as men. They usually appear in childhood or adolescence and tend to persist into adulthood. The causes of specific phobias are not well understood, but there is some evidence that the tendency to develop them may run in families.

If the feared situation or feared object is easy to avoid, people with specific phobias may not seek help; but if avoidance interferes with their careers or their personal lives, it can become disabling, and treatment is usually pursued.

Specific phobias respond very well to carefully targeted psychotherapy.

Generalized Anxiety Disorder (GAD)

People with generalized anxiety disorder (GAD) go through the day filled with exaggerated worry and tension, even though there is little or nothing to provoke it. They anticipate disaster and are overly concerned about health issues, money, family problems, or difficulties at work. Sometimes just the thought of getting through the day produces anxiety.

GAD is diagnosed when a person worries excessively about a variety of everyday problems for at least six months. People with GAD cannot seem to get rid of their concerns, even though they usually realize that their anxiety is more intense than the situation warrants. They cannot relax, startle easily, and have difficulty concentrating. Often they have trouble falling asleep or staying asleep. Physical symptoms that often accompany the anxiety include fatigue, headaches, muscle tension, muscle aches, difficulty swallowing, trembling, twitching, irritability, sweating, nausea, lightheadedness, having to go to the bathroom frequently, feeling out of breath, and hot flashes.

When their anxiety level is mild, people with GAD can function socially and hold down a job. Although they do not avoid certain situations as a result of their disorder, people with GAD can have difficulty carrying out the simplest daily activities if their anxiety is severe.

GAD affects about 6.8 million Americans and about twice as many women as men. The disorder comes on gradually and can begin across the life cycle, though the risk is highest between childhood and middle age. It is diagnosed when someone spends at least six months worrying excessively about a number of everyday problems. There is evidence that genes play a modest role in GAD.

Other anxiety disorders, depression, or substance abuse often accompany GAD, which rarely occurs alone. GAD is commonly treated with medication or cognitive-behavioral therapy, but co-occurring conditions must also be treated using the appropriate therapies.

Treatment Of Anxiety Disorders

In general, anxiety disorders are treated with medication, specific types of psychotherapy, or both. Treatment choices depend on the problem and the person's preference. Before treatment begins, a doctor must conduct a careful diagnostic evaluation to determine whether a person's symptoms are caused by an anxiety disorder or a physical problem. If an anxiety disorder is diagnosed, the type of disorder or the combination of disorders that are present must be identified, as well as any coexisting conditions, such as depression or substance abuse. Sometimes alcoholism, depression, or other coexisting conditions have such a strong effect on the individual that treating the anxiety disorder must wait until the coexisting conditions are brought under control.

People with anxiety disorders who have already received treatment should tell their current doctor about that treatment in detail. If they received medication, they should tell their doctor what medication was used, what the dosage was at the beginning of treatment, whether the dosage was increased or decreased while they were under treatment, what side effects occurred, and whether the treatment helped them become less anxious. If they received psychotherapy, they should describe the type of therapy, how often they attended sessions, and whether the therapy was useful.

Often people believe that they have "failed" at treatment or that the treatment did not work for them when, in fact, it was not given for an adequate length of time or was administered incorrectly. Sometimes people must try several different treatments or combinations of treatment before they find the one that works for them.

Medications

Medication will not cure anxiety disorders, but it can keep them under control while the person receives psychotherapy. Medication must be prescribed by physicians, usually psychiatrists, who can either offer psychotherapy themselves or work as a team with psychologists, social workers, or counselors who provide psychotherapy. The principal medications used for anxiety disorders are antidepressants, anti-anxiety drugs, and beta-blockers to control some of the physical symptoms. With proper treatment, many people with anxiety disorders can lead normal, fulfilling lives.

Antidepressants

Antidepressants were developed to treat depression but are also effective for anxiety disorders. Although these medications begin to alter brain chemistry after the very first dose, their full effect requires a series of changes to occur; it is usually about four to six weeks before symptoms start to fade. It is important to continue taking these medications long enough to let them work.

- **Selective Serotonin Reuptake Inhibitors (SSRIs):** Some of the newest antidepressants are called selective serotonin reuptake inhibitors, or SSRIs. SSRIs alter the levels of the neurotransmitter serotonin in the brain, which like other neurotransmitters helps brain cells communicate with one another. These medications are started at low doses and are gradually increased until they have a beneficial effect. SSRIs have fewer side effects than older antidepressants, but they sometimes produce slight nausea or jitters when people first start to take them. These symptoms fade with time. Some people also experience sexual dysfunction with SSRIs, which may be helped by adjusting the dosage or switching to another SSRI.

- **Tricyclics:** Tricyclics are older than SSRIs and work as well as SSRIs for anxiety disorders other than OCD. They are also started at low doses that are gradually increased. They sometimes cause dizziness, drowsiness, dry mouth, and weight gain, which can usually be corrected by changing the dosage or switching to another tricyclic medication.

- **Monoamine Oxidase Inhibitors (MAOIs):** Monoamine oxidase inhibitors are the oldest class of antidepressant medications. People who take MAOIs cannot eat a variety of foods and beverages (including cheese and red wine) that contain tyramine or take certain medications, including some types of birth control pills, pain relievers (such as Advil®, Motrin®, or Tylenol®), cold and allergy medications, and herbal supplements; these substances can interact with MAOIs to cause dangerous increases in blood pressure. The development of a new MAOI skin patch may help lessen these risks. MAOIs can also react with SSRIs to produce a serious condition called "serotonin syndrome," which can cause confusion, hallucinations, increased sweating, muscle

Anxiety Disorders

stiffness, seizures, changes in blood pressure or heart rhythm, and other potentially life-threatening conditions.

Anti-Anxiety Drugs

High-potency benzodiazepines combat anxiety and have few side effects other than drowsiness. Because people can get used to them and may need higher and higher doses to get the same effect, benzodiazepines are generally prescribed for short periods of time, especially for people who have abused drugs or alcohol and who become dependent on medication easily. One exception to this rule is people with panic disorder, who can take benzodiazepines for up to a year without harm.

Some people experience withdrawal symptoms if they stop taking benzodiazepines abruptly instead of tapering off, and anxiety can return once the medication is stopped. These potential problems have led some physicians to shy away from using these drugs or to use them in inadequate doses.

✔ Quick Tip
Taking Medications

Before taking medication for an anxiety disorder, do the following:

- Ask your doctor to tell you about the effects and side effects of the drug.

- Tell your doctor about any alternative therapies or over-the-counter medications you are using.

- Ask your doctor when and how the medication should be stopped. Some drugs cannot be stopped abruptly but must be tapered off slowly under a doctor's supervision.

- Work with your doctor to determine which medication is right for you and what dosage is best.

- Be aware that some medications are effective only if they are taken regularly and that symptoms may recur if the medication is stopped.

Beta-Blockers

Beta-blockers, such as propranolol (Inderal®), which is used to treat heart conditions, can prevent the physical symptoms that accompany certain anxiety disorders, particularly social phobia. When a feared situation can be predicted (such as giving a speech), a doctor may prescribe a beta-blocker to keep physical symptoms of anxiety under control.

Psychotherapy

Cognitive-Behavioral Therapy

Cognitive-behavioral therapy (CBT) is very useful in treating anxiety disorders. The cognitive part helps people change the thinking patterns that support their fears, and the behavioral part helps people change the way they react to anxiety-provoking situations.

For example, CBT can help people with panic disorder learn that their panic attacks are not really heart attacks and help people with social phobia learn how to overcome the belief that others are always watching and judging them. When people are ready to confront their fears, they are shown how to use exposure techniques to desensitize themselves to situations that trigger their anxieties.

People with OCD who fear dirt and germs are encouraged to get their hands dirty and wait increasing amounts of time before washing them. The therapist helps the person cope with the anxiety that waiting produces. After the exercise has been repeated a number of times, the anxiety diminishes. People with social phobia may be encouraged to spend time in feared social situations without giving in to the temptation to flee and to make small social blunders and observe how people respond to them. Since the response

> ♣ **It's A Fact!!**
> Psychotherapy involves talking with a trained mental health professional, such as a psychiatrist, psychologist, social worker, or counselor, to discover what caused an anxiety disorder and how to deal with its symptoms.

Anxiety Disorders

is usually far less harsh than the person fears, these anxieties are lessened. CBT therapists also teach deep breathing and other types of exercises to relieve anxiety and encourage relaxation.

Exposure-based behavioral therapy has been used for many years to treat specific phobias. The person gradually encounters the object or situation that is feared, perhaps at first only through pictures or tapes, then later face-to-face. Often the therapist will accompany the person to a feared situation to provide support and guidance.

CBT is undertaken when people decide they are ready for it and with their permission and cooperation. To be effective, the therapy must be directed at the person's specific anxieties and must be tailored to his or her needs. There are no side effects other than the discomfort of temporarily increased anxiety.

CBT or behavioral therapy often lasts about 12 weeks. It may be conducted individually or with a group of people who have similar problems. Group therapy is particularly effective for social phobia. Often "homework" is assigned for participants to complete between sessions. There is some evidence that the benefits of CBT last longer than those of medication for people with panic disorder, and the same may be true for OCD and social phobia. If a disorder recurs at a later date, the same therapy can be used to treat it successfully a second time.

Medication can be combined with psychotherapy for specific anxiety disorders, and this is the best treatment approach for many people.

How To Get Help For Anxiety Disorders

If you think you have an anxiety disorder, the first person you should see is your family doctor. A physician can determine whether the symptoms that alarm you are due to an anxiety disorder, another medical condition, or both.

If an anxiety disorder is diagnosed, the next step is usually seeing a mental health professional. The practitioners who are most helpful with anxiety disorders are those who have training in cognitive-behavioral therapy and/or behavioral therapy and who are open to using medication if it is needed.

You should feel comfortable talking with the mental health professional you choose. If you do not, you should seek help elsewhere. Once you find a mental health professional with which you are comfortable, the two of you should work as a team and make a plan to treat your anxiety disorder together.

Remember that once you start on medication, it is important not to stop taking it abruptly. Certain drugs must be tapered off under the supervision of a doctor or bad reactions can occur. Make sure you talk to the doctor who prescribed your medication before you stop taking it. If you are having trouble with side effects, it is possible that adjusting how much medication you take, and when you take it, can eliminate them.

Most insurance plans, including health maintenance organizations (HMOs), will cover treatment for anxiety disorders. Check with your insurance company and find out. If you do not have insurance, the Health and Human Services division of your county government may offer mental health care at a public mental health center that charges people according to how much they are able to pay. If you are on public assistance, you may be able to get care through your state Medicaid plan.

✔ Quick Tip

Ways To Make Treatment More Effective

Many people with anxiety disorders benefit from joining a self-help or support group and sharing their problems and achievements with others. Talking with a trusted friend or member of the clergy can also provide support, but it is not a substitute for care from a mental health professional.

Stress management techniques and meditation can help people with anxiety disorders calm themselves and may enhance the effects of therapy. There is preliminary evidence that aerobic exercise may have a calming effect. Since caffeine, certain illicit drugs, and even some over-the-counter cold medications can aggravate the symptoms of anxiety disorders, they should be avoided. Check with your physician or pharmacist before taking any additional medications.

The family is very important in the recovery of a person with an anxiety disorder. Ideally, the family should be supportive but not help perpetuate their loved one's symptoms. Family members should not trivialize the disorder or demand improvement without treatment.

Chapter 43

Posttraumatic Stress Disorder (PTSD)

What is posttraumatic stress disorder?

Posttraumatic stress disorder is an anxiety disorder that can occur after you have been through a traumatic event. A traumatic event is something horrible and scary that you see or that happens to you. During this type of event, you think that your life or others' lives are in danger. You may feel afraid or feel that you have no control over what is happening.

Anyone who has gone through a life-threatening event can develop PTSD. These events can include the following:

- Combat or military exposure
- Child sexual or physical abuse
- Terrorist attacks
- Sexual or physical assault
- Serious accidents, such as a car wreck
- Natural disasters, such as a fire, tornado, hurricane, flood, or earthquake

---

About This Chapter: Information in this chapter is from "What is Posttraumatic Stress Disorder (PTSD)," National Center for Posttraumatic Stress Disorder, United States Department of Veterans Affairs, May 2007.

After the event, you may feel scared, confused, and angry. If these feelings do not go away or they get worse, you may have PTSD. These symptoms may disrupt your life, making it hard to continue with your daily activities.

How does PTSD develop?

All people with PTSD have lived through a traumatic event that caused them to fear for their lives, see horrible things, and feel helpless. Strong emotions caused by the event create changes in the brain that may result in PTSD.

Many people who go through a traumatic event do not get PTSD. It is not clear why some people develop PTSD and others do not. How likely you are to get PTSD depends on many things. These include the following:

- How intense the trauma was
- If you lost a loved one or were hurt
- How close you were to the event
- How strong your reaction was
- How much you felt in control of events
- How much help and support you got after the event

PTSD symptoms usually start soon after the traumatic event, but they may not happen until months or years later. They also may come and go over many years. About half (40% to 60%) of people who develop PTSD get better at some time, but about one out of three people who develop PTSD always will have some symptoms.

What are the symptoms of PTSD?

Symptoms of posttraumatic stress disorder (PTSD) can be terrifying. They may disrupt your life and make it hard to continue with your daily activities. It may be hard just to get through the day.

PTSD symptoms usually start soon after the traumatic event, but they may not happen until months or years later. They also may come and go over many years. If the symptoms last longer than four weeks, cause you

Posttraumatic Stress Disorder (PTSD)

great distress, or interfere with your work or home life, you probably have PTSD.

Even if you always have some symptoms, counseling can help you cope. Your symptoms do not have to interfere with your everyday activities, work, and relationships. Most people who go through a traumatic event have some symptoms at the beginning but do not develop PTSD.

There are four types of symptoms: reliving symptoms, avoidance symptoms, numbing symptoms, and feeling keyed up.

Reliving The Event (Also Called Re-Experiencing Symptoms)

Bad memories of the traumatic event can come back at any time. You may feel the same fear and horror you did when the event took place. You may feel like you are going through the event again. This is called a flashback. Sometimes there is a trigger: a sound or sight that causes you to relive the event. Triggers might include the following:

- Hearing a car backfire, which can bring back memories of gunfire and war for a combat veteran
- Seeing a car accident, which can remind a crash survivor of his or her own accident
- Seeing a news report of a sexual assault, which may bring back memories of assault for a woman who was raped

Avoiding Situations That Remind You Of The Event

You may try to avoid situations or people that trigger memories of the traumatic event. You may even avoid talking or thinking about the event.

- A person who was in an earthquake may avoid watching television shows or movies in which there are earthquakes.
- A person who was robbed at gunpoint while ordering at a hamburger drive-in may avoid fast-food restaurants.
- Some people may keep very busy or avoid seeking help. This keeps them from having to think or talk about the event.

Feeling Numb

You may find it hard to express your feelings. This is another way to avoid memories.

- You may not have positive or loving feelings toward other people and may stay away from relationships.
- You may not be interested in activities you used to enjoy.
- You may forget about parts of the traumatic event or not be able to talk about them.

Feeling Keyed Up (Also Called Arousal Or Hyper-Arousal Symptoms)

You always may be alert and on the lookout for danger. This is known as increased emotional arousal. It can cause the following:

- You suddenly become angry or irritable.
- You have a hard time sleeping.
- You have trouble concentrating.
- You fear for your safety and always feel on guard.

♣ **It's A Fact!!**
Acupuncture May Help Symptoms Of Posttraumatic Stress Disorder

Michael Hollifield, M.D., and colleagues conducted a clinical trial examining the effect of acupuncture on the symptoms of posttraumatic stress disorder (PTSD). The researchers analyzed depression, anxiety, and impairment in 73 people with a diagnosis of PTSD. The participants were assigned to receive either acupuncture or group cognitive-behavioral therapy over 12 weeks or were assigned to a wait list as part of the control group. The people in the control group were offered treatment or referral for treatment at the end of their participation.

The researchers found that acupuncture provided treatment effects similar to group cognitive-behavioral therapy; both interventions were superior to the control group. Additionally, treatment effects of both the acupuncture and the group therapy were maintained for three months after the end of treatment.

The limitations of the study are consistent with preliminary research. For example, this study had a small group of participants that lacked diversity, and the results do not account for outside factors that may have affected the treatments' results.

Source: National Center for Complementary and Alternative Medicine, National Institutes of Health, September 2007.

Posttraumatic Stress Disorder (PTSD)

- You become very startled when someone surprises you.

PTSD In Children And Teens

Children can have PTSD too. They may have the symptoms above or other symptoms depending on how old they are. As children get older their symptoms are more like those of adults.

- Young children may become upset if their parents are not close by, have trouble sleeping, or suddenly have trouble with toilet training or going to the bathroom.

- Children who are in the first few years of elementary school (ages 6 to 9) may act out the trauma through play, drawings, or stories. They may complain of physical problems or become more irritable or aggressive. They also may develop fears and anxiety that do not seem to be caused by the traumatic event.

What are other common problems?

People with PTSD may also have other problems. These include the following:

- Drinking or drug problems
- Feelings of hopelessness, shame, or despair
- Employment problems
- Relationship problems including divorce and violence
- Physical symptoms

What treatments are available?

Today, there are good treatments available for PTSD. When you have PTSD, dealing with the past can be hard. Instead of telling others how you feel, you may keep your feelings bottled up, but talking with a therapist can help you get better.

Cognitive-behavioral therapy (CBT) is one type of counseling. It appears to be the most effective type of counseling for PTSD. There are different types of cognitive behavioral therapies such as cognitive therapy and

Acute Stress Disorder

♣ It's A Fact!!

What is acute stress disorder?

Acute stress disorder (ASD) is a psychiatric diagnosis that can be given to individuals in the first month following a traumatic event. The symptoms that define ASD overlap with those for PTSD, although there are a greater number of dissociative symptoms for ASD, such as not knowing where you are or feeling as if you are outside of your body.

How common is ASD?

Because ASD is a relatively new diagnosis, research on the disorder is in the early stages. Rates range from 6% to 33% depending on the type of trauma as follows:

- Motor vehicle accidents: Rates of ASD range from approximately 13% to 21%.
- Typhoon: A study of survivors of a typhoon yielded an ASD rate of 7%.
- Industrial accident: One study found a rate of 6% in survivors of an industrial accident.
- Violent assault: A rate of 19% was found in survivors of violent assault, and a rate of 13% was found among a mixed group consisting of survivors of assaults, burns, and industrial accidents. A recent study of victims of robbery and assault found that 25% met criteria for ASD, and a study of victims of a mass shooting found that 33% met criteria for ASD.

Who is at risk for ASD as a result of trauma?

A few studies have examined factors that place individuals at risk for developing ASD.

One study found that individuals who (1) had experienced other traumatic events, (2) had PTSD previously, and (3) had prior psychological problems were all more likely to develop ASD as the result of a new traumatic stressor.

A study of motor vehicle accident survivors found that those individuals (1) with depression symptoms, (2) who had previous mental health treatment, and (3) who had been in other motor vehicle accidents were more likely to have more severe ASD.

A final study suggests that people who dissociate when confronted with traumatic stressors may be more likely to develop ASD.

How predictive of PTSD is ASD?

A diagnosis of ASD appears to be a strong predictor of subsequent PTSD. In one study, more than three quarters of the individuals who were in motor vehicle accidents and met criteria for ASD went on to develop PTSD. This finding is consistent with other studies that found that over 80% of people with ASD developed PTSD by the time they were assessed six months later.

Are there effective treatments for ASD?

- **Cognitive-Behavioral Interventions:** At present, cognitive-behavioral interventions during the acute aftermath of trauma exposure have yielded the most consistently positive results in terms of preventing subsequent posttraumatic psychopathology.

- **Psychological Debriefing:** Psychological debriefing is an early intervention that was originally developed for rescue workers but has been widely applied in the acute aftermath of potentially traumatic events. It has received much attention in the wake of 9/11. However, there is little evidence to support the continued use of debriefing with acutely traumatized individuals.

Source: "Acute Stress Disorder: A Brief Description," by Laura E. Gibson, Ph.D., The University of Vermont, National Center for Posttraumatic Stress Disorder, United States Department of Veterans Affairs, May 2007.

exposure therapy. There is also a similar kind of therapy called eye movement desensitization and reprocessing (EMDR) that is used for PTSD. Medications have also been shown to be effective. A type of drug known as a selective serotonin reuptake inhibitor (SSRI), which is also used for depression, is effective for PTSD.

Chapter 44

Stress, Substance Abuse, And Addiction

What Is Stress?

- Stress is a term that is hard to define because it means different things to different people. Stress is a normal occurrence in life for people of all ages. The body responds to stress in order to protect itself from emotional or physical distress or, in extreme situations, from danger.

- Stressors differ for each of us. What is stressful for one person may or may not be stressful for another, and each of us responds to stress in different ways. How a person copes with stress—by reaching for a beer or cigarette or by heading to the gym—also plays an important role in the impact that stress will have on our bodies.

- By using their own support systems, some people are able to cope effectively with the emotional and physical demands brought on by stressful and traumatic experiences. However, individuals who experience prolonged reactions to stress that disrupt their daily functioning may require treatment by a trained and experienced mental health professional.

About This Chapter: Information in this chapter is excerpted from "NIDA Community Drug Alert Bulletin—Stress And Substance Abuse," National Institute on Drug Abuse, U.S. National Institutes of Health, February 2006.

> ♣ **It's A Fact!!**
> **How Addiction Changes The Body's Response To Stress**
>
> Heroin and morphine inhibit the stress hormone cycle and presumably the release of stress-related neurotransmitters just as the natural opioid peptides do. Thus, when people take heroin or morphine, the drugs add to the inhibition already being provided by the opioid peptides. This may be a major reason that some people start taking heroin or morphine in the first place, suggests Dr. Mary Jeanne Kreek, of Rockefeller University in New York City. "Every one of us has things in life that really bother us," she says. "Most people are able to cope with these hassles, but some people find it very difficult to do so. In trying opiate drugs for the first time, some people who have difficulty coping with stressful emotions might find that these drugs blunt those emotions, an effect that they might find rewarding. This could be a major factor in their continued use of these drugs."
>
> When the effects of opiate drugs wear off, the addict goes into withdrawal. Research has shown that, during withdrawal, the level of stress hormones rises in the blood and stress-related neurotransmitters are released in the brain. These chemicals trigger emotions that the addict perceives as highly unpleasant, which drive the addict to take more opiate drugs. Because the effects of heroin or morphine last only four to six hours, opiate addicts often experience withdrawal three or four times a day. This constant switching on and off

The Body's Response To Stress

- The stress response is mediated by a highly complex integrated network that involves the central nervous system, the adrenal system, the immune system, and the cardiovascular system.

- Stress activates adaptive responses. It releases the neurotransmitter norepinephrine, which is involved in memory. This may be one reason why people remember stressful events more clearly than they do non-stressful situations.

- Stress also increases the release of a hormone known as corticotropin-releasing factor (CRF). CRF is found throughout the brain and initiates our biological response to stressors. During all stressful experiences, certain regions of the brain show increased levels of CRF.

> of the stress systems of the body heightens whatever hypersensitivity these systems may have had before the person started taking drugs, Dr. Kreek says. "The result is that these stress chemicals are on a sort of hair-trigger release. They surge at the slightest provocation," she says.
>
> Studies have suggested that cocaine similarly heightens the body's sensitivity to stress, although in a different way. When a cocaine addict takes cocaine, the stress systems are activated, much like when an opiate addict goes into withdrawal, but the person perceives this as part of the cocaine rush because cocaine is also stimulating the parts of the brain that are involved in feeling pleasure. When cocaine's effects wear off and the addict goes into withdrawal, the stress systems are again activated—again, much like when an opiate addict goes into withdrawal. This time, the cocaine addict perceives the activation as unpleasant because the cocaine is no longer stimulating the pleasure circuits in the brain. Because cocaine switches on the stress systems both when it is active and during withdrawal, these systems rapidly become hypersensitive, Dr. Kreek theorizes.
>
> Source: Excerpted from "Studies Link Stress And Drug Addiction," by Steven Stocker, *NIDA Notes*, National Institute on Drug Abuse, April 1999. Reviewed February 22, 2008 by David A. Cooke, M.D., Diplomate, American Board of Internal Medicine.

Interestingly, almost all drugs of abuse have also been found to increase CRF levels, suggesting a neurobiological connection between stress and drug abuse.

- Mild or acute stress may cause changes that are useful. For example, stress can actually improve our attention and increase our capacity to store and integrate important and life-protecting information; but if stress is prolonged or chronic, the changes it produces can become harmful.

Stress And Substance Abuse

- Stressful events can profoundly influence the abuse of alcohol or other drugs. Stress is a major contributor to the initiation and continuation of alcohol or other drug abuse, as well as to substance abuse relapse after periods of abstinence.

- Stress is one of the major factors known to cause relapse to smoking, even after prolonged periods of a smoke-free lifestyle.
- Children exposed to severe stress may be more vulnerable to drug abuse.

♣ **It's A Fact!!**

Handling Stress Without Smoking

What To Expect

- After you quit smoking, handling the normal stresses in your life may become more of a challenge.
- Quitting smoking itself is stressful and adds to your stress load.

Did You Know?

- Most smokers report that one reason they smoke is to handle stress.
- You may become more aware of stress during withdrawal. This happens because smoking cigarettes actually relieves some of your stress by releasing powerful chemicals in your brain.
- As you go longer without smoking, you will get better at handling stress, especially if you learn relaxation techniques.

Nicotine And Your Body And Mind

- Everyday worries, responsibilities, and hassles can all contribute to stress.
- It is thought that once nicotine enters your brain, it stimulates production of a number of the brain's most powerful chemical messengers.
- These chemicals (epinephrine, norepinephrine, dopamine, arginine, vasopressin, beta-endorphin, and acetylcholine) are involved in alertness, pain reduction, learning, memory, pleasure, and the reduction of both anxiety and pain.
- When you smoke, your brain chemistry changes temporarily so that you experience decreased anxiety, enhanced pleasure, and alert relaxation. This is why it feels good when you smoke.

Source: Excerpted from "Quitting Tobacco: Handling Stress...Without Smoking," National Cancer Institute, U.S. National Institutes of Health, November 2004.

A number of clinical and epidemiological studies show a strong association between psychosocial stressors early in life (for example, parental loss, child abuse) and an increased risk for depression, anxiety, impulsive behavior, and substance abuse in adulthood.

Stress, Drugs, And Vulnerable Populations

- Stressful experiences increase the vulnerability of an individual to relapse to drug use, even after prolonged abstinence.

- Individuals who have achieved abstinence from drugs must continue to sustain their abstinence by avoiding environmental triggers, recognizing their psychosocial and emotional triggers, and developing healthy behaviors to handle life's stresses.

- A number of relapse prevention approaches have been developed to help clinicians address relapse. Treatment techniques that foster coping skills, problem-solving skills, and social support play a role in successful treatment.

- Physicians should be aware of which medications their patients are taking. Some people may need medications for stress-related symptoms or for treatment of depression and anxiety.

What Is Posttraumatic Stress Disorder (PTSD)?

- Posttraumatic stress disorder (PTSD) is an anxiety disorder that can develop in some people after exposure to a terrifying event or ordeal in which grave physical harm occurred or was threatened.

- Generally, PTSD has been associated with the violence of combat. However, PTSD is not limited to battlefield soldiers. PTSD can result from tragic incidents in which people become witnesses, victims, or survivors of violent personal attacks, natural or human-caused disasters, or accidents.

- PTSD can develop in people of any age, including children and adolescents.

- Symptoms of PTSD can include re-experiencing the trauma; emotional numbness; avoidance of people, places, and thoughts connected

♣ It's A Fact!!
High Stress Teens Twice As Likely To Smoke, Get Drunk, Use Illegal Drugs

The risk that teens will smoke, drink, get drunk, and use illegal drugs increases sharply if they are highly stressed, frequently bored, or have substantial amounts of spending money, according to The National Survey of American Attitudes on Substance Abuse VIII: Teens and Parents, an annual back-to-school survey conducted by The National Center on Addiction and Substance Abuse (CASA) at Columbia University. This was the first time in its eight-year history that the survey measured the impact of these characteristics on the likelihood of teen substance abuse.

Among CASA's survey findings:

- High stress teens are twice as likely as low stress teens to smoke, drink, get drunk, and use illegal drugs.

- Often bored teens are 50 percent likelier than not often bored teens to smoke, drink, get drunk, and use illegal drugs.

- Teens with $25 or more a week in spending money are nearly twice as likely as teens with less to smoke, drink, and use illegal drugs, and more than twice as likely to get drunk.

- Teens exhibiting two or three of these characteristics are at more than three times the risk of substance abuse as those exhibiting none of these characteristics.

- More than half the nation's 12-to-17 year olds (52 percent) are at greater risk of substance abuse because of high stress, frequent boredom, too much spending money, or some combination of these characteristics.

Source: Excerpted from "CASA 2003 Teen Survey: High Stress, Frequent Boredom, Too Much Spending Money: Triple Threat That Hikes Risk of Teen Substance Abuse," August 19, 2003, National Center on Addiction and Substance Abuse (CASA) at Columbia University, http://www.casacolumbia.org. © 2003. All rights reserved. Reprinted with permission.

Stress, Substance Abuse, And Addiction

to the event; and hyper-arousal, which may involve sleeping difficulties, exaggerated startle response, and hyper-vigilance.

- It is not uncommon for people to experience some or all of these symptoms after exposure to a traumatic event; however, if the symptoms persist beyond one month and are associated with impaired functioning, then PTSD may be diagnosed.

PTSD And Substance Abuse

- Emerging research has documented a strong association between PTSD and substance abuse. In some cases, substance use begins after the exposure to trauma and the development of PTSD, thus making PTSD a risk factor for drug abuse.

- Early intervention to help children and adolescents who have suffered trauma from violence or a disaster is critical. Children who witness or are exposed to a traumatic event and are clinically diagnosed with PTSD have a greater likelihood for developing later drug and/or alcohol use disorders.

- Among individuals with substance use disorders, 30 to 60 percent meet the criteria for co-morbid PTSD.

- Patients with substance use disorders tend to suffer from more severe PTSD symptoms than do PTSD patients without substance use disorders.

Helping Those Who Suffer From PTSD And Drug Abuse

- Healthcare professionals must be alert to the fact that PTSD frequently co-occurs with depression, other anxiety disorders, and alcohol and other substance abuse. Patients who are experiencing the symptoms of PTSD need support from physicians and healthcare providers to develop coping skills and reduce substance abuse risk.

- The likelihood of treatment success increases when these concurrent disorders are appropriately identified and treated.

- For substance abuse, there are effective medications and behavioral therapies.

- For symptoms of PTSD, some anti-anxiety and antidepressant medications may be useful.

- Several behavioral treatments can help individuals who suffer from PTSD. Improvements have been shown with some forms of group therapy and with cognitive-behavioral therapy, especially when it includes an exposure component for trauma victims. Exposure therapy allows patients to gradually and repeatedly re-experience the frightening event(s) under controlled conditions to help them work through the trauma. Exposure therapy is thought to be one of the most effective ways to manage PTSD when a trained therapist conducts it.

- Although not widely used for co-morbid PTSD and substance abuse, several studies suggest that exposure therapy may be helpful for individuals with PTSD and co-morbid cocaine addiction.

- *Seeking Safety* is another example of a cognitive-based behavioral treatment, tested mainly among women with co-morbid PTSD and drug abuse. It is currently being evaluated among different populations for its efficacy.

- Treatment of patients with co-morbid PTSD and addictions will vary; and for some patients, successful treatment may require initial inpatient hospitalization.

- Finally, support from family and friends can play an important role in recovery from both disorders.

Chapter 45

Eating Disorders

What Are Eating Disorders?

"Mirror, Mirror on the wall, who's the thinnest one of all?" According to the National Eating Disorders Association, the average American woman is 5'4" tall and weighs 140 pounds. The average American model is 5'11" tall and weighs 117 pounds. All too often, society associates being "thin," with "hard-working, beautiful, strong, and self-disciplined." On the other hand, being "fat" is associated with being "lazy, ugly, weak and lacking will-power." Because of these harsh critiques, rarely are people completely satisfied with their image. As a result, they often feel great anxiety and pressure to achieve and/or maintain an imaginary appearance.

Eating disorders are more than just a problem with food. Food is used to feel in control of other feelings that may seem overwhelming. For example, starving is a way for people with anorexia to feel more in control of their lives and to ease tension, anger, and anxiety. Purging and other behaviors to prevent weight gain are ways for people with bulimia to feel more in control of their lives and to ease stress and anxiety.

About This Chapter: Information under the heading "What Are Eating Disorders?" is from "Eating Disorders," June 2007. The chapter continues with "Anorexia Nervosa," September 2006, "Bulimia Nervosa," January 2007, and "Binge Eating Disorder," January 2005, National Women's Health Information Center, U.S. Department of Health and Human Services, Office on Women's Health.

While there is no single known cause of eating disorders, several things may contribute to the development of these disorders. They are as follows:

- **Culture:** The U.S. has a social and cultural ideal of extreme thinness. People partially define themselves by how physically attractive they are.

- **Personal Characteristics:** Feelings of helplessness, worthlessness, and poor self-image often accompany eating disorders.

- **Other Emotional Disorders:** Other mental health problems, like depression or anxiety, occur along with eating disorders.

- **Stressful Events Or Life Changes:** Things like starting a new school or job or being teased to traumatic events like rape can lead to the onset of eating disorders.

- **Biology:** Studies are being done to look at genes, hormones, and chemicals in the brain that may have an effect on the development of, and recovery from eating disorders.

- **Families:** The attitude of parents about appearance and diet affects their kids' attitudes. Also, if your parent or sibling has bulimia, you are more likely to have it.

♣ **It's A Fact!!**
Eating disorders are serious medical problems. Anorexia nervosa, bulimia nervosa, and binge eating disorder are all types of eating disorders. Eating disorders frequently develop during adolescence or early adulthood, but can occur during childhood or later in adulthood. Females are more likely than males to develop an eating disorder.

Source: Excerpted from "Eating Disorders," National Women's Health Information Center.

Anorexia Nervosa

What is anorexia nervosa?

A person with anorexia (a-neh-RECK-see-ah) nervosa, often called anorexia, has an intense fear of gaining weight. Someone with anorexia thinks

Eating Disorders

about food a lot and limits the food she or he eats, even though she or he is too thin. Most people with anorexia are female. An anorexic:

- has a low body weight for her or his height;
- resists keeping a normal body weight;
- has an intense fear of gaining weight;
- thinks she or he is fat even when very thin; and
- misses three (menstrual) periods in a row for girls/women who have started having their periods.

> ♣ **It's A Fact!!**
> Anorexia is more than just a problem with food. It is a way of using food or starving oneself to feel more in control of life and to ease tension, anger, and anxiety.
>
> Source: Excerpted from "Anorexia Nervosa," National Women's Health Information Center.

Who becomes anorexic?

While anorexia mostly affects girls and women (90–95 percent), it can also affect boys and men. It was once thought that women of color were shielded from eating disorders by their cultures, which tend to be more accepting of different body sizes. Sadly, research shows that as African American, Latina, Asian/Pacific Islander, and American Indian and Alaska Native women are more exposed to images of thin women, they also become more likely to develop eating disorders.

What are signs of anorexia?

Someone with anorexia may look very thin. She or he may use extreme measures to lose weight by doing the following:

- making her or himself throw up
- taking pills to urinate or have a bowel movement
- taking diet pills
- not eating or eating very little
- exercising a lot, even in bad weather or when hurt or tired
- weighing food and counting calories

- moving food around the plate instead of eating it

Someone with anorexia may also have a distorted body image, shown by thinking she or he is fat, wearing baggy clothes, weighing her or himself many times a day, and fearing weight gain.

Anorexia can also cause someone to not act like her or himself. She or he may talk about weight and food all the time, not eat in front of others, be moody or sad, or not want to go out with friends.

What happens to your body with anorexia?

With anorexia, your body does not get the energy from foods that it needs, so it slows down. Anorexia affects your health in the following ways:

- **Brain And Nerves:** Cannot think right, fear of gaining weight, sad, moody, irritable, bad memory, fainting, changes in brain chemistry
- **Hair:** Hair thins and gets brittle
- **Heart:** Low blood pressure, slow heart rate, fluttering of the heart (palpitations), heart failure
- **Blood:** Anemia and other blood problems
- **Muscles, Joints, And Bones:** Weak muscles, swollen joints, bone loss, fractures, and osteoporosis
- **Kidneys:** Kidney stones, kidney failure
- **Body Fluids:** Low potassium, magnesium, and sodium
- **Intestines:** Constipation, bloating
- **Hormones:** Periods stop, problems growing, and trouble getting pregnant. If pregnant, higher risk for miscarriage, having a C-section, baby with low birth weight, and post partum depression.
- **Skin:** Bruise easily, dry skin, growth of fine hair all over body, get cold easily, yellow skin, nails get brittle

Can someone with anorexia get better?

Yes. Someone with anorexia can get better. A health care team of doctors, nutritionists, and therapists will help the patient get better. They will help

Eating Disorders

her or him learn healthy eating patterns, cope with thoughts and feelings, and gain weight. With outpatient care, the patient receives treatment through visits with members of their health care team. Some patients may need "partial hospitalization." This means that the person goes to the hospital during the day for treatment but lives at home. Sometimes, the patient goes to a hospital and stays there for treatment. After leaving the hospital, the patient continues to get help from her or his health care team.

Individual counseling can also help someone with anorexia. If the patient is young, counseling may involve the whole family too. Support groups may also be a part of treatment. In support groups, patients and families meet and share what they have been through.

Often, eating disorders happen along with mental health problems such as depression and anxiety. These problems are treated along with the anorexia. Treatment may include medicines that fix hormone imbalances that play a role in these disorders.

Bulimia Nervosa

What is bulimia?

Bulimia (buh-LEE-me-ah) nervosa, often called bulimia, is a type of eating disorder. A person with bulimia eats a lot of food in a short amount of time (binges) and then tries to prevent weight gain by getting rid of the food, called purging. Purging might be done by doing the following:

- making yourself throw up
- taking laxatives—pills or liquids that speed up the movement of food through your body and lead to a bowel movement

A person with bulimia may also exercise a lot, eat very little or not at all, or take pills to pass urine to prevent weight gain.

Who becomes bulimic?

Many people think that eating disorders affect only young, upper class white females. It is true that most bulimics are women (90 percent of people with bulimia are women), but bulimia affects people from all walks of life, including males, women of color, and even older women. It was once thought that women of color were shielded from eating disorders by their cultures, which tend to be more accepting of different body sizes. Sadly, research shows that as African American, Latina, Asian/Pacific Islander, and American Indian and Alaska Native women are more exposed to images of thin women, they also become more likely to develop eating disorders.

What are signs of bulimia?

A person with bulimia may be thin, overweight, or have a normal weight. This makes it hard to know if someone has bulimia, but there are warning signs to look out for. Someone with bulimia may use extreme measures to lose weight by doing the following:

- using diet pills, or taking pills to urinate or have a bowel movement
- going to the bathroom all the time after eating to throw up
- exercising a lot, even in bad weather or when hurt or tired

Someone with bulimia may show signs of throwing up, such as the following:

- swollen cheeks or jaw area
- calluses or scrapes on knuckles (if using fingers to induce vomiting)
- teeth that look clear
- broken blood vessels in the eyes

Someone with bulimia may also have a distorted body image, shown by thinking she or he is fat, hating her or his body, and fearing weight gain.

Bulimia can also cause someone to not act like her or himself. She or he may be moody or sad, or may not want to go out with friends.

What happens to someone who has bulimia?

Bulimia can be very harmful to the body. Bulimia affects your health in the following ways:

- **Brain:** Depression, fear of gaining weight, anxiety, dizziness, shame, low self-esteem

Eating Disorders

- **Cheeks:** Swelling, soreness
- **Mouth:** Cavities, tooth enamel erosion, gum disease, teeth sensitive to hot and cold foods
- **Throat And Esophagus:** Sore, irritated, can tear and rupture, blood in vomit
- **Blood:** Anemia
- **Heart:** Irregular heartbeat, heart muscle weakened, heart failure, low pulse, and blood pressure
- **Body Fluids:** Dehydration, low potassium, magnesium, and sodium
- **Muscles:** Fatigue
- **Stomach:** Ulcers, pain, can rupture, delayed emptying
- **Intestines:** Constipation, irregular bowel movements (BM), bloating, diarrhea, abdominal cramping
- **Hormones:** Irregular or absent period
- **Skin:** Abrasion of knuckles, dry skin

Can someone with bulimia get better?

Yes. Someone with bulimia can get better. A health care team of doctors, nutritionists, and therapists will help the patient recover. The team will help the patient learn healthy eating patterns and cope with her or his thoughts and feelings.

Different types of therapy have worked to help people with bulimia. These may include individual, group, or family therapy. Some medicines, including ones used to treat depression, have been shown to be effective when used with therapy.

Binge Eating Disorder

What is binge eating disorder?

People with binge eating disorder often eat an unusually large amount of food and feel out of control during the binges. People with binge eating disorder also may do the following:

- eat more quickly than usual during binge episodes
- eat until they are uncomfortably full
- eat when they are not hungry
- eat alone because of embarrassment
- feel disgusted, depressed, or guilty after overeating

What causes binge eating disorder?

No one knows for sure what causes binge eating disorder. Researchers are looking at the following factors that may affect binge eating:

- **Depression:** As many as half of all people with binge eating disorder are depressed or have been depressed in the past.

- **Dieting:** Some people binge after skipping meals, not eating enough food each day, or avoiding certain kinds of food.

- **Coping Skills:** Studies suggest that people with binge eating may have trouble handling some of their emotions. Many people who are binge eaters say that being angry, sad, bored, worried, or stressed can cause them to binge eat.

- **Biology:** Researchers are looking into how brain chemicals and metabolism (the way the body uses calories) affect binge eating disorder. Research also suggests that genes may be involved in binge eating, since the disorder often occurs in several members of the same family.

Certain behaviors and emotional problems are more common in people with binge eating disorder. These include abusing alcohol, acting quickly without thinking (impulsive behavior), and not feeling in charge of themselves.

What are the health consequences of binge eating disorder?

People with binge eating disorder are usually very upset by their binge eating and may become depressed. Research has shown that people with binge eating disorder report more health problems, stress, trouble sleeping, and suicidal thoughts than people without an eating disorder. People with

Eating Disorders

binge eating disorder often feel badly about themselves and may miss work, school, or social activities to binge eat.

People with binge eating disorder may gain weight. Weight gain can lead to obesity, and obesity raises the risk for these health problems:

- type 2 diabetes
- high blood pressure
- high cholesterol
- gallbladder disease
- heart disease
- certain types of cancer

What is the treatment for binge eating disorder?

People with binge eating disorder should get help from a health care provider, such as a psychiatrist, psychologist, or clinical social worker. There are several different ways to treat binge eating disorder. They are as follows:

- **Cognitive-Behavioral Therapy** teaches people how to keep track of their eating and change their unhealthy eating habits. It teaches them

---

✎ What's It Mean?

Anorexia Nervosa: An eating disorder caused by a person having a distorted body image and not consuming the appropriate calorie intake resulting in severe weight loss.

Binge Eating Disorder: An eating disorder caused by a person being unable to control the need to overeat.

Bulimia Nervosa: An eating disorder caused by a person consuming an extreme amount of food all at once followed by self-induced vomiting or other purging.

Source: "Womenshealth.gov Glossary," National Women's Health Information Center, June 2007.

how to cope with stressful situations. It also helps them feel better about their body shape and weight.

- **Interpersonal Psychotherapy** helps people look at their relationships with friends and family and make changes in problem areas.
- **Drug Therapy**, such as antidepressants, may be helpful for some people.

Other treatments include dialectical behavior therapy, which helps people regulate their emotions; drug therapy with the anti-seizure medication topiramate; exercise in combination with cognitive-behavioral therapy; and support groups.

Many people with binge eating disorder also have a problem with obesity. There are treatments for obesity, like weight loss surgery (gastrointestinal surgery), but these treatments will not treat the underlying problem of binge eating disorder.

Chapter 46
Self-Harm

What is self-harm?

"Self-harm" refers to the deliberate, direct destruction of body tissue that results in tissue damage. When someone engages in self-harm, they may have a variety of intentions; these are discussed below. However, the person's intention is not to kill themselves. You may have heard self-harm referred to as "parasuicide," "self-mutilation," "self-injury," "self-abuse," "cutting," "self-inflicted violence," and so on.

How common is self-harm?

Self-harm is not well understood and has not yet been extensively studied. The rates of self-harm revealed through research vary tremendously depending on how researchers pose their questions about this behavior. One widely cited estimate of the incidence of impulsive self-injury is that it occurs in at least 1 person per 1,000 annually. A recent study of psychiatric outpatients found that 33% reported engaging in self-harm in the previous three months. A recent study of college undergraduates asked study participants about specific self-harm behaviors and found alarmingly high rates. Although the high rates may have been due in part to the broad spectrum of

---

About This Chapter: National Center for Posttraumatic Stress Disorder, United States Department of Veterans Affairs, May 2007.

self-harm behaviors that were assessed (for example, severe scratching and interfering with the healing of wounds were included), the numbers are certainly cause for concern:

- Eighteen percent reported having harmed themselves more than ten times in the past.
- Ten percent reported having harmed themselves more than 100 times in the past.
- Thirty-eight percent endorsed a history of deliberate self-harm.
- The most frequently reported self-harm behaviors were needle sticking, skin cutting, and scratching, endorsed by 16%, 15%, and 14% of the participants, respectively.

It is important to note that research on self-harm is still in the early stages, and these rates may change as researchers begin to utilize more consistent definitions of self-harm and more studies are completed.

> ♣ **It's A Fact!!**
> Teens who hurt themselves on purpose—called "self-injury"—often keep painful or confusing feelings bottled up inside. Teens that self-injure say that it helps them to feel better, but self-injury is very dangerous. It can lead to infections, scars, hospital stays, and even death. If you cut yourself, burn yourself, pull out your hair, or hurt your body in other ways, get help right away. Talk to a parent or guardian, counselor, or other trusted adult. You can learn, with help, healthy ways to cope with the things that bother you.
>
> Source: Excerpted from *Teen Survival Guide: Health Tips for On-the-go Girls*, Girls Health.gov, U.S. Department of Health and Human Services, Office on Women's Health, June 2007.

Who engages in self-harm?

Only a handful of empirical studies have examined self-harm in a systematic, sound manner. Self-harm appears to be more common in females than in males, and it tends to begin in adolescence or early adulthood. While some people may engage in self-harm a few times and then stop, others engage in it frequently and have great difficulty stopping the behavior. Several studies have

Self-Harm

found that individuals who engage in self-harm report unusually high rates of histories of the following:

- Childhood sexual abuse
- Childhood physical abuse
- Emotional neglect
- Insecure attachment
- Prolonged separation from caregivers

At least two studies have attempted to determine whether particular characteristics of childhood sexual abuse place individuals at greater risk for engaging in self-harm as adults. Both studies reported that more severe, more frequent, or a longer duration of sexual abuse was associated with an increased risk of engaging in self-harm in one's adult years.

Also, individuals who self-harm appear to have higher rates of the following psychological problems:

- High levels of dissociation
- Borderline personality disorder
- Substance abuse disorders
- Posttraumatic stress disorder
- Intermittent explosive disorder
- Antisocial personality
- Eating disorders

Why do people engage in self-harm?

While there are many theories about why individuals harm themselves, the answer to this question varies from individual to individual.

The following are some reasons why people engage in self-harm:

- To distract themselves from emotional pain by causing physical pain
- To punish themselves

- To relieve tension
- To feel real by feeling pain or seeing evidence of injury
- To feel numb, zoned out, calm, or at peace
- To experience euphoric feelings (associated with release of endorphins)
- To communicate their pain, anger, or other emotions to others
- To nurture themselves (through the process of healing the wounds)

How is self-harm treated?

Self-harm is a problem that many people are embarrassed or ashamed to discuss. Often, individuals try to hide their self-harm behaviors and are very reluctant to seek needed psychological or even medical treatment.

Psychological Treatments

Because self-harm is often associated with other psychological problems, it tends to be treated under the umbrella of a co-occurring disorder like a substance abuse problem or an eating disorder. Sometimes the underlying feelings that cause the self-harm are the same as those that cause the co-occurring disorder. For example, a person's underlying feelings of shame may cause them to abuse drugs and cut themselves. Often, the self-harm can be addressed in the context of therapy for an associated problem. For example, if people can learn healthy coping skills to help them deal with their urges to abuse substances, they may be able to apply these same skills to their urges to harm themselves.

There are also some treatments that specifically focus on stopping the self-harm. A good example of this is dialectical behavior therapy (DBT), a treatment that involves individual therapy and group skills training. DBT is a therapy approach that was originally developed for individuals with borderline personality disorder who engage in self-harm or "parasuicidal behaviors." Now the treatment is also being used for self-harming individuals with a wide variety of other psychological problems, including eating disorders and substance dependence. The theory behind DBT is that individuals tend to engage in self-harm in an attempt to regulate or control their strong emotions. DBT teaches clients alternative ways of managing their emotions and

Self-Harm

tolerating distress. Research has shown that DBT is helpful in reducing self-harm.

Pharmacological Treatments

It is possible that psychopharmacological treatments would be helpful in reducing self-harm behaviors, but this has not yet been rigorously studied. As yet, there is no consensus regarding whether or not psychiatric medications should be used in relation to self-harm behaviors. This is a complicated issue to study because self-harm can occur in many different populations and co-occur with many different kinds of psychological problems. If you are wondering about the use of medications for the emotions related to your self-harm behaviors, it is recommended that you discuss this with your doctor or psychiatrist.

> ✔ **Quick Tip**
> **How To Find A Qualified Psychologist Or Psychiatrist**
>
> If you are trying to find a psychologist or psychiatrist, you should ask them whether they are familiar with self-harm. Consider which issues are important to you and make sure you can talk to the potential therapist about them. Remember that you are the consumer. You have the right to interview therapists until you find someone with whom you feel comfortable. You may want to ask trusted friends or medical professionals for referrals to psychologists or psychiatrists. Consider asking your potential provider questions, such as the following:
>
> - How do you treat self-harm?
> - What do you think causes self-harm?
> - Do you have experience in treating self-harm?
>
> Source: United States Department of Veterans Affairs

Self-Help Resources

There are a variety of self-help books on the market for people who engage in self-harm. Most of these provide practical advice, support, and coping skills that may be helpful to individuals who engage in self-harm. These approaches have not been studied in research trials, so it is not known how effective they are for individuals who self-harm.

My friend or relative self-harms. What should I do to be supportive?

If you have a friend or relative who engages in self-harm, it can be very distressing and confusing for you. You may feel guilty, angry, scared, powerless, or any number of things. Some general guidelines are as follows:

- Take the self-harm seriously by expressing concern and encouraging the individual to seek professional help.

- Don't get into a power struggle with the individual. Ultimately, they need to make the choice to stop the behavior. You cannot force them to stop.

- Don't blame yourself. The individual who is self-harming initiated this behavior and needs to take responsibility for stopping it.

- If the individual who is self-harming is a child or adolescent, make sure the parent or a trusted adult has been informed and is seeking professional help for them.

- If the individual who is engaging in self-harm does not want professional help because he or she does not think the behavior is a problem, inform them that a professional is the best person to make this determination. Suggest that a professional is a neutral third party who will not be emotionally invested in the situation and so will be able to make the soundest recommendations.

Part Four
Managing Stress

Chapter 47

Fitting In And Finding Yourself

If you are a teenager, or about to become one, you have a lot to look forward to. Maybe more than at any other time of life, your world is wide open, and the possibilities are endless. Of course, just as in other times of life, you will have both bad and good experiences. The ideas in this chapter can help you learn to deal with the tough times and enjoy the good times by finding the people and places that are right for you. You might find these ideas useful in your everyday life, or read them to see if they might be helpful to a friend.

Freedom And Responsibility

The teenage years are full of change. You might get a job to earn money of your own. You may get a driver's license and graduate from high school. You also might begin doing the following:

- Questioning more of what you hear
- Learning the skills you will need to pursue a job or a career
- Spending more time with your friends and others outside your family

About This Chapter: Information in this chapter is from "Express Yourself: A Teenager's Guide to Fitting in, Getting Involved, Finding Yourself," National Clearinghouse on Families and Youth, 2000; http://www.ncfy.com/publications/expseng.htm, accessed October 2007. Despite the older date of this document, the information presented is still appropriate for readers seeking to understand this issue.

- Hearing from teachers, parents, and other adults about taking more responsibility

Those changes do not mean that your teenage years have to be harder than others. In fact, this can be the time when you get what you need to have fun and be happy now and in the future. Obviously, what you go through will depend on the following:

- Whether or not the adults responsible for you are loving and supportive
- Whether or not the neighborhood you live in offers you many opportunities
- Whether or not you feel close to people your age and are connected with your school and community

That means everyone's experience is different; but no matter what your experience, you still can figure out how to be happy.

One thing that most people find satisfying is figuring out what they do well.

Deciding what you do well often is a matter of knowing what you like to do. Most people like to do what they are good at.

So, think about what you enjoy. Then try asking people how you might get involved in those activities. You might talk to your parents, other relatives, friends, and neighbors. Check with people at your school like a teacher, a guidance counselor, or the school librarian. If school is not the most comfortable place for you, get help at the public library. Look on the internet or check the newspaper.

Get Connected

Better yet, get involved in a youth organization.

Youth agencies exist across the country. Their mission is to support young people and link them with activities they are interested in. Wherever you are, one of these organizations usually is close by.

Youth organizations have all kinds of programs. Some offer activities. Others can give you support when you have a problem or are in trouble, or they can be helpful when you just need someone to talk to.

Fitting In And Finding Yourself

Youth agencies like the Boys and Girls Clubs, 4-H Clubs, and the YMCA can help you find the following:

- Recreational activities
- Volunteer opportunities
- Other people who share your interests

To learn more about youth agencies in your area, call them.

When you call, tell the person you talk to your age and your area of interest. Ask questions to find out more about their programs, for example:

- What types of programs and activities does your organization offer for someone my age?
- Do these programs cost anything? What if I do not have money to pay a fee?
- Do I need my parents' permission to become involved? What if I would like to join but cannot get a signed permission slip from my parents?

✔ Quick Tip

Here are two ways to locate a youth organization near you. (If there is not a youth organization where you live, find one in a nearby area.)

1. Check the Yellow Pages. Look under "Youth Organizations," "Youth Centers," or "Teenage Activities."

2. Contact the national offices of youth agencies to find their local organization. Here are three you can start with:

    - **Boys and Girls Clubs of America:** Phone: (404) 487-5700; E-mail: info@bgca.org; Website: www.bgca.org.
    - **National 4-H Council:** Phone: (301) 961-2800; E-mail: info@fourhcouncil.edu; Website: www.fourhcouncil.edu (Note: If you are 12 years old or younger, 4-H requires you to involve your parents when you contact them.)
    - **YMCA of the USA:** Phone: (800) 872-9622; E-mail: fulfillment@ymca.net; Website: www.ymca.net

- What do I do next to get involved?

The best youth organization for you has people you feel comfortable with. One of the bonuses of being involved in a youth club or program is meeting all kinds of people. Some agencies even have "mentoring programs." These link you with someone your age or an adult. You can discuss ideas with that person and learn about new ways to deal with everyday problems, or you can try out new activities together.

In fact, getting to know people is often what makes life fun and interesting, and the best people to have around are those who do care about you. They can be helpful when you feel pressure to do things that you do not want to do. They can offer advice on how to be yourself and still fit in. These are signs that a person does care about you and questions to help you identify those signs. Think about how real friends treat you.

- They are interested in your well-being, not in something that you might give them or do for them.
    - Do they value your health and safety (including never asking you to do something that puts you in danger or is illegal)?
    - Do they suggest that you do things that help you, not them?
    - Do other people you respect and trust also trust this person?
- They listen. They care about what you have to say.
    - Are they paying attention to you when you talk to them?
    - Do they ask questions when they do not understand something you tell them?
    - Do they make sure they understand your situation before they offer advice?
- They are interested in your success and are happy for you when things go well.
    - Do they praise you when something good happens or you have done something well?
    - Do they ask about your goals and interests?

Fitting In And Finding Yourself

- They say they are sorry when they make a mistake.
    - Do they admit when they are wrong (just as you or anyone else should be able to do)?
- They do not expect you to be perfect.
    - Would you feel comfortable telling them when you have made a mistake and need help knowing what to do next?
    - Do they help you recognize and work through mistakes? (Or do they use words that make you feel ashamed or worthless?)
    - Do you have a feeling that no matter what happens, they will look out for your well-being (since everyone makes mistakes)?
- When they give you guidance, they do so in a way that shows they care.
    - Does this person make you feel encouraged and motivated?
    - When they are talking or asking about a mistake you made, do you still feel that they are trying to help you?
    - Do they make you feel comfortable (including never physically or emotionally hurting you)?
- They let you think things through on your own when you want to and respect your privacy.
    - Do they accept that sometimes you might prefer to think through a problem or situation on your own? (Most people do sometimes.)
    - Do they keep things you say private when you ask them to?

Keep in mind, though, that a person you confide in may not have a choice about whether to keep something you tell them private. They may be required under the law to report a problem to authorities if what you tell them involves a legal issue.

So if you go to someone for assistance, you might want to ask them about whether they can keep a problem to themselves. They may say that they will report legal issues to someone else. If so, ask them how they have handled situations like this in the past. Ask what happened to the teenagers involved and talk with them about your choices before you tell them your story. So ask questions and trust your feelings.

Sometimes you may still feel unsure about whether you trust someone. If so, follow your instinct and talk to someone else. Explain why you feel uncertain. That is one of the best things about having a circle of people to turn to. They can help you think through the doubts all of us have sometimes.

Of course, nobody's perfect. Most people do not always do all the right things. Just remember that people who say they care about you prove that by their actions over a period of time.

People who you trust can help you make the best of all that life has to offer.

There is not any magical answer that will always make life easy. For all of us, there are both hard times and good times, but having a network of friends, supportive adults, and people to talk to at a youth service organization can help. They will be there for both the unexpected difficulties and life's good surprises.

Here are some ideas to think about no matter how things are going for you:

- Believe in yourself.
- You cannot compare yourself to others.
- Do not let a negative response stop your positive effort.

Enjoy the good times, learn from the difficult ones, and get help when you need it. If you do, you may find that life has great things to offer.

☞ Remember!!

- Expect a lot of yourself.
- Everyone has strengths and limitations.
- Everybody needs help sometimes.
- Express yourself. Your ideas and feelings matter.

Chapter 48

The Importance Of Emotional And Social Support

The wisdom of the ages, anecdotal reports, numerous clinical studies, a wealth of epidemiologic data on death rates in married, single, and divorced individuals, as well as sophisticated psychophysiologic and laboratory testing, all confirm that strong social and emotional support is a powerful stress buster that improves health and prolongs life. But what exactly does strong social support mean? How can it be measured? How can it be developed or improved?

It's possible to be alone but not lonely. Conversely, you can be in the company of others and still feel isolated. Some people may seem to have a large circle of "friends," but the majority are merely acquaintances who do not provide social support. Emotional support can also be obtained from pets, a firm belief in a specific religion, or being involved in supporting a cause, sports team, or celebrity with strangers who have a similar allegiance. Caring for someone can provide mutual emotional support, and even tending to fish or plants may provide benefits.

With respect to just exactly what social support means, perhaps one of the best definitions was given by the psychiatrist Sidney Cobb. He proposed that

---

About This Chapter: Information in this chapter is from "Emotional Support and Social Support," © 2006 The American Institute of Stress (www.stress.org). Reprinted with permission.

social support was a subjective sensation in which the individual feels, "That he is cared for and loved. That he is esteemed and valued. That he belongs to a network of communication and mutual obligation." There are a variety of ways to measure social support. The Social Network Questionnaire includes items about marriage, children, a significant other or confidant, other relatives, friends, and participation in social or community activities that may involve strangers. The Inventory of Socially Supportive Behaviors inquires about the type and amount of support these sources provide with respect to emotional, informational, and financial benefits. It also asks the respondent to rate each item's frequency of occurrence during the preceding month on a scale of 1 to 5. While these results indicate how much and what kind of social support is available, they do not tell us very much about its real significance. This crucial information can be obtained from the Perceived Social Support Quiz, which evaluates the recipient's subjective assessment of the degree to which the emotional support received has enhanced his or her sense of satisfaction and well being. In some studies involving the elderly, the role of religion is factored in based on information about attendance at religious functions, the number of close contacts who were readily available from religious sources, and determining the strength and comfort that were derived from religious activities. This can be important since senior citizens have progressively less social support as they age due to the increased loss of friends and often tend to rely more on religious sources to make up for this.

There are so many reports confirming the stress-reducing and health benefits of social support as assessed by these measures that only a few can be mentioned here.

> ♣ **It's A Fact!!**
> Social support buffers the adverse effects of stress on cardiovascular and immune responses, which can provide numerous health benefits.

Laboratory studies show that when subjects are subjected to stress, emotional support reduces the usual sharp rise in blood pressure and increased secretion of damaging stress-related hormones. One report demonstrated that middle aged men who had recently endured high levels of emotional stress but had little social support were three times more likely to die over the next seven years.

The Importance Of Emotional And Social Support 303

Lack of social support has been found to increase death rates following a heart attack and to delay recovery following cardiac surgery. Conversely, a happy marriage or good long-term relationship at age 50 was a leading indicator of being healthy at age 80, whereas having a low cholesterol level had very little significance. Emotional support also reduces the risk of coronary events in individuals with Type A behavior.

Strong emotional support reduces the immune system abnormalities that contribute to numerous disorders due to the stress of caregivers for spouses with Alzheimer disease. It also boosts immune system function in acquired immune deficiency syndrome (AIDS) and human immunodeficiency virus (HIV)-positive patients. Breast cancer and malignant melanoma patients who receive group emotional support from strangers also live longer and have a better quality of life. Similar emotional support is responsible for the success of Alcoholics Anonymous, Gamblers Anonymous, Shoppers Anonymous, and other groups that deal with addictions to drugs, smoking, or reducing compulsive behaviors.

This comes from sharing things with strangers, getting things of your chest, and learning how others have been able to deal with or conquer the same problem you have. Such groups often provide additional emotional support by utilizing a "buddy system"—someone you can call at any time if you feel you are slipping into your old habits and who can provide support when you need it the most.

Chapter 49

Tips For Dealing With Stress

Put your body in motion. Moving from the chair to the couch while watching television is not being physically active. Physical activity is one of the most important ways to keep stress away by clearing your head and lifting your spirits. Physical activity also increases endorphin levels—the natural "feel-good" chemicals in the body that leave you with a naturally happy feeling.

Whether you like full-fledged games of football, tennis, or roller hockey, or you prefer walks with family and friends, it is important to get up, get out, and get moving.

Fuel up. If your body was a car, you would not go for a long drive without filling up the gas tank first. Likewise, begin each day by eating breakfast to give you the energy you need to tackle the day. Eating regular meals (this means no skipping dinner) and taking time to enjoy them (nope, eating in the car on the way to practice does not count) will make you feel better too.

Make sure to fuel up with fruits, vegetables, proteins (peanut butter, a chicken sandwich, or a tuna salad), and grains (wheat bread, pasta, or some crackers). These will give you the power you need to make it through those hectic days.

Do not be fooled by the jolt of energy you get from sodas and sugary snacks. This only lasts a short time, and once it wears off, you may feel sluggish and

About This Chapter: Information in this chapter is from "11 Tips for Dealing with Stress," GirlsHealth.gov, sponsored by the National Women's Health Information Center, U.S. Department of Health and Human Services, April 2007.

more tired than usual. For that extra boost of energy to sail through history notes, math class, and after school activities, grab a banana, some string cheese, or a granola bar for some power-packed energy.

Laugh out loud. Some say that laughter is the best medicine—well, in many cases, it is. Did you know that it takes 15 facial muscles to laugh? Lots of laughing can make you feel good, and that good feeling can stay with you even after the laughter stops. So, head off stress with regular doses of laughter by watching a funny movie, reading a joke book (you may even learn some new jokes), or even make up your own riddles. Laughter can make you feel like a new person.

Everyone has those days when they do something really silly or stupid. Instead of getting upset with yourself, laugh out loud. No one is perfect. Life should be about having fun. So, lighten up.

Have fun with friends. Being with people you like is always a good way to ditch your stress. Get a group together to go to the movies, shoot some hoops, listen to music, play a board game, or just hang out and talk. Friends can help you work through your problems and let you see the brighter side of things.

Spill to someone you trust. Instead of keeping your feelings bottled up inside, talk to someone you trust or respect about what is bothering you. It

---

Stress And Time Management Tips ✔ **Quick Tip**

- **Choose your own goals.** Do not live out choices that others have made for you.

- **Become part of a support system.** Look out for yourself by letting friends help you when you are under too much stress and by helping them when they are overloaded.

- **Make decisions.** In general, any decision, even consciously deciding to do nothing, is better than no decision.

- **Keep your expectations realistic.** Expect some problems reaching your goals and realize that you can solve most of them with practice.

- **Accept what you cannot change.** If a situation is beyond your control, you are better off accepting it than spinning your wheels.

Tips For Dealing With Stress

could be a friend, a parent, a friend's parent, someone in your family or from your religious community, or a teacher. Talking out your problems and seeing them from a different view might help you figure out ways to deal with them. Just remember, you do not have to go at it alone.

Take time to chill. Pick a comfy spot to sit and read, daydream, or even take a snooze. Listen to your favorite music. Work on a relaxing project like putting together a puzzle or making jewelry.

Stress can sometimes make you feel like a tight rubber band stretched to the limit. If this happens, take a few deep breaths to help yourself unwind. If you are in the middle of an impossible homework problem, take a break. Finding time to relax after (and sometimes during) a hectic day or week can make all the difference.

Catch some sleep. Fatigue is a best friend to stress. When you do not get enough sleep, it is hard to deal. You may feel tired, cranky, or you may have trouble thinking clearly. When you are overtired, a problem may seem much bigger than it actually is. You may have a hard time doing a school assignment that usually seems easy, you do not do your best in sports or any physical activity, or you may have an argument with your friends over something really stupid.

- **Anticipate potentially stressful situations and prepare for them.** Decide whether the situation is one you should deal with, postpone, or avoid.
- **Live in the present.** Learn from the past and move on.
- **Communicate effectively.** If someone is causing you stress, make the time to discuss with him/her the problem or situation that is causing you stress.
- **Manage your time.** Prioritizing and planning can help keep the demands of life from becoming overwhelming.
- **Take care of your health.** Exercise regularly, eat a balanced diet, get enough sleep, and avoid alcohol and other mood-altering drugs.
- **Take the time for yourself.** Make yourself a priority. Find time to relax, even if only for a few minutes, each day.

Source: Excerpted from "Stress and Time Management Tips," Student Health Services, Texas A & M University, © 2005. Reprinted with permission.

Sleep is a big deal. Getting the right amount of sleep is especially important for kids your age. Most teens need between eight and one half and just over nine hours of sleep each night. Because your body (and mind) is changing and developing, it requires more sleep to re-charge for the next day. So do not resist, get some sleep.

Keep a journal. If you are having one of those crazy days when nothing goes right, it is a good idea to write things down in a journal to get it off your chest—like how you feel, what is going on in your life, and things you would like to accomplish. You could even write down what you do when you are faced with a stressful situation, and then look back and think about how you handled it later. So, find a quiet spot, grab a notebook and pen, and start writing.

Get it together. Too much to do but not enough time? Forgot your homework? Feeling overwhelmed or forgetful? Being unprepared for school, practice, or other activities can make for a very stressful day.

Getting everything done can be a challenge, but all you have to do is plan a little and get organized.

Lend a hand. Get involved in an activity that helps others. It is almost impossible to feel stressed out when you are helping someone else. It is also a great way to find out about yourself and the special talents you never knew you had. Signing up for a service project is a good idea, but helping others is as easy as saying hello, holding a door, or volunteering to keep a neighbor's pet. If you want to get involved in a more organized volunteer program, try working at a local recreation center, or helping with an after school program. The feeling you will get from helping others is greater than you can imagine.

Learn ways to better deal with anger. It is totally normal to be angry sometimes. Everyone gets mad at some point, and as a teen, the changing hormones in your body can cause you to feel mad for what seems like no good reason sometimes. The important thing is to deal with your anger in a healthy way. It will help to cool down first and then focus on positive solutions to problems. This will help you to communicate better with the people in your life, and you can even earn more respect along the way.

Chapter 50

Build Resilience

What Is Resilience?

In some video games you have to get your character through all sorts of obstacles to the next level, and then do the same sort of things again. On the way you can "power up" by hitting or jumping on something, and that would give you the strength to keep going.

Well, life is a bit like that. You go through life trying to "get to the next level", and there are all sorts of obstacles to stop you, and times when you can "power up" to help you keep going.

Coping with everything, keeping on going, and collecting something to help you is what resilience is all about.

What Helps You To Become Resilient?

Where is it that you get your "power"?

- A caring and supportive family
- Caring friends who you can trust

About This Chapter: Information in this chapter is from "Resilience," reprinted with permission, © 2005 Children, Youth and Women's Health Service, Government of South Australia.

- Being encouraged to try
- Setting yourself realistic goals and reaching them
- Being confident in your own abilities
- Being able to communicate with others
- Successfully using your problem-solving skills
- Managing strong feelings like anger

How To Build Up Your Own Resilience

If you have all these "power builders," that's great. But what if you don't? You can still build up your own resilience and create the kind of caring support that everyone needs by:

- **Getting connected.** Make friends, get to know people, join in with teams, clubs, and organizations. Talk to and help people and allow them to help you.

- **Don't give up.** Everyone has to deal with a crisis from time to time. Just go into "automatic mode" and work your way through it. Things will get better. It isn't easy, but you do get through eventually.

- **Change is here to stay—accept it.** Of course, it's unsettling when you feel comfortable with something, and then it all changes. Try to see change as a chance to alter the future, not the end of the world, as you know it.

- **Get good at making realistic goals.**
    - Make long-term goals, and then work out the steps you have to take to achieve them.
    - Set these as your short-term goals, and work your way through all the short-term goals that will get you where you want to be.
    - Remember that being realistic doesn't mean accepting second best. As you reach each goal, you can aim higher.

- **Face up to problems.** Think about how you can solve them instead of wishing that they would go away.

Build Resilience

- **Learn from the bad times.** Often people find that they have developed better skills, made new friends, and got to know themselves better after they have gone through some crisis.
- **Trust yourself.** Develop your skills (for example, communication, problem solving, conflict resolving) and instincts, and then develop confidence in your ability to use them.
- **Don't turn every small setback into a "10 act drama,"** unless of course you are practicing to be a stand-up comedian.
- **Practice thinking positive thoughts.** Always be hopeful of your ability to get through, and that things will improve.
- **Look after yourself.** Exercise and eat well for a healthy body and learn to relax.
- **Get to know yourself.** Some people do this by meditation or writing down their thoughts. It's helpful to know what your opinions are, and also to reflect on how you handle life, what works for you and what doesn't.

How You Can Destroy Your Resilience

All you need to do is to look at all the ways in which you can build your resilience, and then do the opposite.

- **Don't** connect with others, allow them to help you, care about yourself, develop skills, be positive, face up to problems, or have confidence in yourself.
- **Do** put yourself down, give up, become a loner, neglect your body and mind, and be miserable and unhappy.

Then, like the video game, you will be knocked out by every obstacle, and without the "power builders," you will be out of the game.

Learn, Adapt, And Move On

We need resilience to cope with the challenges life throws at us. Looking at how you have managed and survived past events can help you become more resilient at managing future events.

Ask yourself:

- What were the bad times?
- How was I affected?
- Who helped me?
- Who did I help?
- Did I overcome obstacles and how did I do it?
- What did I learn that would help in the future?
- What did I learn about myself?

> **☞ Remember!!**
> Every time you face a crisis, deal with a disappointment, or lose someone or something you love, you use your resilience to help yourself recover and move on with your life.

Chapter 51

Boost Your Self-Esteem

Feeling Good About Yourself

Part of being a teen is having thoughts and feelings about different parts of your life, such as how you feel about the following:

- Your friends and other kids your age
- How you are doing in school and in other activities
- Your parents
- The way you look

While having these new feelings, many changes are also taking place in your body. It is normal to feel self-conscious or shy about the changes in your body and emotions, but there are also changes to celebrate.

Having a healthy or high self-esteem can help you to think positively, deal better with stress, and boost your drive to work hard. Having low self-esteem can cause you to feel uneasy and may get in the way of doing things you might enjoy. For some, low self-esteem can contribute to serious problems such as depression, drug and alcohol use, and eating disorders.

About This Chapter: Information in this chapter is from "Feeling Good about Yourself," "Find Out If You Have Low or Poor Self-Esteem," and "Try These Steps to Boost Your Self-Esteem," GirlsHealth.gov, sponsored by the National Women's Health Information Center, U.S. Department of Health and Human Services, April 2007.

> ### 🕮 What's It Mean?
>
> <u>Self-Confidence:</u> Self-confidence is having a positive and realistic opinion of yourself and being able to accurately measure your abilities.
>
> <u>Self-Esteem:</u> Self-esteem describes the value and respect you have for yourself. If you have a healthy self-esteem, you feel good about yourself as a person and are proud of what you can do. However, it is normal to feel down sometimes.
>
> Source: Excerpted from "Feeling Good about Yourself," GirlsHealth.gov.

Self-confidence is also an important part of feeling good about yourself. Self-confidence is that little voice inside of you that tells you that you are okay, that you are a good person, and that you know how to deal with things in good times and in bad.

You are not born confident; confidence is learned. As a baby, you started to learn self-confidence from knowing your family loved you. As you learned to walk, play and talk, you also learned self-confidence. Now as a teen, you are learning to be more self-confident in school, playing sports, and in other social settings; but sometimes it is not easy. Participating in class, talking to new teachers or students, or trying out for an after-school activity may make you feel stressed or anxious, but that is normal. The good news is, as you try these new things, you are gaining confidence in spite of your fears. In fact, that is what real self-confidence is—your belief that you can do things well even when you have doubts.

Find Out If You Have Low Or Poor Self-Esteem

If you have low or poor self-esteem, you might agree with the following statements:

- I cannot do anything right.
- I am ugly or dumb.
- I do not have any friends.
- I do not like to try new things.
- It really upsets me to make mistakes.

Boost Your Self-Esteem

- I do not think I am as nice or smart as the other people in my class.
- I have a hard time making friends.
- I have a hard time making friends because I end up getting angry and fighting with people.
- It makes me uncomfortable when people say nice things about me.
- Sometimes I feel better if I say mean things to other people.

If many or all of these items sound like you, it will be helpful for you to work on raising your self-esteem.

Try These Steps To Boost Your Self-Esteem

- Tell yourself that it is okay not to be the best at everything.
- Help out by doing chores around the house and volunteering in your community.
- Do things that you enjoy or learn about new things you would like to try.
- Understand that there will be times when you will feel disappointed in yourself and other people. No one is perfect.
- If you are angry, try talking it over with an adult you trust (parents/guardians, relatives, or a school counselor).
- Think positively about yourself and the things you can do. Think: "I will try."
- If you still find that you are not feeling good about yourself, talk to your parents/guardian, a school counselor, or your doctor because you may be at risk for depression. (You can also ask the school nurse for help through tough times. Some schools offer counseling.) Learn more about depression and other health issues that can affect your mind.

How you feel about yourself can help you through tough times when other kids are not so nice.

Thinking positively about yourself—who you are and the things you can do—can help boost your self-esteem.

Chapter 52

Control Your Anger

Everybody Gets Angry

Anger is a natural emotion and not necessarily bad. It can give you information about situations, and it can make you feel strong. It is the behavior that follows anger that often gets people into trouble. Reacting to being cut off in traffic by provoking an altercation with the other driver can get you into trouble. Screaming at your brother or sister at the top of your lungs can get you into trouble. Telling your parents that they are jerks, ditto. All of these reactions to anger will probably lead to a negative outcome. And while we can't always control our feelings, our behavior is something over which we have some control. And learning to control our behavior when we are angry is a goal that is attainable.

Identifying Your Anger

The first step in learning to control your anger is to know when you are angry. This may not be as easy as it sounds. It is not unusual for people to feel a certain emotion without realizing what they are feeling. A quick way to help determine if you are holding angry feelings without realizing it is to do

---

About This Chapter: Information in this chapter is adapted from "Anger Management," © Counseling Center at the University of Massachusetts Lowell. Reprinted with permission; cited August 2007.

a body scan. Are your fists clenched? Are you frowning? Are your muscles tensed in general? These are often signs of anger.

In addition, monitor your thinking. If thoughts like, "I hate that jerk!" or "That's unfair," or "I'm gonna get that guy!" are in your head, that's a sure sign you are feeling angry. It may be helpful to write down some of your thoughts and feelings when you are feeling upset. Besides providing a way to vent, this can help you figure out if you are feeling angry or sad or something else.

Trigger Thoughts

Trigger thoughts are thoughts that automatically enter your head and trigger certain emotions. This can happen with any emotion, but anger is particularly vulnerable to triggering. For example, if you see people across the room laughing and looking in your direction, you may think, "Those people are ridiculing me!" This could lead to angry feelings, which could lead to retaliatory behavior, such as starting a fight with the people. It is important to remind yourself that trigger thoughts may or may not be based on accurate perceptions. In the example above, the people across the room may or may not have actually been ridiculing you. They may have been laughing at something else entirely.

Trigger thoughts fall into two categories:

1. The belief that you've been harmed, ridiculed, or victimized.
2. The belief that the other person means to do you harm.

The key point about trigger thoughts is that they may escalate an angry situation without any basis in reality. It is important that we try to recognize our trigger thoughts, so that we can step back and assess how accurate they are. In this way, we can halt any escalating event that may lead to intense feelings that are difficult to control. Again, keeping a record or journal of our thoughts when we get angry is a first step towards changing patterns of anger.

Alternative Behaviors

The next step after identifying your anger and the cognitions that perpetuate it is to find alternative behaviors to express anger. This means substituting behaviors that will help the situation for behaviors that will make the situation worse. Of course, it is not easy to be so rational when you are upset. The key is practice. Practicing alternative behaviors to angry situations that may arise is the best way of helping yourself be in control of what you do. It may sound silly, but actually making a list of and then acting out possible productive behaviors helps keep you in control of how you act.

Assertive Versus Aggressive Behavior

Using assertive behavior results in positive outcomes. This is true in most situations, but especially ones involving anger. It is important to distinguish between assertive behavior and aggressive behavior. Assertive behavior involves standing up for personal rights and expressing yourself in direct ways that do not violate another person's rights. The goal of assertive behavior is communication with mutuality. Aggressive behavior involves standing up for personal rights as well, but in a manner that is indirect and in violation of the rights of others. Its goal tends to be domination and "winning." Some of the components of each are listed below.

Assertive Style

- Uses "I" statements and takes responsibility for one's feelings
- Negotiates clearly for what is wanted
- Cites specific problem behaviors and what changes are desired
- Avoids exaggerating with words such as always and never
- Repeats appropriate requests in a calm manner

Aggressive Style

- Uses "you" statements to blame or intimidate
- Uses threats, put-downs, and name-calling
- Sets up "win-lose" situations instead of negotiating
- Does not listen to the other side
- Tries to use power to manipulate others

Where Does Anger Come From?

As mentioned in the beginning of this section, anger is a natural emotion and is not necessarily "bad." It can let you know when things are not right. Everybody feels anger sometimes. Do some people experience it more often than others? Maybe. Do people tend to express it differently? Definitely. There are many theories as to why this is, but it does seem true that people can learn patterns of emotional expression from their family while growing up. Recognizing this can give us a better understanding of why we express anger (or any emotion) the way we do.

You can think about this for yourself by asking yourself the following questions:

- How was anger expressed by my parents?
- How did my family react when I expressed anger? Was it acceptable?
- Were there subtle messages controlling how anger was expressed?
- Was anger quickly forgotten, or did it linger on?

Looking at your answers to these questions, you may be able to better understand your own feelings about anger and how you let others know that you are angry.

♣ **It's A Fact!!**
Sometimes, excessive irritability and anger is a symptom of depression or anxiety. If you are also having difficulty with sleep, mood, appetite, or other emotional difficulties, consult with a mental health professional to assess this possibility.

Chapter 53

Proper Nutrition And Exercise Can Help Relieve Stress

Stress is our bodies' reaction to change. Every time we experience a new situation our bodies produce more adrenaline (a stimulant), which gives us energy to deal with the challenge at hand. This energy is "fueled" by the nutrients we store from the food we eat. Too much stress can drain our supplies of these nutrients, leaving us with little or no food fuel for our daily energy needs. This can result in feelings of weakness, fatigue, and yes—more stress. The key for eating for less stress is to avoid foods that aggravate our stress response and to increase our bodies' storage of the nutrients we need to handle stressful situations.

Limit Caffeine And Alcohol

Like adrenaline, caffeine is a stimulant. Too much caffeine acts in the same way as too much stress. So caffeine can make your stress symptoms worse. Caffeine is found in coffee, tea, chocolate, and many sodas (especially colas). It's wise to limit caffeine in general, but it's particularly beneficial to avoid caffeine when you're under stress. Alcohol is a depressant and can aggravate stress. All too often, people rely on caffeine to "pick them up" and

---

About This Chapter: Information in this chapter is from "Eating for Less Stress," © Wellness Council of Arizona. Reprinted with permission; cited December 2007.

> ♣ **It's A Fact!!**
> ## Exercise Fuels The Brain's Stress Buffers
>
> Exercise may improve mental health by helping the brain cope better with stress, according to research into the effect of exercise on neurochemicals involved in the body's stress response.
>
> Preliminary evidence suggests that physically active people have lower rates of anxiety and depression than sedentary people. But little work has focused on why that should be. So to determine how exercise might bring about its mental health benefits, some researchers are looking at possible links between exercise and brain chemicals associated with stress, anxiety, and depression.
>
> So far there's little evidence for the popular theory that exercise causes a rush of endorphins. Rather, one line of research points to the less familiar neuromodulator norepinephrine, which may help the brain deal with stress more efficiently.
>
> Work in animals since the late 1980s has found that exercise increases brain concentrations of norepinephrine in brain regions involved in the body's stress response.
>
> Norepinephrine is particularly interesting to researchers because 50 percent of the brain's supply is produced in the locus coeruleus, a brain area that connects most of the brain regions involved in emotional and stress responses. The chemical is thought to play a major role in modulating the action of other more prevalent neurotransmitters that play a direct role in the stress response. And

alcohol to bring them down. Avoid this stress seesaw by restricting your use of both caffeine and alcohol.

Eat Vitamin C-Rich Foods

Your adrenal glands (which produce adrenaline) use Vitamin C during episodes of physical stress. Illness or injury can deplete Vitamin C. Eating a variety of fresh fruits and vegetables, especially citrus fruits, can help ensure

> although researchers are unsure of exactly how most antidepressants work, they know that some increase brain concentrations of norepinephrine.
>
> But some psychologists don't think it's a simple matter of more norepinephrine equals less stress and anxiety, and therefore, less depression. Instead, they think exercise thwarts depression and anxiety by enhancing the body's ability to respond to stress.
>
> Biologically, exercise seems to give the body a chance to practice dealing with stress. It forces the body's physiological systems—all of which are involved in the stress response—to communicate much more closely than usual: The cardiovascular system communicates with the renal system, which communicates with the muscular system. And all of these are controlled by the central and sympathetic nervous systems, which also must communicate with each other. This workout of the body's communication system may be the true value of exercise; the more sedentary we get, the less efficient our bodies in responding to stress.
>
> Source: Copyright © 2004 by the American Psychological Association. Reprinted with permission. The official citation used in referencing this material is: American Psychological Association Practice Directorate, Exercise Fuels the Brain's Stress Buffers, 2004, http://apahelpcenter.org/articles/article.php?id=25.

that your body has adequate Vitamin C. You might also ask your physician or nutritionist about a Vitamin C supplement.

Eating Protein And Complex Carbohydrates

Your body also uses more protein and complex carbohydrates when you're under stress. Good sources of protein include peas, beans, fish, poultry, and lean meats. Complex carbohydrates are found in fruits, vegetables, and whole grain products such as breads, cereals, and pasta. (Avoid refined flours and sugars as these can aggravate your stress response).

Stress-Less Eating Is Healthy Eating

What you can eat can affect how you feel. By following these nutritional tips for stress management, you'll be helping your body to handle stress more effectively, and you'll also be improving your nutritional health in general.

Chapter 54

The Benefits Of Journaling, Stress Logs, And Other Action Plans For Stress Management

Journaling

What is journaling?

Journaling is a term coined for the practice of keeping a diary or journal that explores thoughts and feelings surrounding the events of one's life. Journaling, as a stress management and self-exploration tool, is not the same as simply recording the happenings in one's life, like keeping a log. To be most helpful, one must write in detail about feelings and cognitions related to stressful events, as one would discuss topics in therapy.

What are the benefits of journaling?

Journaling allows people to clarify their thoughts and feelings, thereby gaining valuable self-knowledge. It's also a good problem-solving tool;

> About This Chapter: Information under the heading "Journaling," is from "The Benefits of Journaling for Stress Management," http://stress.about.com/od/generaltechniques/p/profilejournal.htm. © 2007 by Elizabeth Scott, M.S. Used with permission of About, Inc., which can be found online at www.about.com. All rights reserved. Text under the heading "Stress Logs" is excerpted from "Stress Management—Taking Charge," © 1997 Clemson University Cooperative Extension Service. Reprinted with permission. Despite the older date of this document, the information presented is still appropriate for readers seeking to understand stress logs.

oftentimes, one can hash out a problem and come up with solutions more easily on paper. Journaling about traumatic events helps one process them by fully exploring and releasing the emotions involved, and by engaging both hemispheres of the brain in the process, allowing the experience to become fully integrated in one's mind.

As for the health benefits of journaling, they've been scientifically proven. Research shows the following:

- Journaling decreases the symptoms of asthma, arthritis, and other health conditions.
- It improves cognitive functioning.
- It strengthens the immune system, preventing a host of illnesses.
- It counteracts many of the negative effects of stress.

What are the drawbacks to journaling?

Those with learning disabilities may find it difficult to deal with the act of writing itself. Perfectionists may be so concerned with the readability of their work, their penmanship, or other periphery factors that they can't focus on the thoughts and emotions they're trying to access. Others may get tired hands or be reluctant to relive negative experiences. And, journaling only about your negative feelings without incorporating thoughts or plans may actually cause more stress.

How does journaling compare to other stress management practices?

Unlike more physical stress management techniques such as yoga or exercise, journaling is a viable option for the disabled. And, although some prefer to use a computer, journaling requires only a pen and paper, so it's less expensive than techniques that require the aid of a class, book, teacher, or therapist, like techniques such as biofeedback or yoga. Journaling doesn't release tension from your body like progressive muscle relaxation, guided imagery, and other physical and meditative techniques, however. But it's a great practice for overall stress reduction as well as self-knowledge and emotional healing.

The Benefits Of Journaling

> ✔ **Quick Tip**
>
> - Do not plan what you are going to write. Just write. Vent. Write down everything that comes to you. The words you write may be funny, sad, angry, silly, or happy. These are your emotions so just write like you feel.
>
> - Try to write every day. If your writing becomes routine, this can help you put stress in its place.
>
> - Do not share your journal. It is yours and holds your private thoughts. If you share, you might start worrying about what others would think. Use it to express yourself without any fear or worries.
>
> - Keep your journal pages in a notebook. After a few weeks of writing, look back at what you have written. See what things you have accomplished, what stressors you have solved, and those that you have not. Use your journal as a tool to help you explore your emotions, self-esteem, and self-confidence.
>
> Source: Excerpted from "Mind—Create a Journal," GirlsHealth.gov, sponsored by the National Women's Health Information Center, U.S. Department of Health and Human Services, April 2007.

Stress Logs

A helpful way of monitoring your stress level is to keep a daily stress log. Record how often, causes of, and reactions to stressful events, people, places, and situations. As you take steps to manage stress, the daily stress log provides a before and after check on your progress. Use Figure 54.2 to help you monitor your own levels of stress.

Plan Of Action

To take charge of stress, it is important to identify sources of stress and skills that you have for managing it. Use Figure 54.1 [beginning on the next page] as a guide to set up your own plan of action for stress management—take charge.

Figure 54.1. Plan of Action

Plan of Action

To take charge of stress, it is important to identify sources of stress and skills that you have for managing it. **Use the following fuide to set up your own plan of ation for stress management—take charge.**

I. Identify your three strongest sources of stress and the degree of stress you feel regarding each.

1 _____
2 _____
3 _____

II. How do you respond to each source of stress?

Physical _____
Emotional _____
Mental _____
Social _____

III. Why are you dissatisfied or unhappy with each of the three stressors?

1 _____
2 _____
3 _____

IV. What would you like to change in each of the three situations?

1 _____
2 _____
3 _____

V. Identifying skills you possess that could help in managing stress.
Physical skills (energy, strength, agility)

1 _____
2 _____
3 _____

Emotional strengths (self-confidence, empathy, calm)

1 _____
2 _____
3 _____

The Benefits Of Journaling

Support from others (family, friends, clubs)

1 _____
2 _____
3 _____

Mental resources (humor, problem-solving, insight)

1 _____
2 _____
3 _____

Present lifestyle (rituals, hobbies, health)

1 _____
2 _____
3 _____

VI. Develop a plan of action. Describe each step you will take to reduce the level of stress and solve the situation.

1 _____
_____

2 _____
_____

3 _____
_____

VII . What goals would you hope to achieve and when?

Ideal goal: _____

Challenging goal: _____

Acceptable goal: _____

VIII. Act on your plans.

Stress Information For Teens

Figure 54.2. Daily Stress Log Worksheet

Daily Stress Log
(worksheet)

Date _____

Time	Place	Source of Stress	Tension Level*	Coping Stragegy

*Tension Level   1=Slight 2=Moderate 3=Strong 4=Intense

Major source of stress today: _____

_____

Assessment of how you managed stress today: _____

_____

_____

Today's exercise: _____   Duration: _____

Chapter 55

Owning A Dog Or Cat Can Reduce Stress

When thinking of ways to reduce stress in life, usually techniques like meditation, yoga, and journaling come to mind. These are great techniques, to be sure. But getting a new best friend can also have many stress relieving and health benefits. While human friends provide great social support and come with some fabulous benefits, this chapter focuses on the benefits of furry friends: cats and dogs. Research shows that, unless you're someone who really dislikes animals or is absolutely too busy to care for one properly, pets can provide excellent social support, stress relief, and other health benefits—perhaps more than people. Here are more health benefits of pets:

- **Pets can improve your mood.** For those who love animals, it's virtually impossible to stay in a bad mood when a pair of loving puppy eyes meets yours or when a super-soft cat rubs up against your hand. Research supports the mood-enhancing benefits of pets. A recent study found that men with acquired immunodeficiency syndrome (AIDS) were less likely to suffer from depression if they owned a pet. (According to a study, men with AIDS who did not own a pet were about three times more likely to report symptoms of depression than men who did not have AIDS. But men with AIDS who had pets were only

---

About This Chapter: © 2007 by Elizabeth Scott, M.S., "How Owning a Dog or Cat Can Reduce Stress," http://stress.about.com/od/lowstresslifestyle/a/petsandstress.htm. Used with permission of About, Inc., which can be found online at www.about.com. All rights reserved.

about 50 percent more likely to report symptoms of depression, as compared to men in the study who did not have AIDS.)

- **Pets control blood pressure better than drugs.** Yes, it's true. While angiotensin converting enzyme (ACE)-inhibiting drugs can generally reduce blood pressure, they aren't as effective on controlling spikes in blood pressure due to stress and tension. However, a group of hypertensive New York stockbrokers who got dogs or cats were found to have lower blood pressure and heart rates than those who didn't get pets. When they heard of the results, most of those in the non-pet group went out and got pets.

- **Pets encourage you to get out and exercise.** Whether we walk our dogs because they need it, or are more likely to enjoy a walk when we have companionship, dog owners do exercise more than non-pet owners, at least if we live in an urban setting. Because exercise is good for stress management and overall health, owning a dog can be credited with increasing these benefits.

- **Pets can help with social support.** When we're out walking, having a dog with us can make us more approachable and give people a reason to stop and talk, thereby increasing the number of people we meet, giving us an opportunity to increase our network of friends and acquaintances, which also has great stress management benefits.

- **Pets stave off loneliness and provide unconditional love.** Pets can be there for you in ways that people can't. They can offer love and companionship, and can also enjoy comfortable silences, keep secrets, and are excellent snugglers. And they could be the best antidotes to loneliness. In fact, research shows that nursing home residents reported less loneliness when visited by dogs than when they spent time with other people. All these benefits can reduce the amount of stress people experience in response to feelings of social isolation and lack of social support from people.

- **Pets can reduce stress—sometimes more than people.** While we all know the power of talking about your problems with a good friend who's also a good listener, recent research shows that spending time with a pet may be even better. Recent research shows that, when conducting a task that's stressful, people actually experienced less stress when their pets were with them than when a supportive friend or even their spouse was present. (This may be partially due to the fact that pets don't judge us; they just love us.)

> **☞ Remember!!**
> It's important to realize that owning a pet isn't for everyone. Pets do come with additional work and responsibility, which can bring its own stress. However, for most people, the benefits of having a pet outweigh the drawbacks. Having a furry best friend can reduce stress in your life and bring you support when times get tough.

Chapter 56
Using Your Senses To Relieve Stress: Aromatherapy And Music

What is aromatherapy?

Aromatherapy is the ancient practice of using plant oils for health and wellbeing. Using the distilled oils from roots, leaves, and flowers, aromatherapists promote physical and psychological wellness through baths, inhalations, facials, candles, and massage.

What is the history of aromatherapy?

Plant oils have been used by many different cultures for both medicinal and cosmetic purposes.

Ancient Chinese cultures burned incense to foster harmony and wellbeing. The Egyptians used plant oils for cosmetic reasons and are credited for inventing perfume. They also used oils from plants such as myrrh, cedarwood, clove, and nutmeg to embalm their dead.

The Greeks and the Romans used the oils as perfumes, as anti-inflammatories, and to heal wounds.

About This Chapter: Information in this chapter is from "Aromatherapy," by Jillian Graham, © 2007 University of New Hampshire Health Services. Reprinted with permission.

In the 11th century, an Arab physician, named Avicenna, developed distillation, as we know it today. This enhanced the use of essential oils through the Middle Ages, where distilled oils were used as both medicine and perfume.

Today, aromatherapy is used in North America and Europe, particularly in France, for its therapeutic qualities.

What are the principles of aromatherapy?

Plant oils are distilled without the use of chemicals by heating the plant through boiling or steaming until the oil vaporizes. The oil is then used in a variety of different ways, such as for massage, as a steam inhalation, as bath oil, or as vaporizers for a living space.

The oils react with the hypothalamus in the brain, affecting mood and emotion. Oils applied to the skin travel through the bloodstream, contributing to physical health and hygiene, and oils inhaled through the lungs are also thought to have a physical benefit.

What are the benefits of aromatherapy?

Different oils have different properties and can cause a variety of reactions depending on the individual client. For instance, lavender oil is thought to have relaxing properties, so aromatherapists tend to use lavender oil on a client who is suffering from stress or anxiety. Lavender is also thought to act as an antiseptic on burns, acne, and insect stings.

Aromatherapy can be used to treat or lessen symptoms of stress-related conditions such as headaches and insomnia and to ease discomfort associated with pregnancy and childbirth. Topical treatments of certain essential oils can be used to treat skin problems, cuts, and burns, and steam inhalations can be used for asthma and colds. When used in massage, the therapy can also improve circulation.

Is aromatherapy safe?

If done correctly, aromatherapy is a very safe practice. However, because some plants contain harmful toxins, it is important to understand the oil and how to apply it. Never put undiluted oils directly on the skin (except lavender

Using Your Senses To Relieve Stress

and tea tree oil for certain skin conditions), and keep them away from the eyes and from open flames. Oils should also never be swallowed.

What happens in an aromatherapy session?

There is no current state licensing program to train aromatherapists. However, many massage therapists, naturopaths, acupuncturists, and cosmeticians will become trained in aromatherapy and use it within their practice.

Aromatherapy is most commonly used in conjunction with a massage. The aromatherapist will interview you on your lifestyle, medical history, diet, and sleeping patterns. He or she will then ask you about any specific conditions you may wish to address before choosing the oil, or allowing you to choose pleasing oil for the massage. He or she should use high quality oils from organically grown plants and often mixed with carrier oils such as grape seed or almond oil, or made into a cream or lotion for skin applications.

Can I use aromatherapy on my own?

Yes, aromatherapy can be a useful tool for stress relief and relaxation at home. Many people take aromatherapy baths by adding a few drops of certain oils such as lavender, geranium, rose, sandalwood, or spruce oil to a hot bath and soaking for at least ten minutes.

Another technique to try at home is a steam inhalation. Add four drops of oil such as peppermint, eucalyptus, tea tree, or chamomile to a bowl of steaming hot water. Place a towel over your head to keep the steam from dispersing too quickly and lean over the bowl, inhaling deeply for about ten minutes. This can help with relaxation and also to relieve stuffy noses and congestion associated with colds and the flu.

What are some common essential oils?

Lavender oil has a fresh and floral scent. Its relaxing fragrance is used for depression, anxiety, and stress.

Rosemary oil smells herbaceous and fresh. Its uplifting scent is commonly used for exhaustion.

Rose oil smells floral and sweet. It is used for stress and depression.

> ♣ **It's A Fact!!**
>
> ## Music Relaxation:
> ## A Healthy And Convenient Stress Management Tool
>
> With all the ways music affects your body, you can probably already clearly see how music can be used as an effective relaxation and stress management tool. In addition to the many physical changes that music can bring (go to http://stress.about.com/od/tensiontamers/a/music_therapy.htm for more information), music is especially helpful in relaxation and stress management because it can be used in the following ways:
>
> - **Music And Physical Relaxation:** Music can promote relaxation of tense muscles, enabling you to easily release some of the tension you carry from a stressful day (or week).
>
> - **Music As An Aid In Stress Relief Activities:** Music can help you get "into the zone" when practicing yoga, self hypnosis, or guided imagery, can help you feel energized when exercising, help dissolve the stress when you're soaking in the tub, and be a helpful part of many other stress relief activities. It can take an effective stress reliever and make it even more effective.
>
> - **Music And A Meditative State:** As mentioned before, music can help your brain get into a meditative state, which carries wonderful stress relief benefits with it. For those who find it intimidating, music can be an easier alternative.

Patchouli oil is a deep golden brown and smells earthy and woody. It is commonly used for stress and fatigue.

Sandalwood oil smells rich, earthy, and sweet. The oil is clear and slightly yellowish, and it is used for depression and stress, and for promoting happiness and peace.

Lemon oil has a bright, citrus scent. It is used for fatigue and exhaustion, memory and concentration, and happiness and peace.

- **Music To Promote A Positive Focus:** Music, especially upbeat tunes, can take your mind off what stresses you and help you feel more optimistic and positive. This helps release stress and can even help you keep from getting as stressed over life's little frustrations in the future.

- **Music And Affirmations:** The way you see the world and the type of self talk you habitually use can also have a profound effect on your stress level, which is why positive affirmations that create more positive self talk are so helpful. Music that has affirming lyrics can bring the double benefit of music and positive affirmations, helping you to surround yourself with positive energy and more often look on the bright side, letting stressful events more easily roll off your back.

These are some of the reasons that music relaxation is among the easiest and most effective forms of relaxation available, and music is such a great stress management tool.

Source: © 2007 by Elizabeth Scott, M.S., "Music Relaxation: A Healthy and Convenient Stress Management Tool," http://stress.about.com/od/tensiontamers/a/musicrelaxation.htm. Used with permission of About, Inc., which can be found online at www.about.com. All rights reserved.

Sage oil is a bright, earthy, and herbaceous oil that is used for stress, anxiety, depression, fatigue, and feelings of loneliness.

Peppermint oil has a concentrated minty scent and is used for exhaustion, vertigo, nausea, headaches, and to help with memory and concentration.

How do I find an aromatherapist?

Many massage therapists are also trained in aromatherapy, and if not, they might be able to direct you to someone.

Chapter 57

Breathing Techniques For Stress Management

During stressful situations we rarely stop to think about what is happening within our bodies. Indeed, the pressures of the moment keep our minds occupied on almost everything but our physiological functions. Consequently, those functions often become irregular, leaving us in an unhealthy state of being. When we are in this state, we have fewer chances to succeed in whatever we try to accomplish.

Among the many physiological functions adversely affected by stress is our breathing. Even when stress is minimal, few people retain a habit of natural, full breathing, which is required for maintaining a good mental and physical state. Proper breathing is essential for sustaining life and cleansing inner body systems.

Breathing: The Importance Of Oxygen

Oxygen plays a vital role in the circulatory and respiratory systems. As we breathe, oxygen that is inhaled purifies our blood by removing poisonous waste products circulating throughout our blood systems. Irregular breathing

---

About This Chapter: Information in this chapter is from "Breathing Techniques," reprinted with permission from the Counseling Center, University of South Florida Lakeland. © 2002 University of South Florida Lakeland.

will hamper this purification process and cause waste products to remain in circulation. Digestion will then become irregular, leaving tissues and organs undernourished. Improper oxygen consumption will thus ultimately lead to fatigue and heightened anxiety states. The irregular breathing elicited during stressful situations not only make them hard to cope with but also contribute to a general deterioration of health. By the careful control of our breathing pattern, we may not only rejuvenate our systems, but also counter the unhealthy effects of stress.

Breathing Methods

Breathing methods are useful to settle the body and mind and induce a heightened sense of awareness. Breathing exercises have been practiced for thousands of years in the East. The West began studying the effectiveness and importance of them several years ago. By this time, sufficient research has taken place in the West to verify the usefulness of these techniques.

> ♣ It's A Fact!!
> By learning proper breathing techniques, stressful situations may be handled better, and overall mental and physical health will be improved.

The following breathing methods can be helpful for reducing anger, anxiety, depression, fatigue, irritability, muscular tension, and stress.

Proper Breathing

Before beginning any technique, it is essential that you learn how to breathe properly and fully:

- Lie down on a rug or blanket on the floor with your legs straight and slightly apart, your toes pointed comfortably outwards, arms at your sides not touching your body, your palms up, and your eyes closed. This is called a "relaxed body" position. Take time to relax your body and breathe freely.

- It is best to breathe through your nose, as the tiny hairs and mucous membranes filter out dust and toxins from the inhaled air. Keep your mouth closed as you breathe.

- As you breathe, your chest and abdomen should move together. If only the chest seems to rise and fall, your breathing is shallow, and you are not making good use of the lower part of your lungs. As you inhale, you should feel your abdomen rising; it is as if your stomach is filling with air. As you exhale, the abdomen comes back in, like a balloon releasing all of its air. This inhale and exhale process should continue comfortably and smoothly. The chest and abdomen should rise as you inhale and fall as you exhale. The chest should move only slightly.

Deep, Relaxed Breathing

Although this exercise can be practiced in a variety of poses, the following is recommended for beginners:

- Lie down on a blanket or rug on the floor. Bend your knees and move your feet about eight inches apart, with your toes turned outward slightly. Make sure your spine is straight.

- Place one hand on your abdomen and one hand on your chest.

- Inhale slowly and deeply through your nose into your abdomen to push up your hand as much as feels comfortable. Your chest should move only a little and only with your abdomen.

- Continue step three until it becomes rhythmic and comfortable. Now smile slightly, inhale through your nose, and exhale through your mouth, making a quiet, breezy sound as you gently blow out. Your mouth, tongue, and jaw will be relaxed. Take long, slow, deep breaths raising and lowering your abdomen. Hear the sound and feel the texture of breathing as you become more and more relaxed.

- When you first begin this technique, do it for five minutes. When you become more comfortable with it, you may extend it up to 20 minutes.

- Upon ending a session, stay still for a few minutes and try to keep the entire body relaxed.

> ♣ **It's A Fact!!**
> While breathing is a function most people take for granted, rarely is it practiced in a proper fashion.

- The purpose of this technique is to develop a good, relaxing breathing method. It may be practiced anytime, especially during stressful situations.

The Relaxing Sigh

Sighing and yawning during the day are signs that you are not getting enough oxygen. A sigh releases a bit of tension and can be practiced at will as a means of relaxing.

- Sit or stand up straight.
- Sigh deeply, letting out a sound of deep relief as the air rushes out of your lungs.
- Let new air come in naturally.
- Repeat this procedure eight to twelve times whenever you feel the need for it, and experience the feeling of relaxation.

The Clenched Fist

This exercise will stimulate your breathing, circulation, and nervous system.

- Stand up straight, hands at your sides.
- Inhale and hold a complete natural breath as described above.
- Raise your arms out in front of you, keeping them up and relaxed.
- Gradually bring your hands to your shoulders. As you do, slowly contract your hands into fists, so that when they reach your shoulders, they are clenched as tight as possible.
- Keep the fists tense as you push your arms out straight again very slowly.
- Pull your arms back to your shoulders and straighten them out, fists tense, as fast as you can, several times.

Imaginative Breathing

This exercise combines the relaxing benefits of deep, relaxed breathing with the curative value of positive autosuggestions.

Breathing Techniques For Stress Management

- Lie down on a rug or blanket on the floor in a "relaxed body" pose.

- Place your hands gently on your solar plexus (that point where your ribs start to separate above your abdomen) and practice deep, relaxed breathing for a few minutes.

- Imagine that, with each incoming breath of air, energy is rushing into your lungs and being immediately stored in your solar plexus. Imagine that as you exhale, this energy is flowing out to all parts of your body. Form a mental picture of this energizing process.

- Continue on a daily basis for at least five to ten minutes a day.

The Rolling Breath

The following exercise requires a partner and is effective in relaxing and energizing you.

- Lie on your back. Have your partner put one hand on your abdomen and one hand on your chest.

- Inhale and exhale as in deep, relaxed breathing, but each inhale is taken in two stages—abdomen, then chest. Imagine that you are breathing into your partner's hand as you fill your belly with air. When your abdomen feels full, continue breathing into your chest. Watch your partner's hands as it rises.

- Exhale fully through the chest and belly simultaneously.

- Repeat. It is important to keep a rhythmic rolling effect between abdomen and chest. Breathe at your natural pace, however.

Any of the above techniques can and should be practiced everyday. Being a natural preventive measure for stress, there are very few side effects. It will take some time before you observe any profound changes taking place within your body and mind, but practice diligently and patiently. You will eventually realize that you have more energy and are much more relaxed.

Chapter 58

Massage Therapy

What is massage therapy?

Many physicians have been recommending massage therapy for years—nearly 2,400 years. The Greek physician Hippocrates first documented the medical benefits of "friction" in Western culture around 400 BC. Today, massage therapy is being used as a means of treating painful ailments, decompressing tired and overworked muscles, reducing stress, rehabilitating sports injuries, and promoting general health. This is accomplished by manipulating a client's soft tissues in order to improve the body's circulation and remove waste products from the muscles.

While massage therapy is done for medical benefit, a massage can be given to simply relax or rejuvenate the person being massaged. It is important to note that this type of massage is not intended for a medical purpose, and provides medical value only through general stress reduction and increased energy levels. Thoroughly trained individuals who provide specialized care with their client's medical health in mind, on the other hand, practice massage therapy.

About This Chapter: Information in this chapter is excerpted from "Massage Therapists," Bureau of Labor Statistics, U.S. Department of Labor, *Occupational Outlook Handbook, 2006-2007 Edition*.

Most massage therapists specialize in several modalities, which require different techniques. Some use exaggerated strokes ranging the length of a body part, while others use quick, percussion-like strokes with a cupped or closed hand. A massage can be as long as two hours or as short as five or ten minutes. Usually, the type of massage therapists give depends on the client's needs and the client's physical condition. For example, they use special techniques for elderly clients that they would not use for athletes, and they would use approaches for clients with injuries that would not be appropriate for clients seeking relaxation. There are also some forms of massage that are given solely to one type of client, for example prenatal massage and infant massage.

> ♣ **It's A Fact!!**
> Massage therapists can specialize in over 80 different types of massage, called modalities. Swedish massage, deep tissue massage, reflexology, acupressure, sports massage, and neuromuscular massage are just a few of the many approaches to massage therapy.

Massage therapists work by appointment. Before beginning a massage therapy session, therapists conduct an informal interview with the client to find out about the person's medical history and desired results from the massage. This gives therapists a chance to discuss which techniques could be beneficial to the client and which could be harmful. Because massage therapists tend to specialize in only a few areas of massage, customers will often be referred, or seek a therapist with a certain type of massage in mind. Based on the person's goals, ailments, medical history, and stress- or pain-related problem areas, a massage therapist will conclude whether a massage would be harmful, and if not, move forward with the session while concentrating on any areas of particular discomfort to the client. While giving the massage, therapists alter their approach or concentrate on a particular area as necessary.

Many modalities of massage therapy use massage oils, lotions, or creams to massage and rub the client's muscles. Most massage therapists, particularly those who are self-employed, supply their own table or chair, sheets, pillows, and body lotions or oils. Most modalities of massage require clients to be covered in a sheet or blanket and require clients to be undressed or to wear loose-fitting clothing. The therapist only exposes the body part on which

Massage Therapy 349

he or she is currently massaging. Some types of massage are done without oils or lotions and are performed with the client fully clothed.

Massage can be a delicate issue for some clients, and those clients may indicate that they are comfortable with contact only in specified areas. For this reason, and also for general-purpose business risks, about half of all massage therapists have liability insurance, either through a professional association membership or through other insurance carriers.

Massage therapists must develop a rapport with their clients if repeat customers are to be secured. Because those who seek a therapist tend to make regular visits, developing a loyal clientele is an important part of becoming successful.

What is the typical environment when getting a massage?

Massage therapists work in an array of settings both private and public: private offices, studios, hospitals, nursing homes, fitness centers, sports medicine facilities, airports, and shopping malls, for example. Some massage therapists also travel to clients' homes or offices to provide a massage. It is not uncommon for full-time massage therapists to divide their time among several different settings, depending on the clients and locations scheduled.

Most massage therapists give massages in dimly lit settings. Using candles and/or incense is not uncommon. Ambient or other calm, soothing music is often played. The dim lighting, smells, and background noise are meant to put clients at ease. On the other hand, when visiting a client's office, a massage therapist may not have those amenities. The environment depends heavily on a therapist's location and what the client wants.

What are the training standards and requirements for massage therapists?

Training standards and requirements for massage therapists vary greatly by state and locality. In 2004, 33 states and the District of Columbia had passed laws regulating massage therapy in some way. Most of the boards governing massage therapy in these states require practicing massage therapists to complete a formal education program and pass the national certification examination or a state exam. Some state regulations require that therapists keep up on their knowledge and technique through continuing education. It is best to check information on licensing, certification, and accreditation on a state-by-state basis.

Chapter 59

Mind-Body Therapies: Guided Imagery, Meditation, Progressive Muscle Relaxation, Yoga, And Spirituality And Religion

Guided Imagery

What is guided imagery?

Guided imagery (directing the images/pictures we experience through any of our sensory perceptions) is an ancient therapy. Providers of health care extending back to the beginning of human history have used guided

> About This Chapter: Information under the heading "Guided Imagery," is from "Guided Imagery," © Hartford Hospital. All rights reserved. Reprinted with permission; cited September 2007. Text under the heading "Meditation" is excerpted from "Meditation for Health Purposes," National Center for Complimentary and Alternative Medicine, National Institutes of Health, June 2007. Information under the heading "Progressive Muscle Relaxation" is from "Progressive Muscle Relaxation," © 2007 American Lung Association. Reprinted with permission. For more information about the American Lung Association or to support the work it does, call 1-800-LUNG-USA (1-800-586-4872) or log on to http://www.lungusa.org. Text under the heading "Yoga" is from "The Benefits of Yoga for Stress Management," http://stress.about.com/od/tensiontamers/p/profileyoga.htm. © 2007 by Elizabeth Scott, M.S. Used with permission of About, Inc., which can be found online at www.about.com. All rights reserved. Information under the heading "Spirituality And Religion" is from "Spirituality and Mental Health: Benefits of Spirituality," http://stress.about.com/od/optimismspirituality/a/22307_God_power.htm. © 2007 by Elizabeth Scott, M.S. Used with permission of About, Inc., which can be found online at www.about.com. All rights reserved.

imagery as a reflecting point in assisting people to reconnect to their inner resources for healing. Recalled sights, tastes, smells, and feelings are inner resources containing images and energy important to a healthy recovery.

Helping others to direct their imaginations and daydreams to a greater awareness of their overall health and well-being has been increasingly established by research to demonstrate a positive impact in the healing process.

What are the effects?

In addition to inducing a relaxation response and reducing chronic pain, guided imagery has been effective in many areas for the mind, body, and spirit by lowering cholesterol, reducing blood pressure, and lessening the adverse effects of chemotherapy, etc.

What are the benefits?

"Guided imagery can be used," writes Katherine Brown-Saltzman, "to reacquaint patients with their healthy side, give them back a measure of control, enhance their immunologic response to stress, reduce side effects of treatment, and diminish anxiety and fear. For persons with cancer, guided imagery has been found to reduce or arrest the side effects of nausea and vomiting, create a relaxation response, affect the immune system, and assist in the management of anxiety, pain, and terminal illness."

Who guides you?

Professionals certified in performing guided imagery define their role as others have down through the centuries: like that of a companion or partner accompanying another on a journey. An important assumption in the practice of this ancient technique is that people intuitively know what images will serve them most as powerful resources in their healing process.

What is the experience like?

Assisting others through guided imagery can go in many different directions, but generally all of the various techniques include efforts to produce a sense of general relaxation.

Mind-Body Therapies

For example, recipients are encouraged to release physical tensions and to be mindful of their breathing and heart rate. They may then be asked to locate a safe or familiar place where they feel secure and protected, empowered, relaxed, or at peace.

This technique enables recipients to experience themselves with greater awareness while providing opportunities for greater stress management. In addition, recipients are often encouraged and reminded to draw upon this resource when situations of stress, anxiety, and pain reoccur.

Other guided imagery techniques include focusing on a specific area that is causing a problem or pain and imagining an inner guide or wise person assisting in the healing process.

Meditation

What Meditation Is

The term meditation refers to a group of techniques, most of which started in Eastern religious or spiritual traditions. These techniques have been used by many different cultures throughout the world for thousands of years. Today, many people use meditation outside of its traditional religious or cultural settings for health and wellness purposes.

In meditation, a person learns to focus his attention and suspend the stream of thoughts that normally occupy the mind. This practice is believed to result in a state of greater physical relaxation, mental calmness, and psychological balance. Practicing meditation can change how a person relates to the flow of emotions and thoughts in the mind.

Most types of meditation have four elements in common. They are as follows:

- **A Quiet Location:** Many meditators prefer a quiet place with as few distractions as possible. This can be particularly helpful for beginners. People who have been practicing meditation for a longer period of time sometimes develop the ability to meditate in public places, like waiting rooms or buses.

- **A Specific, Comfortable Posture:** Depending on the type being practiced, meditation can be done while sitting, lying down, standing, walking, or in other positions.

- **A Focus Of Attention:** Focusing one's attention is usually a part of meditation. For example, the meditator may focus on a mantra (a specially chosen word or set of words), an object, or the breath.

- **An Open Attitude:** Having an open attitude during meditation means letting distractions come and go naturally without stopping to think about them. When distracting or wandering thoughts occur, they are not suppressed; instead, the meditator gently brings attention back to the focus. In some types of meditation, the meditator learns to observe the rising and falling of thoughts and emotions as they spontaneously occur.

Meditation is practiced both on its own and as a component of some other therapies, such as yoga, tai chi, and qi gong. This chapter focuses on meditation practiced on its own.

Meditation For Health Purposes

Meditation used as complementary and alternative medicine (CAM) is a type of mind-body medicine (one of the four domains, or areas of knowledge, in CAM). Generally, mind-body medicine focuses on the following:

- the interactions among the brain, the rest of the body, the mind, and behavior

- the ways in which emotional, mental, social, spiritual, and behavioral factors can directly affect health

People use meditation for various health problems, such as the following:

- anxiety
- pain
- depression
- mood and self-esteem problems
- stress

Mind-Body Therapies

- insomnia

- physical or emotional symptoms that may be associated with chronic illnesses and their treatment, such as cardiovascular (heart) disease, human immunodeficiency virus/acquired immune deficiency syndrome (HIV/AIDS), and cancer

Meditation is also used for overall wellness.

Examples Of Meditation

Mindfulness meditation and the transcendental meditation technique (also known as TM) are two common approaches to meditation.

Mindfulness meditation originated in Buddhism. It is based on the concept of being mindful, or having an increased awareness and total acceptance of the present. While meditating, the meditator is taught to bring all her attention to the sensation of the flow of the breath in and out of the body. The intent might be described as focusing attention on what is being experienced, without reacting to or judging that experience. This is seen as helping the meditator learn to experience thoughts and emotions in normal daily life with greater balance and acceptance.

TM originated in the Vedic tradition in India. It is a type of meditation that uses a mantra (a word, sound, or phrase repeated silently) to prevent distracting thoughts from entering the mind. The intent of TM might be described as allowing the mind to settle into a quieter state and the body into a state of deep rest. This is seen as ultimately leading to a state of relaxed alertness.

Looking At How Meditation May Work

Practicing meditation has been shown to induce some changes in the body, such as changes in the body's "fight or flight" response. The system responsible for this response is the autonomic nervous system (sometimes called the involuntary nervous system). It regulates many organs and muscles, including functions such as the heartbeat, sweating, breathing, and digestion, and does so automatically.

The autonomic nervous system is divided into two major parts. They are as follows:

- The **sympathetic nervous system** helps mobilize the body for action. When a person is under stress, it produces the fight-or-flight response: the heart rate and breathing rate go up, for example, the blood vessels narrow (restricting the flow of blood), and muscles tighten.

- The **parasympathetic nervous system** creates what some call the "rest and digest" response. This system's responses oppose those of the sympathetic nervous system. For example, it causes the heart rate and breathing rate to slow down, the blood vessels to dilate (improving blood flow), and activity to increase in many parts of the digestive tract.

While scientists are studying whether meditation may afford meaningful health benefits, they are also looking at how it may do so. One way some types

♣ **It's A Fact!!**
Meditation, one of the most common mind-body interventions, is a conscious mental process that induces a set of integrated physiological changes termed the relaxation response. Functional magnetic resonance imaging (fMRI) has been used to identify and characterize the brain regions that are active during meditation. This research suggests that various parts of the brain known to be involved in attention and in the control of the autonomic nervous system are activated, providing a neurochemical and anatomical basis for the effects of meditation on various physiological activities. Recent studies involving imaging are advancing the understanding of mind-body mechanisms. For example, meditation has been shown in one study to produce significant increases in left-sided anterior brain activity, which is associated with positive emotional states. Moreover, in this same study, meditation was associated with increases in antibody titers to influenza vaccine, suggesting potential linkages among meditation, positive emotional states, localized brain responses, and improved immune function.

Source: Excerpted from "Mind-Body Medicine: An Overview," National Center for Complimentary and Alternative Medicine, National Institutes of Health, July 2007.

of meditation might work is by reducing activity in the sympathetic nervous system and increasing activity in the parasympathetic nervous system.

Scientific research is using sophisticated tools to learn more about what goes on in the brain and the rest of the body during meditation and diseases or conditions for which meditation might be useful. There is still much to learn in these areas. One avenue of research is looking at whether meditation is associated with significant changes in brain function. A number of researchers believe that these changes account for many of meditation's effects.

Side Effects And Risks

Meditation is generally safe. There have been a small number of reports that intensive meditation could cause or worsen symptoms in people who have certain psychiatric problems, but this question has not been fully researched. Individuals who are aware of an underlying psychiatric disorder and want to start meditation should speak with a mental health professional before doing so.

Progressive Muscle Relaxation

Ask your buddy or someone else to read this to you. Ideally your buddy will read it slowly, with a low voice tone to encourage relaxation.

Get as comfortable as possible. This exercise will help you relax all of your muscles. It will also teach you to be more aware of parts of your body that are especially tense and show you how to relieve most stress. The object of this exercise is to tense and then release the pressure in different muscles. In this way, you will progressively achieve deeper relaxation.

Start by raising your eyebrows as high as possible, feeling the tension build. Hold that tension for a moment. Now relax, and feel the tension flow out. Now squeeze your eyes shut as tight as you can. Hold that tension. Let it build. Now relax your eyelids. Feel the relief from the tension.

Now clench your teeth together tightly. Let the tension build. Hold it. Now release your jaw, letting it go loose. Now squeeze your whole face up into a knot and hold it there. Hold it. Let the tension build as you squeeze your eyes, mouth, and nose together hard. And now relax. Notice how loose and relaxed your whole face feels.

Now bring your chin slowly down toward your chest, feeling the tension building in your neck and shoulders. Hold it. And now relax. Feel the relief.

Now make your right hand into a tight fist and raise your right arm to shoulder height, stretching it way out. Feel the tension build as you clench your fist and keep your arm stretched. Now relax, letting your arm fall slowly to your side.

Now with your left hand make a hard fist. Raise your left arm to shoulder height, stretching it out as far as you can, straight ahead. Feel the tension build in your clenched fist and arm. Hold it. Now relax, letting your arm fall back to your side. Now, make fists with both hands and raise both arms to shoulder height, stretching straight ahead as far as you can. Let the tension build. Hold it. Now, let your arms fall back to your sides and relax. Feel the relief in these muscles.

Now, to your stomach. Pull these muscles in tight, as tight as you can. Hold it. Let the tension build. And now, relax.

Now, raise your right leg, tensing your thigh and calf muscles and pulling your toes back toward you. Hold it. Feel the tension build. Now, let your leg back down and relax. Now, raise you left leg and tighten your calf and thigh muscles as you pull your toes back. Let the tension build. Hold it. Now, let your leg back down and relax. Now raise both legs together and tighten your calf and thigh muscles as you extend your toes and point them straight forward as far as you can. Let the tension build. Hold it. Now let your legs back down and relax. Feel the sense of relief.

Now, take a few moments to think about how the muscles feel throughout your body. Check your neck, shoulders, arms, chest, stomach, legs, and feet.

Now, spend a few moments experiencing the deeply relaxed restful feeling throughout your body. Sense the quiet and restfulness that comes from releasing the tension in your muscles. Now, take a full deep breath, hold it a moment, and then, as you let out the air allow any remaining anxieties and tensions to just flow away. You are now very deeply relaxed and at ease. Now, open your eyes, stretch your arms and legs, moving them about. Get up when you feel ready.

Mind-Body Therapies

✎ What's It Mean?

<u>Guided Imagery:</u> Directing the images/pictures we experience through any of our sensory perceptions. [1]

<u>Meditation:</u> A conscious mental process using certain techniques, such as focusing attention or maintaining a specific posture, to suspend the stream of thoughts and relax the body and mind. [2]

<u>Mind-Body Medicine:</u> Practices that focus on the interaction among the brain, mind, body, and behavior, with the intent to use the mind to affect physical functioning and promote health. [2]

<u>Progressive Muscle Relaxation:</u> A cognitive-behavioral strategy in which muscles are alternately tensed and then relaxed in a systematic fashion. [3]

<u>Qi Gong:</u> A component of traditional Chinese medicine that combines movement, meditation, and controlled breathing. The intent is to improve blood flow and the flow of qi. [2]

<u>Spirituality:</u> An individual's sense of purpose and meaning of life beyond material values. Spirituality may be practiced in many ways, such as through religion. [2]

<u>Yoga:</u> A practice from Ayurvedic medicine that combines breathing exercises, physical postures, and meditation. It is intended to calm the nervous system and balance the body, mind, and spirit. [2]

Source:

1. © Hartford Hospital.

2. "Mind-Body Medicine: An Overview," National Center for Complimentary and Alternative Medicine, National Institutes of Health, July 2007.

3. "Glossary," From Management of Cancer Pain, Clinical Guideline Number 9, AHCPR Publication No. 94-0592: March 1994. Health Services/Technology Assessment Text, National Library of Medicine; cited February 2008.

Yoga

Introduction

Dating back over 5,000 years, yoga is the oldest defined practice of self-development. The methods of classical yoga include ethical disciplines, physical postures, breathing control, and meditation. Traditionally an Eastern practice, it's now becoming popular in the West. In fact, many companies, especially in Britain, are seeing the benefit of yoga, recognizing that relaxed workers are healthier and more creative, and are sponsoring yoga fitness programs.

Overview Of Yoga

Many of the popular techniques found to reduce stress derive from yoga:

- controlled breathing
- meditation
- physical movement
- mental imagery
- stretching

Yoga, which derives its name from the word, "yoke"—to bring together—does just that, bringing together the mind, body, and spirit. But whether you use yoga for spiritual transformation or for stress management and physical well-being, the benefits are numerous.

Yoga's Effects On The Body

The following is only a partial list of yoga's benefits:

- reduced stress
- sound sleep
- improvement of many medical conditions
- allergy and asthma symptom relief
- lower blood pressure
- smoking cessation help
- lower heart rate

Mind-Body Therapies

- spiritual growth
- sense of well-being
- reduced anxiety and muscle tension
- increased strength and flexibility
- slowed aging process

Yoga's benefits are so numerous; it gives a high payoff for the amount of effort involved.

What's Involved?

The practice of yoga involves stretching the body and forming different poses, while keeping breathing slow and controlled. The body becomes relaxed and energized at the same time. There are various styles of yoga, some moving through the poses more quickly, almost like an aerobic workout, and other styles relaxing deeply into each pose. Some have a more spiritual angle, while others are used purely as a form of exercise.

What Are The Benefits Of Yoga?

Virtually everyone can see physical benefits from yoga, and its practice can also give psychological benefits, such as stress reduction and a sense of well-being, and spiritual benefits, such as a feeling of connectedness with God or Spirit, or a feeling of transcendence. Certain poses can be done just about anywhere, and a yoga program can go for hours or minutes, depending on one's schedule.

What Are The Drawbacks Of Yoga?

Yoga does require some commitment of time and is more difficult for people with certain physical limitations. Some people feel self-conscious doing some of the poses. Also, yoga classes can be expensive, although it is possible, albeit perhaps more challenging, to learn from a book or video.

How Does It Compare To Other Stress Reduction Methods?

As yoga combines several techniques used for stress reduction, it can be said to provide the combined benefits of breathing exercises, stretching exercises, fitness programs, meditation practice, and guided imagery, in one technique. However, for those with great physical limitations, simple breathing exercises, meditation, or guided imagery might be a preferable option and provide similar benefits. Yoga also requires more effort and commitment than taking pills or herbs for stress reduction.

Spirituality And Religion

While people use many different religions and paths to find God, research has shown that those who are more religious or spiritual, and use their spirituality to cope with life, experience many benefits to their health and well-being. For many, this news would come as no surprise; spirituality and religious activity have been a source of comfort and relief from stress for multitudes of people. In fact, according to a study from the University of Florida in Gainesville and Wayne State University in Detroit, older adults use prayer more than any other alternative therapy for health; 96% of study participants use prayer specifically to cope with stress. Here are just a few more of the many positive findings about spirituality and its influence on physical and mental health:

- Canadian college students who are involved with campus ministries visited the doctor less, scored higher on tests of psychological well-being, and coped with stress more effectively.

- Older women are more grateful to God than older men, and they receive greater stress-buffering health effects due to this gratitude.

- Those with an intrinsic religious orientation, regardless of gender, exhibited less physiological reactivity toward stress than those with an extrinsic religious orientation. They were also less afraid of death and had greater feelings of well-being. (Those who were intrinsically oriented dedicated their lives to God or a "higher power," while the extrinsically oriented ones used religion for external ends like making friends or increasing community social standing.)

- Prayer works for young and old alike. Prayer and spirituality have been linked to:
    - better health

Mind-Body Therapies

- less hypertension
- less stress, even during difficult times
- more positive feelings
- less depression
- greater psychological well-being
- superior ability to handle stress

Whether this information inspires you to rediscover a forgotten spiritual path, reinforces your commitment to an already well-established one, or simply provides interesting food for thought, this is just a sample of all the encouraging research that's been done on the topic.

♣ **It's A Fact!!**

Spirituality is personal, and everyone's spiritual path may be unique. However, some spiritual stress relief strategies have been helpful to many, regardless of faith.

Source: Excerpted from "Spirituality and Mental Health: Benefits of Spirituality," © 2007 by Elizabeth Scott, M.S. Used with permission of About, Inc.

Part Five
If You Need More Information

Chapter 60

Directory Of Stress And Stress Management Resources

American Academy of Allergy, Asthma and Immunology
555 East Wells Street, Suite 1100
Milwaukee, WI 53202-3823
Phone: 414-272-6071
Website: http://www.aaaai.org
E-Mail: info@aaaai.org

American Academy of Child and Adolescent Psychiatry
3615 Wisconsin Avenue, NW
Washington, DC 20016-3007
Phone: 202-966-7300
Fax: 202-966-2891
Website: http://www.aacap.org
E-Mail: communications@aacap.org

American Academy of Dermatology
P.O. Box 4014
Schaumburg, IL 60618-4014
Toll Free: 866-503-SKIN (7546)
Fax: 847-240-1859
Website: http://www.aad.org
E-Mail: MRC@aad.org

American Academy of Experts in Traumatic Stress
368 Veterans Memorial Highway
Commack, NY 11725
Phone: 631-543-2217
Fax: 631-543-6977
Website: http://www.aaets.org
E-Mail: info@aaets.org

About This Chapter: Information in this chapter was compiled from many sources deemed reliable; inclusion does not constitute endorsement. All contact information was verified and updated in January 2008.

American Academy of Family Physicians
P.O. Box 11210
Shawnee Mission, KS 66207-1210
Toll Free: 800-274-2237
Phone: 913-906-6000
Website: http://www.aafp.org
E-mail: fp@aafp.org

American Heart Association
7272 Greenville Avenue
Dallas, TX 75231
Toll Free: 800-AHA-USA-1 (800-242-8721)
Website: http://www.americanheart.org

American Institute of Stress
124 Park Avenue
Yonkers, NY 10703
Phone: 914-963-1200
Fax: 914-965-6267
Website: http://www.stress.org
E-mail: Stress125@optonline.net

American Massage Therapy Association
500 Davis Street, Suite 900
Evanston, IL 60201-4695
Toll Free: 877-905-2700
Phone: 847-864-0123
Fax: 847-864-1178
Website: http://www.amtamassage.org
E-Mail: info@amtamassage.org

American Meditation Institute
60 Garner Road, P.O. Box 430
Averill Park, NY 12018
Toll Free: 800-234-5115
Phone: 518-674-8714
Fax: 518-674-8714
Website: http://www.americanmeditation.org
E-Mail: ami@americanmeditation.org

American Psychiatric Association
1000 Wilson Boulevard, Suite 1825
Arlington, VA 22209-3901
Phone: 703-907-7300
Website: http://www.psych.org
E-mail: apa@psych.org

American Psychological Association (APA)
750 First Street, NE
Washington, DC 20002-4242
Toll Free: 800-374-2721
Phone: 202-336-5500
TDD/TTY: 202-336-6123
Website: http://www.apa.org

American Yoga Association
P.O. Box 19986
Sarasota, FL 34276
Phone: 941-927-4977
Fax: 941-921-4977
Website: http://www.amaericanyogaassociation.org

E-Mail: info@americanyogaassociation.org

Anxiety Disorders Association of America (ADAA)
8730 Georgia Avenue, Suite 600
Silver Spring, MD 20910
Phone: 240-485-1001
Fax: 240-485-1035
Website: http://www.adaa.org

Centers for Disease Control and Prevention
1600 Clifton Road
Atlanta, GA 30333
Toll Free: 800-311-3435
Phone: 404-639-3534
Website: http://www.cdc.gov

Cleveland Clinic
9500 Euclid Avenue
Cleveland, OH 44195
Toll Free: 800-223-2273, Ext. 42200
Phone: 216-444-2200
TTY: 216-444-0261
Website: http://www.clevelandclinic.org

International Society for Traumatic Stress Studies
60 Revere Drive, Suite 500
Northbrook, IL 60062
Phone: 847-480-9028
Fax: 847-480-9282
Website: http://www.istss.org
E-Mail: istss@istss.org

Mental Health America
2000 North Beauregard Street, 6th Floor
Alexandria, VA 22311
Toll Free: 800-969-6642
Phone: 703-684-7722
TTY: 800-433-5959
Fax: 703-684-5968
Website: http://www.nmha.org

National Cancer Institute (NCI)
NCI Public Inquiries Office
6116 Executive Boulevard, Room 3036A
Bethesda, MD 20892-8322
Toll Free: 800-4-CANCER (800-422-6237)
TTY: 800-332-8615
Website: http://www.cancer.gov

National Center for Complementary and Alternative Medicine
P.O. Box 7923
Gaithersburg, MD 20898-7923
Toll Free: 888-644-6226
TTY: 866-464-3615
Fax: 866-464-3616
Website: http://nccam.nih.gov
E-mail: info@nccam.nih.gov

National Institute of Child Health and Human Development (NICHD)
P.O. Box 3006
Rockville, MD 20847
Toll Free: 800-370-2943
Fax: 301-984-1473
TTY: 888-320-6942
Website: http://www.nichd.nih.gov

National Institute of Mental Health (NIMH)
Science Writing, Press, and Dissemination Branch
6001 Executive Boulevard, Room 8184, MSC 9663
Bethesda, MD 20892-9663
Toll Free: 866-615-NIMH (866-615-6464)
Phone: 301-443-4513
TTY: 301-402-9612
Website: http://www.nimh.nih.gov
E-Mail: nimhinfo@nih.gov

National Sleep Foundation
1522 K Street, NW, Suite 500
Washington, DC 20005
Phone: 202-347-3471
Fax: 202-347-3472
Website: http://www.sleepfoundation.org
E-Mail: nsf@sleepfoundation.org

National Women's Health Information Center
U.S. Department of Health and Human Services
8270 Willow Oaks Corporate Drive
Fairfax, VA 22031
Phone: 800-994-9662
TDD: 888-220-5446
Website: http://www.womenshealth.gov

Nemours Foundation
1600 Rockland Road
Wilmington, DE 19803
Phone: 302-651-4000
Website: http://www.kidshealth.org
E-mail: info@kidshealth.org

Students Against Destructive Decisions (SADD)
255 Main Street
Marlborough, MA 01752
Toll Free: 877-SADD-INC
Fax: 508-481-5759
Website: http://www.sadd.org
E-Mail: info@sadd.org

U.S. Department of Health and Human Services (HHS)
5600 Fisher Lane
Rockville MD 20857
Toll Free: 877-696-6775
Phone: 202-619-0257
Website: http://www.hhs.gov

Chapter 61

Additional Reading About Stress And Stress Management

Books

Balancing Act: A Teen's Guide to Managing Stress
By Joan Esherick
Published by Mason Crest Publishers, 2005
ISBN: 978-1590848531

Dealing with the Stuff That Makes Life Tough: The 10 Things That Stress Girls Out and How to Cope with Them
By Jill Zimmerman Rutledge
Published by McGraw-Hill, 2004
ISBN: 978-0071423267

About This Chapter: This chapter includes a compilation of various resources from many sources deemed reliable. It serves as a starting point for further research and is not intended to be comprehensive. Inclusion does not constitute endorsement. Resources in this chapter are categorized by type and, under each type, they are listed alphabetically by title to make topics easier to identify.

Don't Worry, You'll Get In:
100 Winning Tips for Stress-Free College Admissions
By Mimi Doe and Michele A. Hernandez
Published by Marlowe and Company, 2005
ISBN: 978-1569243671

Fighting Invisible Tigers: Stress Management for Teens
By Earl Hipp
Published by Free Spirit Publishing Inc., 2008
ISBN: 978-1575422824

Managing Stress:
A Creative Journal
By Brian Luke Seaward
Published by Jones and Bartlett Publishers, 2004
ISBN: 978-0763723781

Posttraumatic Stress Disorder:
Malady or Myth?
By Chris R. Brewin
Published by Yale University Press, 2007
ISBN: 978-0300123746

Re-Defining Stress to Prevent Disease:
Changing Thoughts, Perceptions and
Learned Experiences for Improved Health
By Steven Jaffe
Published by The Mind Diet Group, Inc., 2006
ISBN: 978-0972060585

The Stress Effect
By Richard Weinstein, D.C.
Published by Penguin Group (USA) Inc., 2004
ISBN: 1583331816

Additional Reading About Stress And Stress Management

Stress Free for Good:
10 Scientifically Proven Life Skills for Health and Happiness
By Dr. Frederic Luskin and Dr. Kenneth R. Pelletier
Published by HarperCollins Publishers, Inc., 2005
ISBN: 006058274X

Stress 101: An Overview for Teens
By Margaret O. Hyde and Elizabeth H. Forsyth, M.D.
Published by Twenty-First Century Books, 2007
ISBN: 978-0822567882

Stress Relief: Ultimate Teen Guide
By Mark Powell
Published by The Scarecrow Press, 2007
ISBN: 978-0810858060

10 Simple Solutions to Stress:
How to Tame Tension and Start Enjoying Your Life
By Claire Michaels Wheeler, M.D., Ph.D.
Published by New Harbinger Publications, Inc., 2007
ISBN: 978-1572244764

Too Stressed to Think?:
A Teen Guide to Staying Sane When Life Makes You Crazy
By Annie Fox and Ruth Kirschner
Published by Free Spirit Publishing, 2005
ISBN: 978-1575421735

Turn Stress into Bliss:
The Proven 8-Week Program for Health,
Relaxation, and Stress Relief
By Michael Lee
Published by Fair Winds Press, 2005
ISBN: 978-1592331178

Articles

"Back to Cool," by Kelly White, *Girls' Life*, August-September 2006, p. 34(2).

"Breathing for Life: Shelley Negelow Teaches Us Practical Steps for Letting Go of Stress," by Shelley Negelow, *New Life Journal*, February-March 2004, p. 15(2).

"Busy Bodies: Is Your Life So Hectic That You Can't Remember What Day of the Week It Is? If So, It May Be Time to Slow Things Down," by Leah Paulos, *Scholastic Choices*, November-December 2007, p. 6(6).

"Can You Take the Heat? Pop Quizzes, Buzzer Shots, Split-Second Decisions, Pressure Is Everywhere. Can You Handle It?" by Karen Langley, *Girls' Life*, February-March 2004, p. 56(2).

"Changing the Consequences of Stress," by Frank Sabatino, *Health Science*, Spring 2004, p. 13(5).

"Exam Stress and How to Beat It," by Mike Cardwell, *Psychology Review*, April 2005, p. 10(2).

"Health Rocks!" by Nicole Degli Esposti, *Skipping Stones*, September-October 2005, p. 7(1).

"Maximum Pressure: Teens Face Stress Every Day. Here's How to Calm Down Your Life," by Nancy Fitzgerald, *Scholastic Choices*, September 2004, p. 14(7).

"Mind Over Media: From Summer Blockbusters to 24-Hour News Stations, You're Inundated with Disturbing Sounds, Images, and Ideas. Here's How to Save Your Sanity without Shutting Down," by Robert Pela, *Natural Health*, June 2005, p. 76(3).

"Mind Over Meltdown," by Sarah Bowen Shea, *Natural Health*, October 2004, p. 68(2).

"Music Is Medicine for Body and Soul," by Wendy Priesnitz, *Natural Life*, May-June 2006, p. 10(2).

"New Research Underscores the Benefits of Walking," *Health Science*, Summer 2005, p. 13(1).

Additional Reading About Stress And Stress Management

"Peace of Mind: If You Always Feel Anxious and Stressed, You May Have Generalized Anxiety Disorder. Here's How to Reclaim a Sense of Calm," by Ben Kallen, *Natural Health*, December 2007, p. 57(5).

"RFV It Up: Feeling Fried? We've Got Super Simple Ways to Get Your Ooomph Back—No Red Bull Needed!" by Kara Wahlgren, *Girls' Life*, October-November 2007, p. 84(2).

"The Real-Life Stress Survival Guide," by Sarah Mahoney, *Prevention*, December 2005, p. 140.

"Running from Bears: Beat Stress by Understanding Your Body's Responses to Danger," by John Titan, *Mother Earth News*, February-March 2005, p. 126(3).

"6 Lessons for Handling Stress," by Christine Gorman, *Time*, January 29, 2007, p. 80.

"Stress!?!" by Mackenzie Birkey, *Skipping Stones*, September-October 2007, p. 24(1).

"Stress Busters! Why Get Distressed When You Can De-Stress Instead?" by Mark Rowh, *Current Health 2*, September 2005, p. 26(3).

"Stress Much? Imagine Not Feeling Totally Rushed, Tired, Cranky and Overwhelmed This Year. It's Possible! Really," by Roni Cohen-Sandler, *Girls' Life*, August-September 2005, p. 38(1).

"What Kind of Worrier Are You?" by Traci Mosser, *Scholastic Choices*, September 2005, p. 22(4).

"Your Totally Cool, Stress Free Back-To-School Guide," by Julie Taylor, *Teen People*, September 1, 2004, p. 145.

Index

Index

Page numbers that appear in *Italics* refer to illustrations. Page numbers that have a small 'n' after the page number refer to information shown as Notes at the beginning of each chapter. Page numbers that appear in **Bold** refer to information contained in boxes on that page (except Notes information at the beginning of each chapter).

A

AAAAI *see* American Academy of Allergy, Asthma and Immunology
AAFP *see* American Academy of Family Physicians
abuse
  described 121–25
  effects **124**
  stepparents **140**
"Abuse" (Nemours Foundation) 121n
Academy of General Dentistry, cold sores publication 211n
acne
  chocolate **213**
  stress 211–13
acupuncture, posttraumatic stress disorder **264**
acute stress, described 21–22
acute stress disorder (ASD), described 266–67
ADAA *see* Anxiety Disorders Association of America
addiction
  emotional support 303
  stress hormone 270–71

ADHD *see* attention deficit hyperactivity disorder
"Adolescent Stress and Depression" (Walker) 235n
adrenal glands, stress 3, 22, 270
adrenaline
  fight or flight response 231
  heart disease 232
  test anxiety 64
  see also epinephrine; stress hormones
adrenocorticotropin (ACTH), described 163–71
agoraphobia 250
"Alcohol and Drug Abuse Hurts Everyone in the Family" (SAMHSA) 117n
alcohol use
  parents 117
  prom pressure 104–5
alosetron hydrochloride 203–4
American Academy of Allergy, Asthma and Immunology (AAAAI), contact information 367
American Academy of Child and Adolescent Psychiatry, contact information 367

American Academy of Dermatology, contact information 367
American Academy of Experts in Traumatic Stress, contact information 367
American Academy of Family Physicians (AAFP), contact information 368
American Heart Association, contact information 368
American Institute of Stress
 contact information 368
 publications
  emotional support 301n
  stress effects 13n
American Lung Association, progressive muscle relaxation publication 351n
American Massage Therapy Association, contact information 368
American Meditation Institute, contact information 368
American Osteopathic College of Dermatology, telogen effluvium publication 219n
American Psychiatric Association, contact information 368
American Psychological Association (APA), contact information 368
American Yoga Association, contact information 368–69
amygdala, stress hormones 163
anger
 chronic pain 152
 grief 155
 heart disease 231
 overview 317–20
 stress 6, 27
"Anger Management" (University of Massachusetts) 317n
anger management, abuse 123
angiogenesis, weight gain 207
animal studies
 immune system 177
 psychosocial short stature 166
 stress effects 13–14
 weight gain 207–9
anorexia nervosa
 defined **285**
 described **279**
 overview 278–81
 stress 165

"Anorexia Nervosa" (NWHIC) 277n
antibodies, described 173
anxiety
 anger management **320**
 headache 227
 irritable bowel syndrome 203
anxiety disorders
 blushing **214**
 overview 249–60
 statistics **250**
"Anxiety Disorders" (NIMH) 249n
Anxiety Disorders Association of America (ADAA), contact information 369
anxiety problems, described 5
APA *see* American Psychological Association
arguments
 abuse 124
 family fights 113–16
"Aromatherapy" (Graham) 335n
aromatherapy, stress management 335–39
arthritis, defined **197**
ASD *see* acute stress disorder
assertive behavior, described 319
asthma, emotions **162**
attention deficit hyperactivity disorder (ADHD), stress overload 5
autoimmune diseases, stress response 176–77
autonomic nervous system
 meditation **356**
 stress 166
 stress hormones 163
 stress management 355–56

B

bad stress
 described 4
 immune system 12
BAM! Body and Mind, publications
 acute *versus* chronic stress 21n
 news reports 39n
"Becoming Independent" (NWHIC) 143n
behavioral signs, stress **26**
"The Benefits of Journaling for Stress Management" (Scott) 325n
"The Benefits of Yoga for Stress Management" (Scott) 351n

Index

binge eating disorder
  defined **285**
  overview 283–86
"Binge Eating Disorder" (NWHIC) 277n
blushing, overview **214–15**
Boys and Girls Clubs of America, contact information **297**
Boys Town Press, peer pressure publication 77n
brain
  immune system 173–74
  stress hormones 163, 270
breast cancer
  psychological stress **168–69**
  stress 10
breathing exercises
  mental health **342**
  sports activities 74
  stress management 341–45
  test anxiety 66–67
"Breathing Techniques" (University of South Florida) 341n
Brown-Saltzman, Katherine 352
bulimia nervosa
  defined **285**
  overview 281–83
"Bulimia Nervosa" (NWHIC) 277n
bullying
  abuse 122
  consequences **52, 53, 54**
  crime convictions 55
  overview 51–57
  relationships 87
  stress overload 5
"Bullying" (National Youth Violence Prevention Resource Center) 51n
butterflies
  irritable bowel syndrome 204
  stress 24
  test anxiety 64

C

CAM *see* complementary and alternative medicine
cancer, psychological stress **168–69**
canker sore 213
"Can stress actually be good for you?" (Weaver) 9n
caregivers, stress 175
Carskadon, Mary 35–36
CDC *see* Centers for Disease Control and Prevention
Centers for Disease Control and Prevention (CDC)
  contact information 369
  school violence publication 47n
CFS *see* chronic fatigue syndrome
Childhelp USA, contact information **125**
chocolate, acne **213**
chronic disease
  defined **197**
  overview 143–49
  stress 6
chronic fatigue syndrome (CFS)
  overview 185–89
  stress **186**
"Chronic Fatigue Syndrome" (NWHIC) 185n
chronic pain, stress management 151–54
chronic stress
  described 22–23
  sports activities 75
Chrousos, George 161–71
Clemson University, stress management publication 325n
Cleveland Clinic, contact information 369
cliques, described 87
CLUES acronym **246**
Cobb, Sidney 301
cognitive behavioral therapy
  acute stress disorder **267**
  anxiety disorders 258–59
  binge eating disorder 285–86
  posttraumatic stress disorder 265, 276
cognitive signs, stress **26**
cold sores, overview 213–17
colon, irritable bowel syndrome 200–201, 205
communication
  divorce 129–30
  health problems 146–47
  healthy relationships 88
  stress management 306–7
community organizations
  health problems 148
  school violence 48–49
  youth agencies 296–98

complementary and alternative medicine (CAM), fibromyalgia 196
concentration, stress 24
condoms, sexually transmitted diseases 94
Cooke, David A. 161n, 173n
corticotropin-releasing factor (CRF) 270–71
corticotropin-releasing hormone (CRH) 163–71
CortiSlim **208–9**
cortisol
 described 22, 163
 growth retardation 165
 immune system 167
 reproductive system 164–65
 stress benefits 10
 stress response 174
 weight loss supplement **208–9**
 see also stress hormones
cortisone 174
CortiStress **208–9**
counseling
 anorexia nervosa 281
 anxiety disorders **258**
 anxiety problems 5
 break-ups **99**
 chronic fatigue syndrome 188
 divorce 131
 insomnia 183
 irritable bowel syndrome 205
 loss of pets **158**
 posttraumatic stress disorder 263, 265
 self-injury **288**
CRF *see* corticotropin-releasing factor
CRH *see* corticotropin-releasing hormone
Cushing syndrome 165
cutting *see* self-harm

D

daily schedules, stress 31–33
daily stress log *330*
dating
 break-ups 97–100
 friendships **95**
 healthy relationships 90–92
 saying no **91**
 sexual activity 93–95
 sexually transmitted diseases 93–94
"Dating" (NWHIC) 85n

dating relationships, described 91
DBT *see* dialectical behavior therapy
"Dealing With Divorce" (Nemours Foundation) 127n
"Dealing With Pressure To Have Sex" (NWHIC) 93n
decision making, options **80**
Delisle, James R. 71
Department of Health and Human Services (DHHS; HHS) *see* US Department of Health and Human Services
Department of Labor (DOL) *see* US Department of Labor
depression
 anger management **320**
 binge eating disorder 284
 exercise **322–23**
 versus grief 156–57
 headache 227
 irritable bowel syndrome 203
 moving stress 108
 overview 235–41
 versus panic disorder 251
 quick tips **238**
 suicide 243–47
DHHS *see* US Department of Health and Human Services
dialectical behavior therapy (DBT)
 binge eating disorder 286
 self-harm 290–91
diet and nutrition
 cold sores 217
 fibromyalgia 198
 irritable bowel syndrome 205–6
 stress management 305–6, 321–24
dietary supplements, weight loss **208–9**
DiPietro, Janet 10
disabilities, stress management 143–49
disasters, news reports 39–40
disease, stress 161–71
distress
 defined **74**
 described 15, 33
 sports activities 74
divorce
 good family life **128**
 overview 127–32
 support groups **131**

Index

"Does Stress Really Cause Heart Disease" (Fogoros) 229n
DOL *see* US Department of Labor
drinking *see* alcohol use; substance abuse
drug abuse *see* alcohol use; substance abuse

E

eating disorders
  described **278**
  overview 277–86
  stress 6, 166
"Eating Disorders" (NWHIC) 277n
"Eating for Less Stress" (Wellness Council of Arizona) 321n
"Effects of Stress" (American Institute of Stress) 13n
Ehrensaft, Diane 33
"11 Tips for Dealing with Stress" (NWHIC) 305n
embarrassment, blushing **214**
EMDR *see* eye movement desensitization and reprocessing
emergency supply kits, stress management 41–42
emotional abuse, described 122
emotional concerns
  asthma **162**
  break-ups 97–100
  divorce 128
  grief 155–58
  heart disease **230**
  infections **175**
  stress **26**
emotional disorders, stress effects 19
emotional stress, heart disease 230–34
emotional support, described 301–3
"Emotional Support and Social Support" (American Institute of Stress) 301n
endoscopic thoracic sympathectomy (ETS), blushing **215**
environment, stress 164
epinephrine
  arteries 11
  described 22, 163
  see also adrenaline; stress hormones
epithelium, irritable bowel syndrome 200
erythrophobia **214**
estrogen, breast cancer 10

ETS *see* endoscopic thoracic sympathectomy
eustress
  defined **74**
  described 33
  origin of term 15
  sports activities 74
exercise
  anxiety disorders **260**
  chronic fatigue syndrome 188
  chronic pain 154
  chronic stress **178**
  fibromyalgia 198
  stress hormones 12
  stress management 7, **11**, **305**, **322–23**
"Express Yourself: A Teenager's Guide to Fitting in, Getting Involved, Finding Yourself" (National Clearinghouse on Families and Youth) 295n
eye movement desensitization and reprocessing (EMDR) 268

F

facial tics, overview **224–25**
family issues
  anxiety disorders **260**
  divorce 127–32
  eating disorders 278
  parental fights 113–16
  posttraumatic stress disorder 276
  school violence 49
  step families 133–41
  substance abuse 117–19
  violence 121–25
Federal Trade Commission (FTC), weight loss supplement claims **206–9**
"Feeling Good about Yourself" (NWHIC) 313n
fibromyalgia
  defined **192**, **197**
  overview 191–98
  stress **193**
fight or flight response
  adrenaline 231
  blushing **214**
  described 21–22
  test anxiety 64
  see also stress response

"Find Out If You Have Low or Poor Self-Esteem" (NWHIC) 313n
Fleshner, Monika 10
fMRI *see* functional magnetic resonance imaging
Fogoros, Richard N. 229n
freedom, described 295–96
friends
  bullying 53, 54
  CLUES action steps **246**
  described 298–300
  family violence 125
  good choices **78**
  health problems 147
  moving stress 107, 111
  parental concerns **89**
  peer pressure 81, **82**
  posttraumatic stress disorder 276
  quick tips **86**
  relationships 85–88
  sports activities 75
  stress management 306
  suicidal thoughts 243–47
  suicide 157
"Friendships" (NWHIC) 85n
FTC *see* Federal Trade Commission
functional magnetic resonance imaging (fMRI), meditation **356**

G

GAD *see* generalized anxiety disorder
gastrointestinal tract, stress 166
gender factor
  anorexia nervosa 279
  bulimia nervosa 281–82
  bullying 52
  chronic fatigue syndrome 186
  cortisol 165
  eating disorders **278**
  generalized anxiety disorder 254
  irritable bowel syndrome 199
  panic disorder 250
  self-harm 288
  social phobia 253
generalized anxiety disorder (GAD), described 254
"Getting Over a Break-Up" (Nemours Foundation) 97n

gifted students, stress management 69–71
glucocorticoid *see* cortisol
GnRH *see* gonadotropin-releasing hormone
goal setting, stress management **8**, 310
"Going to the Hospital" (NWHIC) 143n
Gold, Philip 161–62
gonadotropin-releasing hormone (GnRH) 164
good stress
  benefits 10–11
  described 4, 175–76
"Got Butterflies? Find Out Why" (BAM) 21n
Government of South Australia, publications
  resilience 309n
  step families 133n
Graham, Jillian 335n
grief, overview 155–58
growth retardation, stress 165–66
guided imagery
  defined **359**
  stress management 351–53
"Guided Imagery" (Hartford Hospital) 351n

H

hair loss, stress 219–21
"Handling Sports Pressure and Competition" (Nemours Foundation) 73n
Hanson, Richard W. 151n
Hartford Hospital, guided imagery publication 351n
hate crimes, abuse 122
headache
  stress 24–25, 223–27
  test anxiety 64
"Healthy Relationships" (NWHIC) 85n
healthy relationships, described 88–89
heartbreak, described 97–100
heart disease
  emotional stress **230**
  mind-body medicine **233**
  stress 229–34
"Helping Friends in Trouble: Stress, Depression, and Suicide" (Walker) 243n

Index

"Help! My Parents/Guardians Don't Like My Friend(s)" (NWHIC) 85n
heredity
  depression 239
  fibromyalgia 193
  obsessive compulsive disorder 252
  panic disorder 250
  stress 164
herpes simplex virus type 1 (HSV-1) 213–14
Herron, Ron 77n
HHS *see* US Department of Health and Human Services
hippocampus, stress hormones 163
Hollifield, Michael **264**
homework stress
  described 59–62
  schedules 60
  see also school stress; test anxiety
homicides, school hours 49
Hooke's Law (1658) 14
hormones *see* stress hormones
hospitalizations
  chronic diseases 144
  quick tips **145**
"How Owning a Dog or Cat Can Reduce Stress" (Scott) 331n
"How to Deal With Grief" (SAMHSA) 155n
"How to Make Homework Less Work" (Nemours Foundation) 59n
HPA axis *see* hypothalamic-pituitary-adrenal axis
Hunnicutt, Benjamin 32
hyperhidrosis, blushing **215**
hypothalamic-pituitary-adrenal axis (HPA axis), described 162–71
hypothalamus
  corticotropin-releasing hormone 163
  stress 3, 22
  stress response 174

I

IBS *see* irritable bowel syndrome
IGF-1 *see* insulin-like growth factor 1
illness, stress management 143–49
immune system
  emotional support 303
  irritable bowel syndrome **204**
  meditation 356

immune system, continued
  overview 173–79
  psychological stress **168–69**
  social support **302**
  stress 166–67, 270
  stress effects 19
  stress hormones 10
infections
  chronic fatigue syndrome 185
  cold sores 213–17
  emotional traits **175**
  HPA axis 166
  irritable bowel syndrome 201
infectious mononucleosis, chronic fatigue syndrome 185
inflammation, defined **197**
infomercials, weight loss supplement **208–9**
insomnia
  cortisol 170
  overview 181–83
  treatment 38
  see also sleep deprivation
instant messaging, sleep deprivation 36
instincts, peer pressure 81
insulin-like growth factor 1 (IGF-1) 165
insurance coverage, anxiety disorders 260
interleukins, immune system 167
International Society for Traumatic Stress Studies, contact information 369
irritable bowel syndrome (IBS)
  immune system **204**
  overview 199–206
  sensitive colons **201**
"Irritable Bowel Syndrome" (NIDDK) 199n

J

joint, defined **197**
journal writing
  health problems 147
  quick tips **327**
  school stress 44–45
  stress management 41, 308, 325–26

K

Kavey, Neil B. 181n
"Keeping Your Cool Under Prom Pressure" (Nemours Foundation) 101n

knots, stress 24
Kreek, Mary Jeanne **270–71**

L

Lamberg, Lynne 35n
learning disabilities, stress overload 5
learning process, bullying 53
"Learning You Have an Illness or Disability" (NWHIC) 143n
limbic system, stress hormones 163
"Link Found Between Teens' Stress Levels and Acne Severity" (Wake Forest University) 211n
lists, stress management **236**
Long Beach VA Healthcare System, pain management publication 151n
long term stress *see* chronic stress
Lotronex (alosetron hydrochloride) 203–4
luteinizing hormone 164–65
lysine 217

M

Maine Youth Suicide Prevention Program, friends, suicide publication 155n
manipulation, abuse 124
massage therapy
   stress management 347–50
   types, described **348**
"Massage Therapy" 347n
medications
   anxiety disorders 255–58, **257**, 260
   binge eating disorder 286
   chronic fatigue syndrome 188
   cold sores 216–17
   fibromyalgia 194–96
   headache 227
   insomnia 38, 183
   irritable bowel syndrome **203**, 203–4
   posttraumatic stress disorder 268
   self-harm 291
meditation
   chronic stress **178**
   defined **359**
   music therapy 338–39
   relaxation response **356**
   stress management **11**, 311, 353–57

"Meditation for Health Purposes" (NCCAM) 351n
mental health
   abuse 123
   breathing techniques **342**
   bullying **53**
   exercise **322–23**
Mental Health America, contact information 369
mind-body medicine
   coronary artery disease **233**
   defined **359**
   stress management 351–63
Mindell, Jodi 37–38
mindfulness, sports activities 75
mindfulness meditation, described 355
money concerns
   divorce 129
   prom finances **102**
mood disturbances, sleep deprivation 36–37
motility, irritable bowel syndrome 200
motor vehicle accidents, acute stress disorder **266–67**
"The Moving Blues" (Nemours Foundation) 107n
moving stress
   described **108**
   overview 107–11
   step families 137
muscle, defined **197**
muscle relaxation
   defined **359**
   sports activities 75
   stress management 357–58
music therapy, described **338–39**

N

National 4-H Council, contact information **297**
National Cancer Institute (NCI), contact information 369
National Center for Complementary and Alternative Medicine (NCCAM)
   contact information 369
   meditation publication 351n
National Center for Posttraumatic Stress Disorder, posttraumatic stress disorder publication 261n

Index

National Clearinghouse on Families and Youth, finding yourself publication 295n
National Headache Foundation, stress, headache publication 223n
National Institute of Arthritis and Musculoskeletal and Skin Diseases (NIAMS), fibromyalgia publication 191n
National Institute of Child Health and Human Development (NICHD), contact information 370
National Institute of Diabetes and Digestive and Kidney Diseases (NIDDK), irritable bowel syndrome publication 199n
National Institute of Mental Health (NIMH)
　anxiety disorders publication 249n
　contact information 370
National Institute on Drug Abuse (NIDA), substance abuse, stress publication 269n
National Institutes of Health (NIH), disease, stress publication 161n
National Sleep Foundation, contact information 370
National Women's Health Information Center (NWHIC)
　contact information 370
　publications
　　chronic fatigue syndrome 185n
　　chronic illness 143n
　　eating disorders 277n
　　pressure to have sex 93n
　　self-esteem 313n
　　stressful relationships 85n
　　stress management 305n
National Youth Violence Prevention Resource Center, bullying publication 51n
NCCAM *see* National Center for Complementary and Alternative Medicine
NCI *see* National Cancer Institute
neglect, described 121, 122
Nemours Foundation
　contact information 370
　publications
　　break-ups 97n
　　divorce 127n
　　family violence 121n

Nemours Foundation, continued
　publications, continued
　　homework stress 59n
　　moving blues 107n
　　parental fights 113n
　　prom pressure 101n
　　school stress 43n
　　sports pressures 73n
　　stress 3n
　　test anxiety 63n
nervous systems
　fibromyalgia 193
　stress 3, 4, 270
　stress hormones 162
　stress management 355–56
neurological disorders, stress effects 19
neuropeptide Y (NPY) 207–9
news reports
　normal life **40**
　stress 39–42
"News You Can Use" (BAM) 39n
NIAMS *see* National Institute of Arthritis and Musculoskeletal and Skin Diseases
NICHD *see* National Institute of Child Health and Human Development
NIDA *see* National Institute on Drug Abuse
"NIDA Community Drug Alert Bulletin - Stress And Substance Abuse" (NIDA) 269n
NIDDK *see* National Institute of Diabetes and Digestive and Kidney Diseases
NIMH *see* National Institute of Mental Health
norepinephrine
　described 22, 163
　stress management **322–23**
　stress response 270
　see also stress hormones
NPY *see* neuropeptide Y
nutrition *see* diet and nutrition
NWHIC *see* National Women's Health Information Center

O

obsessive compulsive disorder (OCD)
　described 251–52
　psychotherapy 258–59

OCD *see* obsessive compulsive disorder
opiates, addiction **270–71**
optimism, stress management 7
options, making decisions **80**
overbooking, stress 31–33

P

pain, effect of stress **152**
"Pain and Stress" (Hanson) 151n
pain management, stress 151–54
panic disorder
   described 249–51
   psychotherapy 258
parasuicide *see* self-harm
parents
   arguments **115**
   divorce 127–32
   family fights 113–16
   friend relationships 90
   moving stress 108
   peer pressure 81–82
   prom finances **102**
   step families 134–35
   substance abuse 117–19
peer pressure
   cliques 87
   overview 77–83
   prom night **104**
   relationships 86
Perceived Social Support Quiz 302
perfectionism
   gifted students 69–70
   stress management 6
performance anxiety, described 63–64
personality disorders
   abuse 123
   depression 239–40
Peter, Val J. 77n
pet ownership
   benefits *versus* drawbacks **333**
   emotional support 301
   grief **158**
   stress management 331–33
phobias, described 253–54
physical abuse, described 121
physical changes, stress 3–4
physical disorders, stress effects 19
physical signs, stress **26**

physical stress, heart disease 229–30
pituitary gland
   corticotropin-releasing hormone 163
   stress 22
plan of action worksheet *328–29*
popularity, relationships 87
postpartum depression, cortisol 170
posttraumatic stress disorder (PTSD)
   clinical trials **264**
   described 5
   overview 261–68
   substance abuse 273–76
pressure
   dating relationships 91
   gifted students 69–70
   proms 101–5
   sexual activity 93–95, 104
   sports activities 73–76
   see also peer pressure; stress
problem solving
   balance 33
   stress management 7, **8**
progressive muscle relaxation
   defined **359**
   stress management 357–58
"Progressive Muscle Relaxation"
   (American Lung Association) 351n
proms
   financial considerations **102**
   overview 101–5
   peer pressure **104**
PSS *see* psychosocial short stature
psychological stress
   cancer **168–69**
   disease 161–71
   exercise 12
psychosocial short stature (PSS)
   165–66
psychotherapy
   anxiety disorders **258**, 258–59
   binge eating disorder 285–86
   obsessive compulsive disorder 252
   self-harm 290–91
   see also counseling
PTSD *see* posttraumatic stress disorder
puberty
   acne **213**
   sleep need changes 35
purging, eating disorders 277, 279, 281

Index

Q

qi gong, defined **359**
"Questions and Answers About Fibromyalgia" (NIAMS) 191n

R

Rabin, Bruce 12
relationships, overview 85–92
relationship stress, stress overload 5
relaxation response, stress management 7
relaxation techniques
  chronic stress **178**
  insomnia 181–83
  music therapy **338–39**
  smoking cessation **272**
  stress management **8**
  see also meditation; muscle relaxation
religion
  social support 301–2
  stress management 362–63
reproductive system, stress 164–65
resilience
  crises **312**
  overview 309–12
  stress management 8
"Resilience" (Government of South Australia) 309n
respiratory infections, emotional traits **175**
responsibility, described 295–96
rheumatic disorders, fibromyalgia 191–92
Rosch, Paul J. 12
Rosenfield, Alvin 32–33

S

SADD *see* Students Against Destructive Decisions
safety concerns
  bullying 57
  stress management 40–42
SAMHSA *see* Substance Abuse and Mental Health Services Administration
schedules
  sports activities 76
  stress 31–33
  stress management 6
  stress overload 5

school stress
  bullying 52–53
  described 43–45
  see also homework stress; test anxiety
school violence
  bullying **52**
  described 47–49
"School Violence: Tips for Coping with Stress" (CDC) 47n
Scott, Elizabeth 325n, 331n, 351n
seeking safety, posttraumatic stress disorder 276
self-confidence
  bullying 56–57
  defined **314**
  described 314
self-esteem
  abuse 124
  bullying 53
  defined **314**
  healthy relationships 89
  overview 313–15
  prom pressure 102–3
self-expression, overview 295–300
self-harm
  described **288**
  overview 287–92
Self-Management of Chronic Pain: Patient Handbook (Long Beach VA Healthcare System) 151n
Selye, Hans 13–15, 33
serotonin 200–201
sexual abuse, described 122
sexual activity
  gonadotropin-releasing hormone 164
  pressure 93–95, 104
  step siblings 140–41
short term stress *see* acute stress
sickness behavior, described 174
skin disorders
  overview 211–17
  stress effects 19
sleep deprivation
  prevention **37**
  stress 35–38
  test anxiety **65**
  see also insomnia
"Sleep-Deprived Teens Report Stress, Mood Disorders" (Lamberg) 35n

sleep disorders, anger management **320**
sleep hygiene
   described 38
   stress management 307–8
sleeplessness
   stress 25
   stress management 6–7
smoking cessation, stress management **272**
social isolation, bullies 53–54
Social Network Questionnaire 302
social phobia
   described 252–53
   psychotherapy 258
social support
   described 301–3
   health benefits **302**
   pet ownership 332
special education, *versus* mainstream classes **148**
spirituality
   defined **359**
   described **363**
   stress management 362–63
"Spirituality and Mental Health: Benefits of Spirituality" (Scott) 351n
sports activities, competition stress 73–76
statistics
   acne 212
   anxiety disorders **250**
   bullying 51–52
   chronic fatigue syndrome 186
   depression 236
   fibromyalgia 192
   generalized anxiety disorder 254
   irritable bowel syndrome 199
   obsessive compulsive disorder 252
   panic disorder 250
   parental alcohol abuse **118**
   posttraumatic stress disorder 262
   self-harm 287–88
   sleep deprivation 35–36
   social phobia 253
   teen pregnancy **95**
"Step-families" (Government of South Australia) 133n
step families, overview 133–41
Sternberg, Esther 173–79

stress
   avoiding pressure overload **11**
   benefits 9–12
   chronic pain 151–54
   described 269
   different perceptions 13–19
   effects 16–19
   heart disease 229–34, **230**
   origin of term 13–16
   overview 3–8
   physical signs **22**
   scientific definition **16**
   symptoms **26, 178**
"Stress" (National Headache Foundation) 223n
"Stress" (Nemours Foundation) 3n
"Stress, Definition of Stress, Stressor, What Is Stress?, Eustress?" (American Institute of Stress) 13n
"Stress, Obesity Link Found" (Wein) 207n
"Stress and Disease: New Perspectives" (Wein) 173n
"Stress and Insomnia" (Kavey) 181n
stress circuit, described 163–64
stress hormones
   addiction **270–71**
   described 3, 4, 10–11, 22
   good stress 10–11
   nervous system 162
   stress response 161–62
   weight loss supplement **208–9**
   see also adrenaline; cortisol; epinephrine; norepinephrine
stress logs, described 327, *330*
stress management
   anger management 317–20
   anxiety disorders **260**
   aromatherapy 335–39
   breathing techniques 341–45
   diet and nutrition 321–24
   emotional support 301–3
   gifted students 69–71
   heart disease 234
   irritable bowel syndrome 204–5
   journal writing 325–30
   massage therapy 347–50
   mind-body therapies 351–63
   music therapy **338–39**

Index

stress management, continued
  overview 305-8
  pet ownership 331-33
  quick tips **306-7**
  resilience 309-12
  self-esteem 313-15
  social support 301-3
  sports activities 74-75
  suggestions **178**
  test anxiety **67**
"Stress Management - Taking Charge" (Clemson University) 325n
stressors
  acute stress disorder **266-67**
  chronic **178**
  described 4, 269
  origin of term 15
  perceptions 16
  sports activities 74
  substance abuse 273
  temporary problems **8**
stress overload, described 4-6
stress-related disorders, described 167-71
stress response
  described 3-4, 21, 23-24
  disease 161-62
  see also fight or flight response
"Stress System Malfunction Could Lead to Serious, Life Threatening Disease" (NIH) 161n
Students Against Destructive Decisions (SADD)
  contact information 370
  overbooking publication 31n
substance abuse
  break-ups **99**
  bullying 54
  panic disorder 251
  parents 117-19
  posttraumatic stress disorder 265, 275-76
  prom pressure 104-5
  stress 6, 271-73
  stress hormone **270-71**
Substance Abuse and Mental Health Services Administration (SAMHSA), publications
  grief coping strategies 155n
  parental substance abuse 117n

suicide
  bullying 53
  friends 243-47
  grief 157
suicide attempts, depression 236, 238
support groups
  anxiety disorders **260**
  chronic fatigue syndrome 188
  chronic stress **178**
surgical procedures, blushing **215**

T

"Talking about Your Illness or Disability" (NWHIC) 143n
talk therapy, chronic fatigue syndrome 188
Tan, Lynne 10-12
"Teens and Stress: Are You Overbooked?" (SADD) 31n
telogen effluvium
  defined **220**
  described 219-21
"Telogen Effluvium Hair Loss" (American Osteopathic College of Dermatology) 219n
tender points, defined **197**
tension
  bad stress 12
  headache 223, 226
"Tension-Type Headache" (National Headache Foundation) 223n
test anxiety
  described 23
  motivation 5
  overview 63-67
  sleep deprivation **65**
  stress management **67**
  see also homework stress; school stress
"Test Anxiety" (Nemours Foundation) 63n
"Things You Can Do to Become More Independent" (NWHIC) 143n
tics, described **224-25**
time management
  quick tips **306-7**
  stress 32-33
TNF *see* tumor necrosis factor
tragedies
  news reports 39-40
  school violence 47-49

transcendental meditation, described 355
traumatic events
  acute stress disorder **266–67**
  described 261
"Try These Steps to Boost Your Self-Esteem" (NWHIC) 313n
tumor necrosis factor (TNF) 167
tutors, homework stress 62
type A personalities
  emotional support 303
  heart disease 232–33

U

University of Massachusetts, anger management publication 317n
University of South Florida, breathing techniques publication 341n
US Department of Health and Human Services (DHHS; HHS), contact information 370
US Department of Labor (DOL), massage therapy publication 347n

V

violence
  acute stress disorder **266–67**
  bullying 53
  family issues 121–25
visualizations, sports activities 75
volunteer work, stress management 308

W

Wake Forest University, acne, stress publication 211n
Walker, Joyce 235n, 243n
weather reports, stress 39–40
Weaver, Jane 9n

weight management
  binge eating disorder 286
  prom pressure 103–4
  stress 207–9
Wein, Harrison 173n, 207n
"Welcome!" (NWHIC) 143n
Wellness Council of Arizona, diet and nutrition publication 321n
"What Are Cold Sores?" (Academy of General Dentistry) 211n
"What is Posttraumatic Stress Disorder (PTSD)" (National Center for Posttraumatic Stress Disorder) 261n
What's Right for Me? Making Good Choices in Relationships (Herron; Peter) 77n
"What to Do if You Don't Like School" (Nemours Foundation) 43n
"When A Friend Dies By Suicide" (Maine Youth Suicide Prevention Program) 155n
"When Kids Tease" (NWHIC) 143n
"When Parents Fight" (Nemours Foundation) 113n
Whitmore, Joanne Rand 69
worksheets
  daily stress log *330*
  plan of action *328–29*

Y

YMCA of the USA, contact information **297**
yoga, stress management 360–62
Yosipovitch, Gil 211–12
youth organizations, contact information **297**

Z

Zukowska, Zofia 207–9